NORTHEAST

FRUIT & VEGETABLE GARDENING

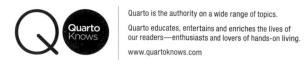

Quarto is the authority on a wide range of topics.

Quarto educates, entertains and enriches the lives of our readers—enthusiasts and lovers of hands-on living.

www.quartoknows.com

First published in 2012 by Cool Springs Press, an imprint of the Quarto Publishing Group USA Inc., 400 First Avenue North, Suite 400, Mineapolis, MN 55401 USA. Telephone: (612) 344-8100 Fax: (612) 344-8692

quartoknows.com
Visit our blogs at quartoknows.com

Cool Springs Press titles are also available at discounts in bulk quantity for industrial or sales-promotional use. For details write to Special Sales Manager at Quarto Publishing Group USA Inc., 400 First Avenue North, Suite 400, Mineapolis, MN 55401 USA.

To find out more about our books, visit us online at www.coolspringspress.com.

ISBN-13: 978-1-59186-529-2

Library of Congress Cataloging-in-Publication Data

Nardozzi, Charlie.
    Northeast fruit & vegetable gardening : plant, grow, and eat the best edibles for Northeast gardens / Charles Nardozzi.
        p. cm.
    Includes index.
    ISBN 978-1-59186-529-2 (pbk.)
    1. Vegetable gardening--Northeastern States. 2. Fruit-culture--Northeastern States. I. Title. II. Title: Northeast fruit and vegetable gardening. III. Title: Plant, grow, and eat the best edibles for Northeast gardens.

    SB321.5.A115N37 2012
    635--dc23

                        2011040650

President/CEO: Ken Fund
Group Publisher: Bryan Trandem
Publisher: Ray Wolf
Senior Editor: Billie Brownell
Editor: Kathy Franz
Creative Director: Michele Lanci
Design Manager: Kim Winscher
Production Manager: Hollie Kilroy
Photo Researcher: Bryan Stusse
Production: S.E. Anderson

Printed in China

10 9 8 7 6 5 4

NORTHEAST
FRUIT & VEGETABLE GARDENING

CHARLIE NARDOZZI

COOL
SPRINGS
PRESS
Growing Successful Gardeners™

MINNEAPOLIS, MINNESOTA

CONTENTS

DEDICATION & ACKNOWLEDGMENTS

To my wife, Wendy, with whom I'm building a garden and a life together.

❃ ❃ ❃

Many thanks to the staff at Cool Springs Press for the opportunity to write this book and for their support during the entire process, including Ray Wolf, Billie Brownell, and Kathy Franz. Thank you to horticulture editor Marty DeHart, who made sure the technicalities of this book reflect the uniqueness of the Northeast, and to Wendy Rowe for her first-rate photography skills. Thanks also to Tracy Stanley and Michele Lanci-Altomare at Quayside, and so many others who contributed to this book.

A special thank you to the late Roger Waynick, president of Cool Springs Press, for his encouragement to gardeners and garden writers everywhere.

USDA COLD HARDINESS ZONE MAP

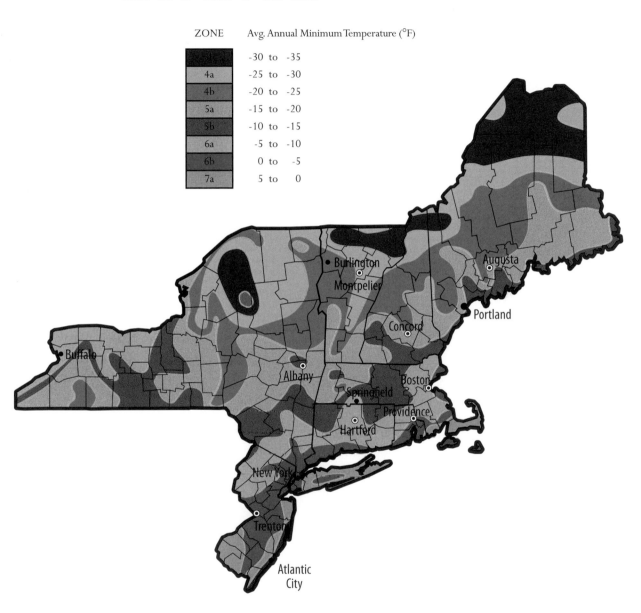

ZONE	Avg. Annual Minimum Temperature (°F)
3b	-30 to -35
4a	-25 to -30
4b	-20 to -25
5a	-15 to -20
5b	-10 to -15
6a	-5 to -10
6b	0 to -5
7a	5 to 0

Cold-hardiness zone designations were developed by the United States Department of Agriculture (USDA) to indicate the minimum average temperature for an area. A zone assigned to an individual plant indicates the lowest temperature at which the plant can be expected to survive over the winter. The Northeast has zones ranging from 3b to 7a. Though a plant may grow (and grow well) in zones other than its recommended cold-hardiness zone, zones are a good indication of which plants to consider for your landscape.

CHAPTER 1

GARDENING IN THE NORTHEAST

We Northeasteners pride ourselves on our self-sufficiency and frugality. Perhaps that's why more of us are growing our own food gardens than ever before. Growing some of our own food helps ensure that the produce we're eating is safe, fresh, and healthy. We know what has been sprayed on it, so we are assured that our kids, family, and friends can enjoy beautiful veggies right out of the garden. Plus, we can save hundreds of dollars a year just by growing our own fruits and vegetables. Those of us with an environment-friendly mindset also know that growing our own food reduces pollution and our carbon footprint because we're not supporting an industry that ships fruits and vegetables 1,500 miles on average from the field to our grocery store. It's a win-win! When I give talks across the country on edible gardening, people young and old, of all different nationalities, religions, and political persuasions, come together on this common ground of eating good, healthy, safe food.

We have a rich history of agriculture in the Northeast. The Northeast is where our European ancestors started gardening and where, for generations before them, Native American tribes grew vegetables and harvested native fruits. The "three sisters" gardens of Native Americans were first discovered here. Varieties of vegetables and fruits, such as 'Long Island Improved' Brussels sprouts and 'Rutgers' tomatoes, started here as well. While much of the commercial production of vegetables and fruits has moved west and overseas, home gardening and farming across this country and in the Northeast is actually making a comeback. For the first time since the USDA started conducting a farm census, over the past five years the number of farms in the United States has actually increased. Much of this increase is due to the renewed interested in fruit and vegetable growing.

I've lived and gardened most of my life in the Northeast, and the variety of terrains, soils, and circumstances where you can garden is amazing. From the sandy pine barrens of New Jersey, to the rocky crags of coastal Maine, and to the mountains of the Adirondacks, the Northeast has a varied topography that makes gardening exciting and sometimes challenging, but also very rewarding. Whether you're an urban gardener in Boston or New York, or a rural gardener in the wide-open spaces of Vermont, the gardening practices, varieties, and methods are similar.

Along the coast, the summer is hot and humid and the winters relatively mild. In these USDA zone 5, 6, and borderline 7 regions (see the USDA Cold Hardiness Zone Map for the Northeast on page 7), you can grow a wide variety of vegetables and fruits for well over two hundred days. That's more than six months of frost-free growing. To determine the number of frost-free days you have, see the table beginning on page 14. You can be planting in April or even March, depending on the winter and vegetable, and have frost-free days right into November. It's easy to grow two or three crops in one season by using a technique called succession planting that I'll talk about later. And the summers are hot and humid, perfect for growing traditional summertime treats such as sweet corn, tomatoes, eggplants, and melons. You can even grow greens through the winter with a little extra care, giving you an almost twelve-month garden. But this climate doesn't come without its downsides. Stormy weather and even hurricanes can blow through in summer, keeping gardeners on their toes.

In colder and more mountainous regions of Maine, New Hampshire, upstate New York, and Vermont, you may have fewer frost-free days to garden, but the season comes on like gangbusters. Mostly in USDA hardiness zone 4, these colder regions have late frosts. You really can't get serious about gardening until Memorial Day. But watch out after that! The combination of long days and warm temperatures makes vegetables and fruits explode with growth in the garden. I often compare the progress of my Vermont garden with my relatives' gardens in Connecticut. While their gardens always begin producing sooner, especially with early crops of greens and peas, by July and August we're both noshing on sweet tomatoes and blueberries. The colder temperatures just challenge the northern gardener to be more creative about season-extending devices such as row covers and cold frames. While warm-weather-loving crops such as watermelons and sweet potatoes may be more of a challenge to grow in the northern parts of this region, cool-season fruits and vegetables, such as apples, peaches, broccoli, carrots, and peas, thrive. They slowly mature during the cool summers to yield sweet-tasting heads, leaves, and roots.

The Northeast is known for its four distinct seasons. Spring can be short, but is often highlighted by windy days with wild temperature extremes. Summer starts in late May or June with heat waves, summer thunderstorms, and sometimes drought. Fall is a classic. October and November days are still warm with cool nights and colorful leaves dropping to the ground. Winter can be severe, with classic nor'easter storms coming up the coast and dumping feet of snow. We gardeners don't mind the snow, though. It's a great cold-temperature insulator for our fruits and perennial vegetables.

While the climate may be somewhat consistent across the Northeast, the weather is not. The old saying, "If you don't like the weather, wait a minute," must have originated here for good reason. I've seen the weather go in one day from sunny, humid, and 80°F to stormy, snowy, and 30°F. But as confused as that might make us feel, the plants seem to roll with it. Fruits, such as apples and blueberries, thrive here. They actually need the cold winters and warm summers to produce the best crop. Some of these plants are so well adapted they can grow for years with little care. I have relatives in the mountains of New Hampshire who have blueberry bushes that are still producing after forty years.

The Northeast doesn't have the deep, fertile soils of the Midwest, but our rocky soils have fed inhabitants for thousands of years. River-bottom silty soils, such as those along the Connecticut, Hudson, and Merrimack rivers, offer some of the best soils for growing. The coastal lowlands in New Jersey, Rhode Island, and Massachusetts have sandy soils that vegetables such as asparagus love. The hills and mountains throughout the rest of the region often provide that ubiquitous clay soil that all gardeners sooner or later come to know. Though hard to work with initially, it is fertile, and I'll

talk about ways to grow a great garden in clay soil in the coming chapters. The key to good soil is organic matter. We have a lot of it in the Northeast. With our consistent rainfall and cool temperatures, we can grow a mean lawn. Lawn clippings are a good source of organic matter if you're bagging and picking them up. Our colorful fall foliage provides truckloads of leaves that can be turned into compost for the garden. Plus, many residents love animals as well as gardens. Horses, cows, sheep, and chickens provide valuable manure that can turn a lifeless sandy soil or hard-to-work clay soil into a vibrant garden soil.

While we have our share of insect pests and diseases, the most troublesome pests that gardeners ask me about are the four-legged types. Because so many people are packed into the Northeast, human development has encroached on animal habitats. The result is that the animals either leave or learn to coexist. Some of our furry friends not only have learned how to coexist, but are thriving. Deer, raccoons, woodchucks, and rabbits are some of the critters that commonly plague a garden. While the threat is real, there are ways to keep Bambi and his friends away and still enjoy your garden and the beautiful natural scenery of our region. I'll talk more about that in the pest control chapter.

Those of you in urban areas might think gardening is a pie-in-the-sky idea because you don't have a big yard or any yard. However, with new technologies, plant varieties, and methods, urban gardens are popping up even in densely populated cities such as New York. And as New Yorkers are famous for saying, "If you can do it here, you can do it anywhere." Community gardens in vacant lots, small raised beds in alleyways, and containers on decks, patios, fire escapes, and balconies can all be used to grow herbs, vegetables, and even some fruits. Self-watering containers, improved potting soil, and dwarf varieties all help make urban gardening in small spaces a success. There are stories of gardeners turning into urban farmers and growing more than enough food to sell at local farmers' markets and grocery stores and directly to restaurants and individuals. So don't be intimidated by the lack of space, animals, poor soil, or cold weather. Gardening in the Northeast has been going on for hundreds of years, so welcome to the party. Throughout this book you'll learn how to design and site your garden; build your soil; handle weeds, water, fertilizer, and pests; and harvest and store the abundance of food you'll soon be producing. The bulk of the book is devoted to common fruits, vegetables, and herbs, with specific information on how to grow them.

So let's get growing in the Northeast and make you a productive and successful gardener.

FIRST AND LAST AVERAGE FROST DATES IN THE NORTHEAST

Connecticut

City	Last Average* Frost Date	First Average Frost Date
Danbury	5/15	9/26
Groton	4/28	10/4
Hartford	5/10	9/26
Stamford	5/11	10/1
Storrs	5/9	9/29

Maine

City	Last Average* Frost Date	First Average Frost Date
Augusta	5/8	9/28
Bangor	5/23	9/26
Portland	5/15	9/26
Presque Isle	6/3	9/8
Rumford	5/21	9/23

Massachusetts

City	Last Average* Frost Date	First Average Frost Date
Amherst	5/24	9/17
Birch Hill Dam	6/13	8/31
Boston	4/21	10/23
Haverhill	5/17	9/23
Hyannis	5/7	10/9
New Bedford	4/26	10/11

New Hampshire

City	Last Average* Frost Date	First Average Frost Date
Concord	6/6	9/8
Hanover	5/25	9/21
Keene	5/27	9/13
Lancaster	6/16	9/1
Mt. Washington	7/24	8/8
Nashua	5/20	9/22

New Jersey

City	Last Average* Frost Date	First Average Frost Date
Atlantic City	5/10	10/4
Newark	4/15	10/22
Newton	5/18	9/20
Pemberton	5/19	9/28
Seabrook Farms	4/23	10/14

New York

City	Last Average* Frost Date	First Average Frost Date
Albany	5/15	9/23
Buffalo	5/6	10/5
Elmira	5/22	9/19
Fredonia	5/14	10/8
Lake Placid	6/22	8/30
New York City	4/13	10/29
Rochester	5/12	9/29
Syracuse	5/8	9/29
Utica	5/17	9/24
Watertown	6/2	9/9

Rhode Island

City	Last Average* Frost Date	First Average Frost Date
Kingston	5/21	9/21
Providence	4/29	10/7

Vermont

City	Last Average* Frost Date	First Average Frost Date
Ball Mountain Lake	6/11	9/2
Burlington	5/20	9/23
Cavendish	6/12	9/7
Montpelier	5/26	9/13
Newport	5/28	9/16
Rutland	5/26	9/14
St. Johnsbury	5/30	9/17

* Please note: These are the last *average* dates, not the absolute last date for a frost. There's a 50 percent chance of a frost beyond this date. It's prudent to wait ten days to two weeks beyond the average spring date to plant warm-weather crops such as tomatoes, peppers, and melons.

CHAPTER 2

LOCATING & DESIGNING YOUR GARDEN

As any good retailer knows, the key to a successful business is location, location, location. This is also true of your garden. *Where* you plant your vegetables, herbs, berries, and tree fruits will have more to do with their success than nearly anything else you'll do to the garden when it's growing. Your garden needs the right light, water, water drainage, ease of access, and design to make it functional. But you obviously want it to look good too. Functionality and beauty are both important, and in my family there's always a healthy back and forth between the two. My wife, Wendy, leans more toward the aesthetics of a garden, while I'm more of a pragmatist. In our yard this works well, as we are always bouncing ideas off each other.

To get started with selecting a location and designing your garden, you need to recognize what you already have in your yard. I've moved a few times now over the past twenty-five years, so what I like to do when I move into a new place is to get a feel for the land and what's already there before I start digging and planting. I find putting that information down on paper to be helpful. On a piece of paper, sketch out the location of the permanent structures in your yard, such as the house, garage, barn, rock walls, utility boxes, fences, and walkways. Also, indicate the locations of trees, shrubs, and other existing landscape plants that you will work around. Mark on the design where the north, south, east, and west directions lie. Notice where overhead and underground power lines run. Don't worry about the sketch being to scale at this point. Next, make a list of the types of gardens and plants you want to install. Once you have a basic sketch of your yard, then you can start matching your plants to the proper location.

Sun in the Garden

The first, and most important, factor in locating your garden is the amount of sun your yard gets. Most vegetables, fruits, and herbs love sun, so when walking around your yard to decide where to grow what plants, look for places that get at least six hours of full sun a day. This can be tricky, especially if you live in a town or near some large trees. The sun's location on the horizon changes throughout the growing season. In April and early May, you might see lots of full-sun sites in your yard. This is mostly due to the absence of leaves on the trees. Once the leaves appear in May, you'll notice where the shadows are falling. Mark the shady places in May to see where you still have full sun. By June the sun is fully overhead, so that's when you'll get the longest days and most light in your yard. However, by August and September, although the days are still warm, the sun is tracking lower on the horizon (like it was in April), so locations that were in full sun in June, can be in part shade in August and September. This is especially true if you have a neighbor's house or garage nearby, or tall trees growing to your south that block the sun during the day. It's important to note where the shady places are in your yard in late summer and fall.

Knowing when and where you'll have full sun is important. Fruits that are trying to mature in August and September, such as apples, pears, melons, winter squash, and tomatoes, will have slower growth and be slower to ripen if they're getting fewer hours of light each day.

On that same piece of paper with the sketch of your house and yard, circle areas that get part sun or full sun in spring, summer, and fall. This will help you determine the best place to site your garden. I did exactly

this at an old house I used to live in. I moved there in early summer and spent the summer and fall watching the shadows in the yard. It was meditative and educational. I found that the place that received the most sun, most often, from July to October, was the front yard. So that's where I planted my vegetable garden, in full sun and in full sight of the neighbors. The pressure was on to keep it looking good, but the rewards were a healthy and productive garden.

You shouldn't get discouraged if your yard has many places that get part sun all summer but has few full-sun locations. Some vegetables are actually adapted to part sun and can still produce even if they don't get six hours of sun a day. Greens, such as lettuce, spinach, Swiss chard, kale, mustard, and mesclun mix, all can grow with only a few hours of direct sun a day. They may not be as productive as those growing in full sun, but you'll be getting something from your patch. Root crops, such as carrots, potatoes, beets, parsnips, and radishes, can grow with three to four hours of direct sun a day and still produce. Again, full sun is ideal, but part sun will work.

If you notice that in May, June, and July your garden has full sun, but come August and September it has only part sun, there is another technique you can use. Grow crops that need full sun, such as bush beans, in May.

By July they will be finished producing. Pull them out and then plant a crop, such as kale, that only needs part sun to mature. It will grow through late summer and fall when the garden area is shadier, but still will give you a good crop. I'll talk more about this technique, called succession planting, in chapter 5.

Part shade in midsummer can be beneficial if you're sowing vegetables in summer for a fall garden. Cool-loving vegetables such as lettuce or carrots will be more likely to germinate and grow, because the soil won't dry out or overheat as quickly as it would in full sun.

Locating the Garden

While finding a spot in your yard that has full sun most of the summer is one of the most important pieces of the puzzle in deciding where to plant, there are other factors too. Finding a spot that has well-drained soil is critical. I'll talk more about soil and water drainage in chapter 3, but if your potential garden spot is flooded part of the year, or the water drains very slowly, you could be setting yourself up for trouble by trying to grow in that

area. This is especially true of fruit trees, berry bushes, and perennial vegetables such as asparagus. They don't grow well in poorly drained soils, so you'll be fighting a losing battle each year.

Also, the old adage, "Out of sight, out of mind," is true with the garden. I am a garden consultant, and many of my customers want to plant a vegetable garden. When someone shows me a site and it's out back, behind a shed, garage, or bushes, I see a red flag, especially with a beginning gardener. If you're not seeing the garden multiple times a day by walking by it or looking at it through a window or off a deck, you're less likely to visit the garden. The surest sign of a healthy garden is a gardener's footprints in it. Locate your garden, raised beds, or containers close to a walkway, driveway, house door, or area where you're going to pass it regularly. That way, you can stop and, even for five minutes, pull a few weeds, pluck a ripe cherry tomato, squish a bug, or water a thirsty plant. I've found over the years that frequent visits to the garden are a more important indicator of a successful garden than almost any other factor.

If you're growing fruits, another factor you need to consider is late-spring frosts. There's nothing worse than growing peaches or apricots in your yard, seeing them bloom, and then watching helplessly as a spring frost kills the blossoms and eliminates the crop for that year. A way to avoid late-spring frost is to plant fruit trees on a slope so the colder air in spring settles in the lowlands away from your trees. Also, plant on an east- or north-facing slope so the trees will be slower to warm up and blossom in spring.

It's also a good idea to locate your garden near a water source. There's nothing more frustrating than dragging garden hoses across a yard to water your garden. If you get sophisticated, you can set up irrigation lines, but that's the next step, and I'll talk more about watering in chapter 5. It's easier to find a spot close to your house to place the garden, one where you can easily bring the hose over for a quick drink or good soak.

On a more serious note, if you have a pre-1980s house, there is a chance it might have been painted with lead-based paints. Also, if you suspect heavy metals or chemicals might have been dumped on your lawn area by previous owners, perform a soil test. See chapter 3 for more on possible soil contaminants.

Don't be discouraged if you do find your soil is contaminated. You can dig up and remove the soil in the garden area and add more topsoil and compost. Or you can seal the soil with a layer of landscape fabric or plastic, build a raised bed, and add more topsoil and compost. These methods will allow you to keep your soil healthy and avoid inadvertently eating tainted foods.

Different Garden Designs

Once you've found the best site for your garden, you need a design. Garden design can seem mysterious, but it's really just about your location, your plants, and matching the right plants to the right site.

With vegetables, fruits, and herbs, design is really about functionality and beauty. You want a design that allows you to move easily in the garden—to plant, weed, water, and harvest without disturbing other plants—and that is beautiful to look at too. Unlike a garden for perennial flowers, a garden for edibles needs to have spaces that allow you to access the plants regularly. The first step is to decide on the orientation of the garden. An east-west orientation is best, so the sun travels across the garden during the day and there is little shading. However, it really depends on your site. The key is to locate the garden in a convenient spot, with full sun, access to water, and easy access for you. Make the pathways wide enough so you can easily

walk down them. If you're using a garden cart, make sure the pathways are at least 3 feet wide; for a wheelbarrow, they can be narrower. I like to mulch my pathways early in the season with everything from cardboard to grass clippings. The mulch not only helps prevent weeds from growing and keeps the soil moist, but makes it clear to newbies what's a garden bed and what's a pathway.

Raised Beds

Now that you have the outline of your garden, it's time to decide how to plant it. For all but gardens in very sandy soil, raised beds are the answer. Raised beds are basically soil that has been raised up at least 8 inches tall. The beds should be no wider than 3 feet, because if they are any wider than that, you'll have to step on the bed to work in its center. That's the beauty of raised beds. You don't step on them and compact the soil. This allows good root penetration into the beds. Raised beds are perfect for root crops such as carrots and beets, but are an advantage for any crops that you grow. Also, raised beds warm up and drain water faster in spring, allowing you to garden in the beds sooner. This is particularly important if you have clay soil. You can concentrate your weeding, watering, and fertilizing in a smaller area in the raised beds, permitting you to grow plants closer together with less work.

There are two basic types of raised beds: temporary and permanent. Temporary raised beds are ones you build in spring by mounding up the soil from pathway areas onto 3-foot-wide rows, circles, or other shapes. The advantage of temporary raised beds is that you can make them any shape you like each spring, based on your whimsy. Some years I'm feeling curvy, so I make S-shaped beds, round beds, and horseshoe-shaped beds. One year I made a heart-shaped bed filled with red beets. How romantic! Other years I'm in a linear mood and go with the traditional squares and rectangles. The shapes don't really matter as long as they're at least 8 inches tall and no more than 3 feet wide. By the end of summer, the beds have naturally flattened out. The downside of temporary raised beds is you have to recreate them each spring.

Permanent raised beds have some type of solid structure holding the beds in shape. Usually it's rot-resistant woods such as cedar or hemlock. Don't use pressure-treated woods in a raised bed, because chemicals in the wood could leak into the soil. But you can use cinder blocks, bricks, stones, or plastic wood. The beauty of this system is that, once installed, it can last for years. All you'll need to do in spring is add compost to fill in where any settling has occurred in winter. However, once the beds are in place, that is the design you have forever. For a beginning gardener, this is a good approach because less maintenance is required. Plus, permanent raised beds keep weeds, kids, and some animals out more easily. It's also clear where the garden and pathway are.

Vertical Gardening

If you have a small garden area, a great way to save space is to design your garden to grow vertically. Vertical gardening takes advantage of a plant's natural desire to grow up. You can save space and plant more than you can imagine by gardening vertically. This is obviously important for urban gardeners or those gardening with containers in cities. But even a gardener with plenty of room will benefit from vertical gardening. Growing plants up takes less room, meaning you don't need as big a garden to be productive. It also keeps the fruits cleaner since they aren't on the ground. It's a great way to thwart some animals that can't reach the high fruits.

The first step is to select vertical-growing vegetables such as peas, pole beans, and cucumbers. If you want to get daring, you can even try growing melons and some summer squash vertically. You'll need a structure to support your plants. For peas, a simple chicken wire fence is easy to construct and maintain (they can also be grown along a chain-link fence). Beans just need something for their tendrils (curlicues) to grab hold of. For pole beans, use single poles or make a tepee out of three to five poles and let the pole beans twine around them. I even used an old basketball pole for beans once. The only problem was that they grew so tall I needed a ladder to pick them! That's a good thing to keep in mind when constructing poles: keep them reachable.

Cucumbers like a 45-degree wooden or metal trellis to trail along. Melons and some summer squash grow well on sturdy fences such as chain-link. The fruits of these will need support. See more about trellising these vegetables in the individual sections on vegetables in chapter 8.

Container Gardening

If you're really tight on space, there are always containers. Container gardening used to be done mostly in clay or plastic pots. However, these materials broke easily and needed constant vigilance for watering. With the new self-watering containers, container gardening has come of age. You can now grow herbs, vegetables, and fruits in a window box, hanging basket, or in a pot on the ground without having to be a slave to watering. Some containers keep plants wet and happy for five days, depending on the weather conditions.

Container gardening is not just for those with little space. A recent National Gardening Association survey showed that almost one-half of the vegetable gardeners in the United States also grow edibles in containers. I like to incorporate some containers in my gardens, even if I have the space for growing everything in the ground. Containers offer some special advantages. They warm up the soil faster in spring, making them perfect for heat-loving veggies such as peppers and tomatoes. Containers have potting soil and compost as their growing medium, so if soilborne diseases are attacking the eggplants growing in your beds, you can grow some in containers. They'll appreciate the heat and clean soil. If slugs are noshing on the lettuce in your beds, try growing some lettuce in containers and protecting the containers by wrapping them with copper wire. See the pest control section for more on this trick. I like the look of containers too. They are artistic and add some color and beauty to my garden.

Of course, containers do require you to purchase potting soil and perhaps some compost. Ideally, each year you'll replace the soil to avoid insect and disease populations building up in the container. For large containers I've gotten away with taking the top third of soil off and replacing just that much. That's probably where most of the bad guys will be hiding anyway. You can also save on potting soil by placing empty water or soda bottles in the bottom third of a large container. Since most plant roots grow only about 12 inches into the container soil, the bottom area doesn't need to be soil, but can be lightweight empty bottles. It makes the container lighter and easier to move and keeps money in your wallet.

Fruits can also be grown in containers. Try growing strawberries in hanging baskets or strawberry pots. Half-high blueberries can fit nicely in containers. Dwarf peaches or apples can also be container grown. I even grow tropical plants like figs in containers. The key to growing fruits in containers is protecting them in winter. Place a container of fruits in a garage, basement, or shed in winter to prevent the soil from freezing too hard and killing the roots. In winter my fig tree lives in the basement, where the temperature stays above 20°F. When the longer days of spring arrive, I move it outside and it starts growing again.

If you're using plastic containers, there's no need to protect them in winter. They can withstand the freezing and thawing of our climate. However, ceramic or clay pots should be emptied of soil or moved into a freeze-free area. They can crack if left outside in winter filled with soil. I'll talk more about care of container plants in chapter 5.

Edible Landscaping
Edible landscaping is one of my favorite gardening styles, and it's becoming more popular across the country. In the simplest terms, edible landscaping

is replacing purely ornamental plants in your yard with attractive, edible ones. Gardeners are turning to edible landscaping to grow fruits, vegetables, and herbs in their yard without sacrificing the beauty of their landscape.

The simplest way to start in an existing yard is to replace an ornamental shrub with an edible one. Some gardeners will plant the wrong plant in the wrong location and it will outgrow the space allotted and become an eyesore, blocking windows, encroaching on other plants, and not looking pretty. Yank it out and replace it with an attractive edible. Here are some ideas.

Replace a burning bush with a blueberry. The blueberry will grow 4 to 6 feet tall, depending on the variety, and produce white flowers in spring, blue fruits in summer, and brilliant red foliage in fall. It's perfect! Pull down that overgrown Virginia creeper on the fence and grow grapes. You can get a good crop in a small area with proper pruning. Pull out that overgrown crabapple and replace it with a dwarf 'Northstar' cherry. One tree is all you need to produce enough sour cherries for pies. It grows 8 feet tall and has pretty flowers in spring. There are many other examples. For more plant ideas, check out my edible landscaping newsletter at www.garden.org/ ediblelandscaping.

You can also mix and match attractive herbs and vegetables in the flower garden. 'Black Pearl' pepper has attractive dark foliage and purple fruits. 'Burgundy' okra has gorgeous hibiscus-like flowers on red stems and leaves. 'Siam Queen' Thai basil has purple-veined leaves with purple flower spikes. It's a looker in any garden. Not only will adding these edibles to your flowers and shrubs add beauty and productivity to your landscape, but it will confuse the pests. Animals and insects will be less likely to find your edible wonders when they are mixed in with other plants.

Hedges

Another way of maximizing space in your edible garden without sacrificing lawn or flower garden space is to use your edible plants as hedges. Berry bushes, such as raspberries, blackberries, and gooseberries, make excellent edible hedges along a property line, the edge of a wooded area, or a fence. These plants will grow and fruit in part sun, provide a visual block in summer, and be a barrier for wildlife, dogs, and neighbors. The thorns on these berry bushes will even deter deer and other large animals from crossing into your yard for lunch. You can enjoy the fruits all summer and the thorny branches will provide a barrier even in winter. Just remember the brambles will spread, so keep them in bounds by mowing around the patch periodically.

Another great hedge plant is asparagus. I remember seeing a row of asparagus placed along a property line. The owners harvested the spears in

spring for six weeks and then let the spears grow into 6-foot-tall ferns. They placed two posts on either end of the row and strung wire between them to help keep the ferns upright. The effect was stunning in summer. The ferns blocked the view of the neighbor's yard and provided privacy for the back deck while looking gorgeous. In fall, the owners cut it down. It didn't block any views in winter, but the summer screening was perfect.

Fruit Orchards

If you want to grow tree fruits, you certainly can plant them in your lawn as part of the overall design of your yard or you can create your own mini fruit orchard. You don't need acres of land to grow a small orchard. Many dwarf trees grow only about 10 feet tall, so you can create a five- to ten-tree orchard in about 1,000 square feet. If you're cramped for space, look for self-pollinating varieties so you only need one tree to get a crop. Locate your orchard on sloping land to avoid damage from spring frosts and away from other trees so it will be easier to protect from squirrels and other critters.

CHAPTER 3

BUILDING GREAT SOIL

Your soil is the soul of your garden. If you treat it well, feed it properly, and care for it, it will reward you with healthy, lush-growing vegetables, herbs, and fruits that are as productive as they are attractive. A healthy soil keeps plants healthy, and a healthy plant is less likely to be attacked by insects or diseases. The laws of nature dictate that weak plants are more likely to be attacked by and succumb to pests.

I learned this lesson the hard way when I was younger. In college, I had a community garden and was so excited about planting that I just dug beds and popped the plants and seeds into the soil. Everything came up, but nothing really thrived. I watched other community gardeners with more experience and saw they were adding bags of compost to each bed before planting. We all planted at the same time with similar plants, but theirs were bigger, lusher, greener, and ultimately more productive. From then on, I've been building my soil before I even plant. In fact, my wife and I recently moved to a new house and instead of planting a garden the first summer, we planted cover crops and added cow manure to build the beds. I'll talk more about these techniques later, but the idea is to build the soil first, and all good things will follow.

Sand   Silt Loam   Clay Soil

Soil Structure

Before you get going on building your soil, you have to understand what your soil is. First of all, promise me you won't call it "dirt." Dirt is something that gets under your couch. Your garden has soil. Soil is a living entity, made not only of various inorganic particles, but also of organic matter and microbes. It's this whole package that makes for a healthy soil and, therefore, healthy plants.

But first you need to know the structure of your soil. What are its building blocks? Your soil is made of different-sized particles called sand, silt, and clay. Rarely will your soil be composed of only one type of particle. Usually it's a mix with one type dominating. Each particle type has some advantages and disadvantages.

Sand has the largest-sized particles. It's great because the particles allow air and water to move freely through the soil. Accordingly, it's described as a well-aerated soil. Sand warms up fast in spring and drains water well. However, it has the least amount of nutrients of any particle size, so it usually needs additions of fertilizer and organic matter to be most productive. However, plants with fine root systems, such as blueberries, or plants that need to send their roots deep into the soil, like carrots, grow well in this type of soil.

Clay is the opposite extreme. The particle size is small, so water and air don't flow freely through clay. It's what we call a heavy soil. When you turn it over, it sticks together, making clods of soil. Clay is great for making bricks, but a little tough to work into a loose, friable garden soil. However, clay holds water and nutrients well, so it's a fertile soil. If you can add enough organic matter to loosen the soil, you can grow a productive garden. Crops that need lots of nutrients can grow well in predominantly clay soils if they are loosened with regular additions of organic matter. Root crops and fine-rooted crops like blueberries have a hard time growing in heavy clay soil.

Silt soil is between sand and clay for all these characteristics. It can hold some water and allows air to move freely in the soil, and it has good nutrient levels. If you've been down by a river, often the banks are loaded with silt soil. Some of the best farmlands in the Northeast are along rivers where silt soil is regularly deposited by seasonal floods.

To determine the type of soil you have, dig a few holes, give the soil a squeeze, and feel it. Sandy soil will feel gritty between your fingers. Clay soil will feel silky smooth. If you're really into it, do a jar test to determine what percentage of sand, silt, and clay you have. Put 1 inch of dry soil in a quart-sized glass jar. Fill the jar two-thirds full with water and add a tablespoon of salt. Cover, shake well, and let the contents settle. The sand in your soil will settle to the bottom of the jar in a few minutes. Measure that layer's depth. Silt will take four to five hours to settle. You'll see the difference in particle size and color. Measure that layer and then subtract to calculate the clay depth. For example, if your sand layer is one-third inch thick, then you have 33 percent sand in your soil. If your silt layer is one-tenth inch thick, then you have 10% silt and the rest (57%) is clay. It's a quick way to know your soil and the dominant characteristics before you get started gardening.

pH

While pH may sound like a rapper DJ's name, it's actually the measure of the alkalinity and acidity of your soil. It's important because your plants will have a difficult time absorbing certain nutrients if the soil pH isn't at the right level for that plant. Most soils in the Northeast tend toward an acidic pH because of all our rainfall. However, there are pockets of alkaline soil that need different attention.

Put in simple terms, the pH is measured on a scale of 1 (highly acid) to 14 (highly alkaline). Seven is considered a neutral pH. Most vegetables, fruits, and herbs grow best with a pH between 6.5 and 7.2. However, some plants, such as blueberries, need a much lower pH (5.0) to thrive. In order to adjust your pH, first do a soil test. You can use a store-bought kit or send a soil sample away to your County Extension service or a private lab for testing. The store-bought kits range from simple and inexpensive to junior science kits. I like to send my soil for a lab test. The basic test gives you pH, organic matter levels, and basic nutrient levels from low to high. It's a good way to get a snapshot view of your garden soil's health.

Most lab soil tests will not only give you the pH value, but also provide recommendations on what to add to the soil to bring that pH to the proper level for the crops you're growing. To raise the pH, add lime. To lower it, add sulfur. Your soil test will have recommendations for the amounts to add.

Organic Matter
Regardless of the soil you have and its pH, organic matter is its savior. Organic matter breaks down into humus, which helps retain and drain water, allows air to move freely, and allows nutrients to be taken up into the plant more efficiently. Organic matter also buffers the pH, making an acidic soil a little more alkaline and an alkaline soil a little more acidic. It's your cornerstone for building great soil.

But building great soil doesn't happen overnight. It's like raising a child. The keys to success are patience and consistency. This means patiently feeding the soil each year and being consistent in what you add. While adding lime or sulfur to raise or lower the pH (soil acidity level) and adding nutrients to get a properly balanced soil are important, adding organic matter is essential.

If there were one mantra to repeat each year to keep your soil healthy, it would be, "Add organic matter." Organic matter is basically any plant material that was once alive. This could be untreated grass clippings, hay, straw, bark mulch, old weeds, dead leaves, or old plants. This organic matter ideally is added the season before planting, so it has a chance to break down before you plant. Forms of organic matter that break down slowly and are high in carbon, such as hay, straw, or bark, may be harmful to plants in the short run. The microbes that break down carbon-based matter like bark need nitrogen to do so, and they'll take it from the soil if needed. This is easily avoided by adding nitrogen fertilizer to the high-carbon-content material. Either incorporate your organic matter into the soil months before planting or build a compost pile and let it break down before adding it to the soil.

Not all organic matter is created equal. It's important to know the advantages and disadvantages of each type of organic matter. Here's a rundown.

➢ **Grass Clippings:** While it's generally better to leave your grass clippings on the lawn to feed your grass, if you do collect them, use the clippings in the garden. Fresh grass clippings are loaded with nitrogen fertilizer and are quick to break down in the soil. Nitrogen is essential for leafy plant growth. It's important to add untreated grass clippings to your garden. Never collect and use grass clippings that have been treated with pesticides. These may harm your plants. Also, if a landscaper offers you grass clippings, again, make sure you know the source. Grass clippings can be used as a mulch on the soil or worked into the garden. Dried grass clippings have lower levels of nitrogen than fresh clippings, but are still a good source of organic matter.

➢ **Compost:** Compost is actually organic matter that's already broken down. It's in a readily available form for your plants to use. All plant- or animal-based material eventually decomposes, or turns into compost. A little later on, I'll talk about how to make your own compost. You can add compost directly to gardens and you won't have to wait to plant.

- **Straw, Hay, and Sea Grass:** You see farmers baling fields all summer long. Straw is the remaining stems of grains like wheat, oats, or rye after threshing, and it is usually cut early in summer before any grass or weeds can go to seed. Therefore, straw is usually weed-free and a great material to use in your garden as a mulch or organic amendment. Hay is cut from a field later in the season, when weeds have set seed. Although still a great source of organic matter, it does have weed seeds, which will sprout in your garden next year. Both straw and hay are slow to break down in the soil. Sea grass is collected along the coast and makes great additions to the garden. You need to wash it or let it sit so the salts will be removed before adding it to your soil.
- **Leaves:** Dead dried leaves are abundant in fall in the Northeast. They make a good addition to the garden as is. Simply rake them into the garden and till them under. Most of them will break down and decompose by spring, adding organic matter and some nutrients to your soil. If you have too many for the garden, or don't want to till them in this fall, pile up your leaves and let them rot naturally. It may take a few years, but eventually they will turn into compost or "leaf mold" that can be added to the garden.
- **Bark Mulch:** Bark mulch, such as pine, hemlock, and cedar, is plentiful in garden centers, where it is sold as mulch. It can also help the soil by adding organic matter, but the big downside of bark is it takes a long time to break down and release its nutrients. It's probably best used as a mulch around fruit trees and berry bushes, where over time it breaks down into rich compost.
- **Old Weeds and Plants:** When you're cleaning up your garden, you may be tempted simply to till or turn under weeds and old plants to add them as organic matter. While they do add organic matter to the soil, you have to use them carefully. If weeds have flowers or have gone to seed, they will spread their seed in the garden. Some weeds, such as quack grass, are spread by root pieces, so they should always be removed from the garden. If your garden plants had insects or diseases on them, they should be removed and not turned under. You'll just be adding more problems to your soil for next year.
- **Peat Moss:** Mined from peat bogs mostly in Canada, this form of organic matter consists of compressed dead plants that have been preserved for thousands of years in the ground. While high in organic matter, peat moss can also acidify the soil, so it should be used carefully on plants that don't like acidic soil. I mostly use it when planting fruit trees and berry bushes.

➤ **Green Manures and Cover Crops:** While most people are familiar with animal manures (I'll talk about those later), green manures are another way to increase your organic matter content. Green manures are crops grown specifically to be turned into the soil while they are still green and actively growing. Buckwheat, oats, vetch, and annual ryegrass are all examples of green manure crops that grow well in the Northeast. Green manures are great for the beginning gardener who isn't in a hurry to plant. If you can spend the first year building the soil's organic matter by growing green manures, you'll be rewarded with a healthier garden the next year. However, you do have to sacrifice your garden or part of your garden each year to keep growing and adding green manures. A solution is to grow a cover crop in fall to overwinter and be tilled under in spring. Some winter-hardy cover crops for the Northeast include winter wheat, winter rye, and oats. Sown in the fall, they grow until winter's cold stalls their growth. They then resume growing in spring. Tilling this crop under a month or so before planting allows it to break down so you can plant.

Why is organic matter important? Organic matter eventually breaks down into humus. Humus is just organic matter in its final state. Most finished composts are loaded with humus, which has many benefits for garden soil.

Humus in clay soils rich in organic matter drain water better. Humus in sandy soils rich in organic matter hold water better. For either type of soil, the organic matter content makes nutrients more readily available to plants. Organic matter also feeds the microorganisms in the soil. These microbes create a healthy balance in the soil so "bad" microbes can't dominate and harm the plants. For most garden soils in the Northeast, 5 to 10 percent organic matter content, depending on a soil test, is sufficient to keep the garden healthy.

Animal Manure

Another form of organic matter that adds fertility to your soil is animal manure. Think of animal manure as organic matter that's already been processed. Depending on the animal, sometimes this is good and sometimes not. Animal manure has the benefit of having higher nutrient levels than straight organic matter, so it can be used to boost the fertility of your soil. While animal manure's fertilizer numbers aren't necessarily high, it can help increase the soil's organic matter and nutrients at the same time. Don't just think of farm animals when you think of animal manure. Birds, bats, earthworms, and even crickets are farmed for their manure. It's that valuable. Like other forms of organic matter, decomposed bagged or bulk manures are best used directly on the garden. Most raw manures are mixed with bedding materials such as sawdust and hay, which take lots of time to break down. They're best applied the fall before planting or added to a compost pile. Here are some common forms of manures to look for.

- **Cow:** Dairy cows are probably one of the best forms of manure because these animals have four stomachs. During digestion, the hay and grass they eat have a chance to really break down and many of the weed seeds they consume are killed. Of course, farmers know this too and will often spread their own dairy manure on their fields.
- **Horse:** This is probably one of the easiest available forms of animal manure in the Northeast. There are lots of horse farms in our area and, as anyone who has worked at a horse stable will attest, there's lots of manure too. Unfortunately, horses only digest one-third of the material they eat, so their manure is usually loaded with weed seeds. However, if you compost it well, it's still useful in the garden.
- **Chicken and Bird:** Chicken and bird manures are high in nitrogen and concentrated. This is good and bad. It's good because of the nutrients this manure can add to plants. It's bad because, unless it's

decomposed, chicken manure is too "hot" for young seedlings and can burn the roots.

➤ **Sheep and Goat:** Sheep and goat manures are drier and don't have as much odor as other manures and are a rich source of nitrogen and potassium nutrients. They do have weed seeds, though.

➤ **Exotic Manures:** If you look in many garden centers in our region, you'll be amazed at the variety of manures available. You could become a connoisseur of manure. Bat manure (or guano), cricket crap (yes, that's what it's called), and worm castings (made from earthworm poop), all can be used to build up your soil. However, they're best used as fertilizer applied directly to soil, instead of as a way to build organic matter. After all, you'll need lots of worms to make enough poop to make a difference. If you're near a zoo, look for "Zoopoo" products. These are bagged manures from zoo animals that can be used in your garden. Usually they're decomposed material that's ready to use in the garden. Don't worry about your garden growing giraffes and elephants.

Making Compost

While adding organic matter in the form of animal manure or plant materials is critical to your garden's success, what you're really after is the finished product, compost. You can certainly buy bags of finished compost and many garden centers now sell it in bulk. Just pull in and load up the truck. You'll be getting a product that has been monitored by professionals, so it should be good quality. But instead of buying compost, why not make it yourself? Remember that everything rots, so you too can become a compost-making machine, producing this black gold for your garden. Here's how to set up your own compost pile in your yard.

1. **Get a bin:** You can purchase a compost bin or a tumbler, or make your own. The goal is to have a container that's no more than 5 feet tall, wide, and deep.

2. **Choose a spot:** Find a naturally well-drained spot in a shady area for composting. It should be someplace out of the way, where the pile won't get too soggy.

3. **Get some brown stuff:** To make compost, you need layers of brown organic materials (high-carbon material) such as dried grass clippings, dead leaves, hay, straw, or old plants. Make a 4- to 6-inch layer of it on the bottom of your compost bin.

4. **Get some green stuff:** The next layer is green organic material (high in nitrogen) such as fresh grass clippings, kitchen veggie scraps, or

fresh leaves. Make a 2- to 4-inch layer of green material on top of the brown.

5. **Keep layering:** Keep making layers of brown stuff and green stuff, just like a lasagna, until you reach the top of the bin. Water each layer as you go. If the layers don't hold together well, consider adding a thin layer of soil to each.

6. **Cover it up:** Cover your pile so it doesn't get too wet from rains or tempt animals to come dig.

Keep the pile evenly moist, but not too wet. Don't overwater. If the pile starts smelling like ammonia, it's probably too wet. Turn it to let it dry out. If it doesn't heat up, there's probably not enough green stuff. Add some organic fertilizer as a starter material to get it going.

After a few weeks, the pile should heat up. You will know because it will begin steaming. Once it cools down, or stops steaming, turn the pile by moving the outside layer into the center and the center to the outside of the pile. Water and it should reheat. Keep repeating this process until it doesn't heat up again. Once your compost is brown and crumbly and smells like soil, it's done. Pop it into the garden.

Water Drainage

Now that you have a handle on your soil's structure and pH and understand the importance of organic matter, let's talk water. Specifically, water drainage. If your soil drains water poorly or, worse yet, becomes flooded during heavy rains, then your plants will suffer. Short of water lettuce (really, it's just an ornamental), there aren't many vegetables, fruits, or herbs that will grow well in a soggy soil.

Make sure your garden is in a location with well-drained soil. What does that mean? Well-drained soil means that when it rains, the water quickly moves out of the upper levels of soil so your plant roots aren't sitting in water for hours or days. Plant roots need water, certainly, but they also need air to survive. This is especially true with long-lived crops such as fruits.

I had a raspberry patch once. One end of the patch produced great berries and the other, slowly over a period of a few years, declined and produced few berries. I treated both sides with the same fertilizers and care. However, I noticed each spring that the side that did poorly was seasonally flooded for a few weeks, while the other side wasn't. That flooding slowly killed the roots and eventually the plants declined. I learned my lesson: be sure the soil is well drained, especially for perennial plants like raspberries, fruit trees, and vegetables such as asparagus, which will be growing in the same spot for years to come.

To calculate if you have poor water drainage, dig a 1-foot-diameter hole, 1 foot deep in the soil. Cover it with plastic to let it dry out. Fill it with water. If it takes longer than four hours for the water to drain completely, then you should look for another location to plant. Another option is to build a raised bed on that site (see chapter 2).

To Till or Not to Till

How you treat your soil can affect its health as much as what you add to it. There's a raging debate in the home gardening world about the topic of tilling. Tilling is using a shovel or a motorized rototiller to turn over your soil. Traditionally this is done in spring a few weeks before you're ready to plant. I must admit, I like the look of a freshly tilled garden. It's smooth, all the soil clods are broken up, and the soil is loose and easy to plant. It's so

fluffy looking I could take a nap in it. Some gardeners have taken the idea of tilling even further. They use their rototiller to weed between rows in summer, till under dead plants or rows of vegetables that are past their peak, and till under the whole garden in fall. While this type of gardening is certainly convenient and helps incorporate that essential organic matter, it has its disadvantages.

When you till or turn over the soil, you are introducing oxygen into the soil. Oxygen feeds the microbes in it, which in turn eat your organic matter. You'll remember I said that adding organic matter should be your mantra. Well, tilling works against that endeavor by encouraging the microbes in the soil to decompose the organic matter quickly. Tilling puts you in a cycle of always having to add large amounts of organic matter each year because the microbes are eating it up. Another problem is weed seeds. Tilling brings dormant weed seeds to the soil surface where they can germinate and grow. This creates an endless cycle of tilling and weeding.

The solution is the no-till gardening method. With no-till, you don't turn under the soil each year. Instead, you add compost to the tops of beds, lightly turn it in, and plant. The idea is that oxygen encouraged the microbes to eat the organic matter faster, causing it to decay quicker. Earthworms and other microbes can create air and water passages by their activity. Also, you're not bringing weed seeds to the soil surface, so fewer weeds grow. The result is a fertile garden soil without having to work as hard.

When I first started gardening I was tiller, but now I'm a no-tiller. I've found that once your soil has a good amount of organic matter and nutrients in it, no-tilling is the way to go. When you're just starting out, certainly till in organic matter, lime, and nutrients based on your soil test. This is a good idea even for raised beds. But after a year or so, once the garden seems to be growing well, transition to no-tilling. It will lead to less work, more production, and a happier gardener.

Soil Contaminants

Another soil consideration is contaminants that might be there. This is especially true if you're gardening near an old house or in a yard where chemicals or car materials could potentially have been dumped on the soil. Petrochemicals and lead are two possible contaminants. Lead-based paints were phased out in the 1970s, but if you have a house older than that, there is a possibility that your soil is contaminated with lead paint chips. Consuming lead with your vegetables can lead to many health problems, especially in children. If you suspect you might have lead in your soil, take a soil sample to your state health department for a test.

Other heavy metals may be in your soil from old tires, cars, or chemical spills. Again, a soil test will help you determine if these chemicals are present. If you have petrochemical-contaminated soils, you may either have to dig and replace the soil in the garden area or seal the soil with plastic and bring in new soil to build a bed on top of it. Either way, you want to limit your plants' exposure to this contaminated soil.

CHAPTER 4

GROWING FROM SEEDS & PLANTS

After doing all the heavy lifting of locating the garden, working up a design, and building your soil, now the real fun begins. It's planting time! But before you go dropping a wad of cash at the local garden center, one key question you need to answer for yourself is, are you a seeder or a transplanter?

With the advent of new technologies, you can purchase almost any vegetable or herb as a transplant at the local garden center or through the mail in spring. There are still a few exceptions, such as carrots and beets, but even these crops can be sown as seeds directly in the garden, so no advance work is necessary. Having a wide range of transplants available has made beginning edible gardeners happy. No longer do they have to think about starting seeds indoors at home weeks before planting in order to have a garden. It can be as simple as going to the garden center on Saturday and planting on Sunday. But as anything in life, there are pluses and minuses to transplanting your plants into the garden as opposed to growing them from seed. Let's look at both methods.

Seeding

Certainly, growing from seed is the most traditional way to grow. There's something satisfying about getting seed catalogs in the mail in December, leafing through them and making lists in January, and receiving the packets in your mailbox a few weeks later. It's the same thrill you get from pawing through seed racks in spring at local garden centers, looking for a new variety. For a Northeast gardener it's a way to live vicariously while the snow is still blowing outside. Beyond the emotional component, there are practical advantages to buying and sowing seeds. As I mentioned earlier, some crops, such as carrots, radishes, and beets, just don't grow well if they're transplanted, so you need to sow seeds outdoors directly in the ground. Others, such as beans, are just easier to plant as seeds in the ground. Also, you'll be able to

get a wider variety of almost any vegetable or herb if you buy seed packets rather than relying on what's available in garden centers. For a beginner this may not be important, but once you get hooked, you'll want to try some of those black tomatoes or self-pollinating zucchini. Also, if you're growing a big garden, it's cheaper to grow plants from seed. One packet of lettuce seeds may cost $4 but can yield forty heads of lettuce, while a pack of just four lettuce plants may be as expensive.

The downside of growing plants from seed is the time and effort that's needed to start them indoors in winter in our climate. Some vegetables have to be planted weeks in advance of spring. Tomatoes, peppers, leeks, onions, and eggplants must be started indoors weeks before being planted outdoors in order to grow and mature before fall. We just don't have enough time in our climate to pop tomato seeds in the ground in May and get much of a yield by September. Some vegetables, such as basil, beans, broccoli, cabbage, lettuce, cucumbers, and squash, don't need to be started indoors beforehand, but you'll get a jump on the season if you do. You can sow these seeds directly in the soil in May, but it will take longer for them to mature.

If you need to start seeds indoors, you'll need seed-starting equipment such as trays, lights, and seed-starting soil. The investment of time and money may be more than beginning gardeners want to handle at this stage. That's why many of these types of plants are better purchased as transplants. However, if you're up for the challenge, here's what to do.

To start seeds indoors, calculate six weeks before your *last* frost date. (See the table on page 14 for average last and first frost dates in your area.) This is always one of the hardest tasks for the eager beginning gardener. In Vermont there's a tradition of sowing tomatoes on town meeting day (the first weekend in March). Unfortunately, this means your seedlings would be ready to go in the ground in mid-April. Vermont often still has snowstorms in mid-April, so that's obviously way too early. To determine the right day to sow seeds, count backward from the last frost date. For example, if that date in your area is May 15, then you should start tomato seeds in pots or trays on April 1. Your plants will thus be large enough to handle the outdoor conditions when transplanted, but not be so overgrown that they will be hard to keep healthy indoors.

Sow seeds in individual pots or seedling trays (flat plastic trays with a lip around the edge) filled with moistened seed-starting mix. Seed-starting soil mix is very lightweight, making it easier for seeds to germinate and grow. Sow a few seeds in each pot or in rows in a tray. Cover the pots and trays with black plastic and place them in a warm spot out of direct sunlight. Check them every few days and as soon as you see some seeds germinating, remove the plastic cover and bring the seedlings into the light. While the traditional way to grow seedlings indoors is on a sunny windowsill, there's just not enough light duration or intensity for them to grow well there. The Northeast is known for stretches of cloudy days, and seedlings grown on a windowsill would reach for the light and get "leggy." Leggy transplants don't grow as well as stocky ones. It's better to have a light setup with a timer that provides your seedlings with artificial lights for fourteen hours a day. Place the lights just a few inches above the seedlings and move them up as the seedlings grow. Keep the plants well watered and fertilize them occasionally with a weak solution of worm poop or fish emulsion. Thin the seedlings to one per pot once their true leaves (second set of leaves) form. Thin the trays to the proper spacing for that vegetable, and transplant into individual pots once the true leaves form. Once the seedling's height is three times the pot diameter, transplant into a larger pot. Keep the seedlings growing until it's time to harden off your transplants before planting. We'll talk about that technique shortly.

Transplanting

When I was younger, if I went to the garden center in spring to look for vegetable transplants for my garden, I would probably find tomatoes, peppers, eggplants, and maybe some lettuce. Now a recent visit to my local garden center revealed everything from fennel to pumpkins, all started as seedlings and available for purchase. This is great, especially for the small-scale, beginning gardener. Many times you'll only need a few of each type of plant to fit in your garden. You can buy individual tomato plants or a six-pack (six plants in a container), each separated with its own rootball. They may be more expensive than a packet of seeds, but since you'll only need a few, it makes a lot more sense. You can always go shopping with a gardening friend and buy together. If you want only three pepper plants, buy a six-pack and split it. I always like to have a few extra of each type of transplant on hand, too, in case the weather, insects, or animals kill a few of them. Some transplants come in biodegradable pots, making them even easier to plant. These pots are made out of coir (coconut husk fiber), peat moss, or manure. Unlike plastic pots, from which you have to gently remove a plant before planting, biodegradable pots allow you simply to plant the pot, with the plant inside it, in the garden. I like to break up a biodegradable pot gently with my fingers before planting to help the roots break out of the pot and into the soil.

When purchasing transplants at a local garden center, look for short, stocky plants that preferably are not in flower. The color should be a healthy green all the way down to the bottom leaves. Pull a seedling out of its pot (without the staff watching you) and check its roots. They should be white, filling the container but not winding around the pot.

Hardening Off

Once you get your bounty home, don't just pop your plants in the garden. Although many greenhouses will expose their transplants to outdoor conditions (wind, rain, sun), you still need to "harden off" your plants before planting so they don't get transplant shock and die. This is especially true for seedlings you've grown at home. Hardening off plants is a way to get them used to the elements. Plants, like people, need to adjust to outdoor temperatures and conditions. To harden off your plants (ones that you started from seed indoors or store-bought ones), set your transplants outdoors on the first day in a partly shaded area for just an hour or two. A cloudy day with little wind is ideal. Then bring them indoors. The next day, extend the amount of time outside by another hour or so and then bring them in. Keep doing this each day, extending the amount of time outdoors, for about seven days, until your transplants are staying outside all night. Then they're ready to face the big world on their own.

Planting

Whether you'll be sowing seeds or transplanting, here are the basic steps for planting your vegetable garden.

1. Add a few inches of compost to the planting area and work it into the soil.
2. On the proper day for planting that vegetable or herb based on your last frost date, loosen the soil in the planting bed or row with a hoe or shovel to a depth of at least 6 inches. Be sure the soil is dry enough to work (see chapter 3).
3. Smooth the soil and create rows for seeds with your trowel. Plant the seeds at the proper depth and spacing as indicated on the seed packet. See chapter 8 for more information on proper spacing for each vegetable.
4. Cover the seeds with soil.
5. For transplants, dig a small hole in the bed or row with your trowel.
6. Remove the plastic pot (or break up the biodegradable pot), and plant the seedling at the same depth as it was in the pot. The exception is tomatoes, which should be planted deeper.
7. Press the soil around the roots while filling the hole.
8. Water the seeds and transplants well. Be careful not to water the seeds (especially small seeds like carrots) heavily or they might wash away.

To plant berry bushes or fruit trees, first, find the correct location in your yard to plant (see chapter 2). Dig a hole as deep as the rootball and twice as wide. Place the shrub or tree in the hole and remove the plastic container or wrap. Water as you fill the soil back into the hole. This will remove any air pockets. Tamp the soil down and create a moat around the drip line of the shrub or tree (about 2 feet away from the trunk). The moat will make is easier to concentrate the watering right where the roots are.

CHAPTER 5

MAINTAINING THE GARDEN

Spring in the vegetable garden is like a new marriage. You're excited about being together, spend extra time with each other, and go the extra yard to make sure everything is just perfect. There's plenty of enthusiasm and endless pleasure in being together. Then comes summer in a marriage and the garden. Other parts of your life start calling. There's less time and energy available, and some parts of your relationship don't get the attention they deserve. If you are married, you know it's a long haul, and to keep things alive and fresh, you need to work at it. If you are new to the vegetable garden, it's the same deal. Don't be lulled to sleep in summer. Your garden needs you to stay involved to make sure all your work of soil building, planning, and planting doesn't go to waste. A healthy marriage needs a time and energy commitment and so does your garden.

But like a strong marriage, maintaining your garden doesn't have to be a chore; it can be very enjoyable. It's all about knowing what to look out for, what to do, and when to do it.

While pests are probably the first concern that comes to mind, they're so important I'll discuss them in another chapter. In this chapter, I'll talk about those everyday chores that can make or break a garden, such as thinning, succession planting, staking, weeding, watering, and fertilizing.

Thinning & Succession Planting

After your seeds start growing, some vegetables and herbs will be a little overcrowded. No matter how meticulous you were when you were sowing the seeds, sometimes you just can't help getting them too close together—especially plants such as basil, carrots, and lettuce that have small seeds. Besides the obvious problem of your plants competing for light, water, and nutrients with their brothers and sisters, some vegetables won't produce at all if they're too close together. That's why you need to thin, or remove, some of your plants while they're young.

Thinning is a brutal concept for the beginning gardener. What I'm asking you to do is pluck and kill the very seedlings you just worked so hard to plant. But for many crops it's essential. Carrots, beets, and radishes, for example, will not form their roots if they're growing too close together. They need to be thinned a few times to get the proper spacing. Lettuce, kale, and other greens also need thinning so plants can grow to their full size. The good thing about thinning greens is you can eat the thinnings. I'll talk more about how to thin each type of vegetable in chapter 8.

Another way to get the most from your garden space is to use a technique called succession planting. Succession planting takes advantage of a plant's natural growth habit. It's planting one crop after another in the same space in your garden in succession. Even in the colder areas of our region, you can plant three crops in one space. For example, you can plant spinach in spring. Once you finish harvesting a month or so later, pull out the spinach plants, add a little compost, and plant some bush beans. They will mature in a few months and will be pulled out of the bed at the end of summer. Then you can plant a fall crop of kale for eating into late fall. One bed or row, three crops. This works very well in containers, too, where you can protect your vegetables from spring and fall frosts, extending the season even longer. The keys to succession planting are being merciless in pulling out your plants once they are done producing and fertilizing with compost after each crop. Even if you still have a few beans on the plant, yank it out and compost it. It might be tough to do, but in the long run you'll get more vegetables from replanting another vegetable than you would from leaving the old plants in the ground. Fertilizing is essential, since your plants are taking nutrients out of the ground and the soil needs to be replenished. Usually you'll be planting cool-weather lovers in spring and fall and hot-weather lovers in early summer. Some other succession planting combinations are mesclun greens in spring, followed by cucumbers, followed by fall spinach. Also, try peas planted in spring, followed by carrots, followed by a fall crop of lettuce.

Another way to save space in the vegetable garden is to intercrop. Intercropping means planting fast-maturing, small-growing vegetables next to slower-maturing, larger-growing vegetables. For example, plant lettuce or

radishes next to tomatoes or broccoli. Because tomatoes and broccoli have to be spaced a few feet apart (they will eventually get large and fill in that space), there's all this room in between plants. Sow seeds of lettuce and radishes in that space. They will grow quickly and be harvested before the tomatoes and broccoli fill in the space to shade them. It's a great way to get a quick crop without having to use extra space.

Staking & Supports

While most vegetables are strong enough to stand on their own, some need help. Some vegetables are upwardly mobile and need something to grab on to. You need to be ready to support your veggies, especially ones grown in containers. Tall veggies in containers don't have the soil mass to help keep them vertical. All it takes is a summer thunderstorm and they'll be flopping on the ground.

Tomatoes, peppers, and eggplants all grow better with supports. Tomatoes can be supported with cages, stakes, or wire. If you're growing indeterminate or large-fruited tomato varieties, make sure your support system will hold up a mature tomato plant. See the tomato section in chapter 8 for details on different support systems you can use. Peppers and eggplants grow fine without support, but I've found the fruits stay cleaner and have fewer disease and insect problems if they are perched above the ground. This is especially true of large-fruited varieties or ones that produce lots of small fruits. The weight of the fruits will pull the plant to the ground. I use small tomato cages to keep my plants erect.

Pole beans and most peas need a fence or stakes to grow on. Use a teepee system or individual poles for your pole beans. For tall-growing peas I use a 6-foot-tall wire fence support and plant on either side of the fence. It's a good way to maximize the yield. Short-growing pea varieties, such as 'Sugar Ann', benefit from a twig fence. To make a twig fence, cut 3-foot-tall saplings from a forest (legally, please) and push the branches into the ground along the pea row. The pea tendrils grab the twigs and that's all these dwarf peas will need to stay upright.

Cucumbers, melons, and squash can also be trellised vertically, but it's not critical. If trellising cucumbers, use a 45-degree-angled platform made of wire or wood that they can grow up. The cuke fruits will hang down through the holes. For melons and squash you may have to support the vines and fruits with cloth slings. These structures are a bit involved, but small-space gardeners may find these gems to be worth the effort.

For more information on trellis, caging, and staking systems for your individual veggies, check out chapter 8.

What's with the Weeds?

When I was a child, I used to help my mom in our vegetable garden. Initially the planting was fun, but then the weeds came. I remember grueling days in the hot summer sun slinging the hoe to kill the weeds that seemed to grow faster and better than any vegetables we sowed. Unfortunately, that's the impression many of us have of vegetable gardening. Pulling weeds on a hot summer day when we really would rather be swimming, biking, or playing baseball. That's certainly not a way to create a lifelong love of gardening for a child or an adult.

But weeding doesn't have to be a chore or even something you have to do often. You just have to understand how weeds work and then apply the right strategies either to prevent them from growing or kill them before they become a jungle. Of course, you can grow vegetables and herbs in containers and reduce the whole weeding issue dramatically, but let's just assume you're planting in the ground and you have weeds.

There are two types of weeds: annual and perennial. Annual weeds grow from seeds lying in the soil each spring. The seeds can last years in the soil, just waiting for the right conditions to germinate. Once a seed has the right temperature, moisture, and light conditions—boom, it's growing. Annual weeds, such as lamb's quarters, pigweed, and purslane, all grow quickly to flower and then set more seed in your garden. The key to controlling these weeds is not to allow the seeds to germinate in the first place, and if they do, to kill the seedlings while they're young. If you can't stay on top of all the weeds, at least don't let the weeds set more seeds to drop into your soil. If you can prevent new weed seeds from entering your soil, there will be fewer and fewer annual weeds in your garden each year.

You can prevent annual weed seeds from germinating by not tilling deeply (see the section on no-till gardening in chapter 3 for more on this idea) and by covering them with mulch. Mulching is one of those techniques that was a revelation to me as a gardener. When I realized that I didn't have to leave the soil exposed and could cover it with a variety of organic or inorganic materials, the angels started to sing. Organic mulches, such as straw, untreated grass clippings, hay, chopped dead leaves, sea grass, or peat moss, will all eventually decompose, feeding the soil. By placing a 2- to 4-inch layer on pathways or around plants, you'll prevent weed seeds from getting the light they need to germinate. The added benefit is that the mulch

will keep the soil cool and moist, so these mulches are perfect for cool-weather-loving crops such as peas, lettuce, broccoli, and carrots, and fruits such as strawberries, raspberries, and blueberries. Look for organic mulches that are prevalent in your area. Along the coast, gardeners often use sea grass to mulch pathways. Near farms, consider straw or hay. In suburban areas, look to your trees for leaves or to your lawn for grass clippings for mulching.

Inorganic mulches, such as plastic and landscape fabric, don't decompose and feed the soil, but do save moisture, heat up the soil, and stop weed growth. However, the material must not let ultraviolet light through; if it does, the weeds will grow. I once made the mistake of using clear plastic mulch in my garden because I heard it warms the soil faster and to a higher temperature than black plastic mulch. The soil baked, but the weeds grew under the plastic and eventually pulled it right off the ground. Inorganic mulches are great for tomatoes, peppers, eggplants, squash, cucumbers, okra, sweet potatoes, and melons—any crop that likes the heat. They do work well for fruits such as strawberries and blueberries because you don't have to weed as often, but they don't feed the soil with the organic matter that these plants crave. However, in pathways among fruits or vegetables, you can use materials that are thick and break down very slowly, such as cardboard, newspaper, and bark mulch. Keep the mulch thick in pathways, since their only purpose is for you to get in and out of the garden. That will make for a lot less space to be weeded.

Use mulches after your plants have germinated or started to put on new growth after transplanting. This leads us to the other way to control annual weeds—cultivating early and often. It's always much easier to cultivate (hoe) early in the season when weeds are small than to wait until they are large. Big weeds are harder to kill. One week or so after planting, start hoeing pathways or the ground around transplants. Simply slicing off the young weeds just below the soil line will kill them quickly (especially during a sunny day) and will not bring up more annual weed seeds from deeper in the soil to germinate. I've found if I cultivate a few times for the first month after planting, then mulch, I spend most of my summer sipping on lemonade, popping cherry tomatoes into my mouth, and harvesting peppers for grilling. You get the idea: less weeding, more fun!

Of course, weeding early in the season will require you to know the difference between a weed and an herb or vegetable. This you'll have to learn from experience or study. There are websites that will show you pictures of young weeds and vegetables. Also, you'll need the right tool for weeding. For most gardens, I like a long-handled, thin-bladed hoe or cultivator. These are lightweight and the blade is sharp enough to slice

the top few inches of the soil without digging deeply. You just walk around scraping the paths and areas between plants. It's more of a scuffling motion than full-fledged hoeing.

Perennial weeds require more diligence. Perennial weeds, such as dandelion, plantain, quack grass, and burdock, grow back from their root system each spring. Even if you kill the tops repeatedly, they're likely to return. Frequent weeding of young perennial weeds does help control them. However, some, like quack grass, thrive on having their roots severed, because just like in some of those alien movies, each severed part will regrow into a new plant. It can be a nightmare!

The three keys to controlling perennial weeds are consistent cultivating to weaken the roots, hand weeding, and mulching. If you can dig up and remove as much of a dandelion or quack grass root system as possible, even if it grows back, it will be weakened and less likely to survive your cultivating and mulching. Hand digging perennial weeds isn't the easiest task, but it's satisfying. It's best to hand weed on a cloudy, cool day after a rain. When the soil is moist, it's easier to get more of the root system out of the ground. Remove the roots and don't compost them. They will just

invade your compost pile and end up back in the garden. Send them off to the landfill or toss them in a vacant area of your yard.

My final word on weeds is to remember to eat them. Yes, many weeds are not only edible, but delicious. I remember my Italian grandmother sautéing wild dandelion greens with olive oil, garlic, and tomatoes. (Almost anything is good sautéed with olive oil, garlic, and tomatoes!) They have a slightly bitter flavor when picked young and are tasty on bread or as a side dish. Purslane, lamb's quarters, and burdock roots are also all edible. Lamb's quarters and purslane make great additions to salads, and I've added them to my "exotic" pestos on occasion. Burdock roots are good roasted with other root crops. You know they must be good because some seed catalog companies now sell varieties of these "weeds" in seed packets. So as you're weeding, remember to save some of the tastier weeds for dinner.

Watering: Infrequent & Deep

Two essential ingredients of a successful garden are sunshine and water. You can't make the sun shine, but you can keep the soil evenly moist. Most vegetables, fruits, and herbs need a moist, well-drained soil to grow their best. Now, that probably sounds like a contradiction. Moist, yet well drained? Well, that's a soil that doesn't have standing water but isn't dry as a bone. The soil has organic matter that will hold water during dry spells but allow it to drain during wet spells. The soil has neither too much, nor too little water.

How you water is different depending on the age of your plant. Young seedlings have small, shallow root systems and need to be watered gently and frequently until they're established. This means a gentle shower, soaking down a few inches into the soil, is probably enough for them. Berry bushes, fruits trees, and established plants with bigger root systems need deep and

infrequent watering to grow their best. Soak the soil around their roots until it's wet to at least 6 inches deep. The deeper the water penetrates, the more likely the roots are to grow deep into the soil. The benefit of deeply rooted plants is that during a hot, dry spell, the roots will be deep in the soil where there's moisture, and the plant will still get enough water to keep it healthy. If you water lightly, so the soil is wet only a few inches deep, the roots will grow to the level of the water and be just below the surface. They will be more likely to dry out during a drought, and your plants will wilt and suffer. To find out how you're doing with your watering, simply dig down after you water to see how deep the moisture has penetrated.

There are a few different ways to water your plants. Most gardeners think of watering as standing with hose in hand, spritzing the garden while sipping a drink. But that's the least efficient way to water. Even though our Northeast climate tends to be wet and water restrictions are infrequent, with the changing climate, more droughts are certainly a possibility in the future and conserving water should be something we're all concerned about.

For young seedlings, a spray wand attached to the hose is a good way to gently apply water right where the plant needs it. A spray wand offers a gentle shower to your seedlings without harming their tender shoots. Hold the wand over an individual plant for a few seconds (count, "one, one thousand; two, one thousand; three, one thousand," and so forth) and then move onto the next one. You'll concentrate water where the plant is and not waste it on pathways or between plants. Also, weeds will be less likely to germinate if the soil between plants stays dry.

As plants get larger, there are some other options. You can build a moat around individual tomato, pepper, eggplant, and squash plants; berry bushes; and fruit trees. Then fill that moat with water once or twice a week. Unless it's really dry or rainy, that should be enough to keep your plants happy. Of course, eventually the roots of big plants, such as pumpkins, blueberries, and apples, will outgrow the moat, but by then your plants will be so well established they may not need as much supplemental watering. Overhead sprinklers are certainly one of the easier ways to water. Just set the sprinkler in the middle of the garden, turn on the water, and walk away. Let the water run long enough to soak down to the required 6 inches. It's best to sprinkle in the morning so the leaves are dry before evening. Wet leaves in the night-time create the perfect environment for diseases. I've used timers to turn the water on and off. It's a great way to avoid overwatering. The disadvantage of overhead sprinklers is that much of the water is wasted on pathways, lawns, and evaporation into the air. Also, watering everything makes weed seeds more likely to grow.

To really focus your watering, try soaker hoses or drip irrigation lines. Soaker hoses, or weeping hoses, have tiny holes in them. When hooked up to a faucet, the water pressure makes the holes leak water to the soil. Soaker hoses keep the soil just around them moist, so are best used along rows of plants such as lettuce, beans, and onions. They work best on flat ground, may clog over time, and will also water areas between plants (where weeds will grow) if used on large vegetables such as tomatoes.

Drip irrigation lines are the most sophisticated watering systems and also the most efficient. Using a series of pipes and tiny emitters (holes), the water is delivered right to the roots of individual plants. It's great for berry bushes, fruit trees, and large individual vegetables, such as tomatoes. When set up with a timer, the water will drip into the soil for the allotted time (usually a few hours a day). Little water is wasted on areas away from plants and little water evaporates into the air. However, there is an initial investment in drip irrigation, and you'll have to take up the lines each season because the freezing winter temperatures in the Northeast can cause the pipes to break.

To keep containers moist, use self-watering pots, moisture-absorbing polymers, and drip irrigation set on timers. The bigger the pot, the less frequently you'll have to water. However, pots of any size (especially clay pots) tend to dry out quickly in summer, so the self-watering container was revolutionary when it was introduced. The container has a reservoir in the bottom that you fill with water. The water is slowly drawn up through capillary action into the dry soil, keeping it moist for up to five days, depending on your crop and the weather. There are self-watering window boxes and hanging baskets as well. There's even a self-watering conversion kit that allows you to transform a regular pot into a self-watering one. Moisture-absorbing polymers are tiny crystals you mix into the soil. As they absorb water, they expand into jelly-like masses that slowly release the water as the soil dries. The masses can look a little weird, but it works.

Now that you know how to deliver the water, how do you know when to water? The best way to know if your soil is moist is to do the finger test. Stick your finger 4 inches deep into the soil. If the soil feels dry on your fingertip at that depth, water. Also, check out the leaves of the plants. Wilting can be a sign of water stress. However, be careful. Check the soil first. If it's moist, the wilting may be due to a disease or even too *much* water in the soil. Too much water causes roots to die. The fewer roots, the less water the plant can take up. Ironically, that can cause leaves to wilt. Wilting may also be due to very high temperatures. When we get days above 90°F, many vegetables, such as eggplants, will naturally droop their leaves. In the cool evening they will perk up again. As long as they bounce back and the soil is moist, your plants are fine.

While keeping the soil evenly moist all the time is the goal, there are times during the life of your veggies that water is critical to getting a good crop. For many vegetables, such as beans, cabbage, cucumbers, squash, peas, melons, and pumpkins, water is essential during flowering and when the fruits are forming. When roots are starting to form on radishes, potatoes, carrots, and beets, that's the time to water well. Once tomatoes or eggplants start fruiting, they'll need consistent water to mature. In fact, one condition affecting tomatoes called blossom end rot (see the tomato section in chapter 8 for more) is caused by fluctuating soil moisture conditions; it's not a disease.

Keeping Your Plants Well Fed

I spent a lot of time discussing the benefits of organic matter and compost in chapter 3. Now it's time to get down to the science of how your plants eat. Certainly, you need to start by building up your soil's organic matter, and adding compost is a great way to do that. But it's also helpful to know a little about the specific nutrients your plants need, how to determine if your plants aren't getting enough of them, and what to apply to fix a nutrient deficiency problem.

So let's take a little trip back in time to high school biology class. I know this may have been a traumatic time for some of you, but stick with me on this one. As you may remember, all plants need carbon, oxygen, and hydrogen along with the miracle of photosynthesis to grow. Photosynthesis occurs when plants take sunlight and transform carbon dioxide from the air and water into sugars that plants use. Those nutrients are in abundant supply in our world, so it's not an issue. Actually, as a little aside, the increased levels of carbon dioxide in our atmosphere due to global warming are projected to increase plant growth rates on some plants. You can see why once you understand photosynthesis. The more carbon dioxide, the more opportunity plants have to produce sugars and new growth.

But our vegetables, fruits, and herbs also need other nutrients to grow. The big three that are needed in largest quantities are nitrogen, phosphorus, and potassium. While plants will need a host of other nutrients as well, such as calcium, magnesium, sulfur, and micronutrients (they aren't little, just needed in very small quantities) such as boron, copper, and zinc, it's the big three that we'll mostly focus on because plants need these the most.

Nitrogen (N)

Nitrogen is the nutrient that keeps plant leaves green. It's a key component of plant proteins and growth. Unfortunately, it's also a very volatile creature. It leaches out of the soil readily, so you often have to insure your plants have a consistent supply in the soil for proper growth. It's easy to know if your plants are lacking nitrogen, the leaves turn a pale yellow and the growth of the plant will be slow. It's particularly noticeable on leafy green crops, such as Swiss chard, lettuce, and spinach. If you add too much nitrogen you'll have lush, dark green leaves. They may look good, but excessive nitrogen can create a nutrient imbalance in the soil and delay flowering and fruiting.

Phosphorus (P)

Phosphorus is a more stable nutrient and stays in the soil for years. It's important for root growth, disease resistance, and seed and fruit development. It's particularly important for onions, carrots, beets, potatoes, and any crops that form edible roots. Phosphorus is also less available in cooler soils and at high and low pH. That's why it's good to do a soil test to determine your nutrient levels. You may see a phosphorus deficiency in your plants, but it may go away once the soil warms if there's adequate phosphorus in the soil. If your pH is below 6 or above 7.5, you may also notice phosphorus deficiencies.

Phosphorus deficiencies show up as a purpling of leaves and stunted growth. Excessive phosphorus in the soil is a problem in many areas because it runs off through soil water into streams and lakes, polluting them. Too much phosphorus creates a zinc and iron deficiency; plants with this condition have misshapen leaves and poor growth.

Potassium (K)

Potassium is the third of the big three nutrients and is essential for vigorous growth, disease resistance, and the overall well-being of your plants. It's particularly important for maturing tree fruits and berries. Like phosphorus, it stays in the soil and doesn't leach out as readily as nitrogen.

If your soil doesn't have adequate amounts of potassium, plants will grow slowly and have deformed yellow leaves with brown edges. If your soil has an overabundance of potassium, like phosphorus, it will create other nutrient imbalances that stunt your plant's growth.

Soil Test

The way to determine your big three levels, as well as pH, organic matter levels, and other nutrients levels, is to do a soil test. I briefly talked about soil tests in chapter 3. While you can purchase a simple home test kit to get general results, I'd suggest looking into testing at a university or private laboratory. For less than $50 you can get a detailed report on your soil organic matter levels, pH, and nutrients, and for an additional fee you can also request other specific tests, such as for heavy metal contaminants. While each laboratory will report the results a little differently, the basic test will generally tell if your major nutrients are at low, medium, or high levels. The report will also recommend materials to add to adjust nutrient levels, pH, and organic matter, and indicate the quantities needed to bring the soil to optimum health. To get accurate information from your soil test, you need to take the samples correctly and indicate what crop is going to be grown in that soil. The recommendations will vary if it's a fruit orchard, berry patch, or vegetable garden. Also, when taking a sample, follow the directions carefully. It's important to dig multiple holes around the garden, take samples from each hole, mix the samples together in a bucket, and then take a sample of the mixture and send to the laboratory.

Choosing the Right Fertilizer

So now that you know the science of your soil's health, what fertilizers should you add to keep your soil healthy? Although soil tests are good indicators of your soil's general health, don't get too obsessive about them. I use them as snapshots to give me a general indication of pH or nutrients that are way out of whack. Once your soil is growing a good garden, doing a soil test every few years is fine. Remember that organic matter in the forms I mentioned in chapter 3 is the best way to feed your soil. Extra fertilizer in a granular or liquid form should be used as a supplement for a specific problem or a general pick-me-up.

I'm an organic gardener, so in this book I'm going to focus on organic additives to your soil. There are many advantages to using organic fertilizers. One benefit is that they release nutrients slowly into the soil as plants need them. Therefore, they last longer in the soil and you don't have to add them as frequently as a chemical fertilizer. Organic fertilizers are also less likely to harm microorganisms in the soil. Microbes are important for breaking down organic matter into humus and other compounds that plants need to grow. See chapter 3 for more on this. Organic fertilizers can be free (in the case of local manures or your own compost) and generally are less processed than chemical fertilizers. So using organic fertilizers can decrease your carbon footprint and your impact on global warming, as you're using less fossil fuel.

Generally, if you have a healthy soil and add a few inches of finished compost to your beds before planting, your soil should be fine to grow most vegetables, fruits, and herbs. However, if you have sandy soils or poor gravelly soils, or are gardening in containers, you may want to supplement your additions of compost with an all-purpose organic fertilizer. These commercial organic fertilizers come in bags or bottles. One I like to use is a granular 5-5-5. The three numbers indicate the big three nutrient percentages in the bag. So a 5-5-5 fertilizer has 5 percent nitrogen, 5 percent phosphorus, and 5 percent potassium. The rest of the bag just has filler material. This is a general all-purpose plant food that gets plants off to a good start. It's also the fertilizer I recommend for sidedressing later in the season, but I'll talk about sidedressing a little later. There are also organic fertilizers that specialize in adding certain nutrients. These you would use based on a soil test.

Here are some easy-to-use commercial organic products that can help keep your plants healthy.

➤ **Bloodmeal:** Well, this isn't a pretty picture. Bloodmeal is a byproduct of the slaughter industry. It's powdered dried blood and is high in nitrogen. The only downside of bloodmeal is that domestic animals may dig in your garden after you apply it because they think there's a dead animal around.

➤ **Bonemeal:** Also from the slaughterhouse, bonemeal is ground animal bones. It's high in phosphorus and has some nitrogen. It's a powder that gets sprinkled and worked into the soil at planting, and it also comes in a liquid form. As with bloodmeal, watch out for animals digging up your plants after applying it. It's best to apply it and let it sit for a few weeks before planting, so the scent will wear off.

➤ **Corn Gluten:** This agricultural byproduct is a little easier to stomach than bloodmeal. It's a pellet and a product of the corn-processing industry. It's also high in nitrogen. Typically used in meal form rather than pellets, corn gluten is a fairly effective pre-emergent herbicide too.

➤ **Fish Emulsion or Mix:** This material is just what it sounds like—ground, fermented fish parts. It's a gentle form of nitrogen fertilizer, and young plants, in particular, respond well to it. It comes in a bottle and can be diluted in water and then applied when watering plants or sprayed right on the foliage. It also comes in a dry, granular form. Although there are versions that are "deodorized," don't make the mistake I once did and use it indoors, unless, of course, you like the odor of rotten fish. Fish emulsion is often mixed with seaweed, because it tends to be made near the ocean. Seaweed adds many micronutrients to the soil.

➤ **Greensand:** Greensand is a soil mineral mined in New Jersey. It's high in potassium and, like rock phosphate, is slow to break down, so it should be added early in the season.

➤ **Lime:** Lime is a mineral that's primarily used to add calcium, and sometimes magnesium, to the soil. It is usually applied to raise the pH to the proper level for vegetables and fruits. Use dolomitic lime to add magnesium.

➤ **Plant Meals:** You'll find these in a granular form in bags. They can be made from cottonseed, alfalfa, or soybean meals. They all are good sources of nitrogen for plants and can be used to boost up young plants or give a shot of nitrogen to older plants. Look for organic versions of these meals because some, such as cotton-seed, may be derived from plants that were heavily sprayed with pesticides.

➤ **Rock Phosphate:** Rock phosphate is literally rock that's been mined and ground. It is high in phosphorus. The phosphorus is released slowly into the soil, so rock phosphate should be added early in the season, before planting, to be effective.

➤ **Sulfur:** This mined material is used specifically to lower the soil's pH. Since many of the soils in the Northeast are already acidic, sulfur is mostly used in our region as an additive to plants such as blueberries that need a really low pH.

➤ **Worm Castings:** Worm castings are the droppings of earthworms. Yes, you can farm earthworms and buy their poop. It's actually a great soil additive, especially for young plants, since this fertilizer is gentle on the root systems. You can also buy a liquid form called worm poop tea that can be watered or sprayed on plants.

➤ **Wood Ashes:** Although this is not a commercial product, I wanted to mention something about wood ashes. Many Northeast gardeners live in rural areas where they burn wood for heat. Wood ashes are a great source of potassium for plants. However, you shouldn't overdo it. Apply only about 10 to 20 pounds of wood ashes per 1,000 square feet of garden. Adding too much can cause nutrient imbalances. Wood ashes also raise the soil pH, so using them is a good way to make an acidic soil a little sweeter.

There are other additives you'll find in garden centers and online for better plant growth. Many of these focus on building the soil's microorganism populations. One that I'm particularly fond of is mycorrhizae. Mycorrhizae are fungi that colonize the soil. They have been proven to help plant roots take up water and nutrients more efficiently. Mycorrhizae occur naturally in many soils in the forest or grasslands. They are a good material to add when planting your berry bushes and tree fruits so they can inhabit the soil and help your plants grow stronger. They need to be applied only once to have a benefit. You can also use them in vegetable gardens, but you'll have to reapply them each spring. If you have poor soil consider selecting mycorrhizae mixes for specific crops you're growing. It's particularly important for container crops grown in potting soil that is devoid of native mycorrhizae.

Sidedressing

Now that you've got your plants off to a good start, you're not done fertilizing. To really get great production, you may want to add more fertilizer as your plants are growing. This is called "sidedressing." Although not always necessary, sidedressing is a good idea if you really want to keep your production coming during the season. It's especially important for container gardens. Containers are watered frequently and the potting soil is naturally low in nutrients. Water leaches out any fertilizers you apply, so you need to reapply them every few weeks to keep your plants growing strong and producing.

The easiest way to side-dress your plants in the garden is with a small handful (a few tablespoons) of a granular organic fertilizer. Just sprinkle it around each plant or along a row of plants close to their roots. Don't worry about tilling it into the soil. It will naturally seep down with watering and rain.

You can also apply liquid fertilizers as a sidedressing. Fish emulsion and worm poop are good examples of organic fertilizers that can be watered around the roots or sprayed onto the plants to give them a boost of nitrogen. Plants do have the ability to take up nutrients right through their leaves, so spraying them does help with immediate nutrient deficiency problems.

When you side-dress depends on the plants. Greens, such as spinach, lettuce, kale, and Swiss chard, and root crops, such as carrots and beets, should get a little boost of fertilizer about three weeks after they germinate or are transplanted into the garden. Potatoes should be side-dressed when they flower, and onions when they start to bulb. Cucumbers, squash, and pumpkins should be side-dressed when they start running (vining) and start blooming. Tomatoes, peppers, and eggplants should get a shot of fertilizer three weeks after transplanting and then monthly after that. Broccoli, cabbage, and cauliflower should be fed about one month after planting.

Some crops, such as mesclun mix, beans, peas, and radishes, don't need any sidedressing. They either make their own fertilizer (in the case of beans and peas) or mature so quickly it's not worth it.

Season Extending
We vegetable gardeners just can't get enough fresh produce. That's why we've developed techniques to extend the season earlier and later, past the last and first frost dates. There are some simple products a beginning gardener can use to extend the growing season. The floating row cover that I suggest for pest control in chapter 6 can also keep plants warm to temperatures in the mid-20s°F. It's great for protecting low-growing crops of greens. Cold frames can also be made or purchased. These are boxes with a clear plastic or glass top that let light in but protect plants from cold. I've used mine to grow spinach, mesclun mix, and parsley into winter. Sometimes I'll even get veggies to survive the winter in my cold frames. So if you really want to push the season longer, try some of these season-extending devices.

CHAPTER 6

PESTS: THE GOOD, THE BAD & THE UGLY

Growing your own fruits, vegetables, and herbs is like setting up a banquet. While you grew this luscious bounty for your family and friends, there are other critters more than willing to crash the party. Insects, diseases, and animals can take the best-looking, healthiest garden and turn it into a war zone. I watched one summer afternoon as a cute little furry woodchuck mowed down row after row of beans in my garden. A few years ago, a blight disease attacked tomatoes

in the Northeast, causing many gardeners to pull up and destroy their plants before they could harvest one fruit. And Japanese beetles have been know to turn my basil plants into lace in a few days. Yes, pests can be frustrating.

So if you're shivering in your boots after all my dire pest warnings and stories, relax. It's really not all that bad. Yes, there are pests that need to be dealt with, and I'll provide a rundown of the most troublesome insects, diseases, and animals in our region and suggest the best controls. But there are also beneficial insects that help keep harmful pests in line, and many new techniques and materials are available to the home gardener. With a little forethought, good observation skills, and decisive action, you can protect and defend your gardens, berry bushes, and fruit trees from the bad guys, without resorting to harmful chemicals. You can then feel safe eating the produce from your garden.

What's Bugging You?

Let's start with the group that most new gardeners fear the most: insects. The fact is that most insects in your garden are neither good guys nor bad guys. They are just living their lives using your garden, trees, and bushes as a place to call home. There are actually a number of good-guy bugs in the garden. These are called beneficial insects and they live to eat other insects. These guys are your allies, so you should do whatever it takes to encourage their presence and appetite. Finally, there is the small minority in question. Some of these bad-guy insects attack a broad range of plants, while others love to feed on specific plants. These are the guys you need to watch out for and be ready to thwart.

You can see there are many types of insects in your garden. The best approach is to grow a healthy, well-nourished garden with strong plants. Healthy plants are more likely to withstand attacks from insects. A strong plant is more likely than a weak one to withstand some leafhoppers chewing on its leaves. So follow the guidelines in chapters 2 and 3 on siting the garden and building healthy soil. All this leads to healthy plants and fewer problems with insects.

But almost as important as having a healthy garden is growing a diverse garden. Mixing flowers and herbs in the vegetables garden, having a nearby water source, and having shrubs and lawn area all contribute to creating a habitat that will attract beneficial insects and animals to your garden. Beneficial insects can help control a pest population before it gets out of hand. Beneficial insects will need some other insects in the garden to encourage their presence, so don't worry if you see a few aphids hanging about. The ladybugs will surely follow soon.

To encourage beneficial insects in your garden, plant flowers such as dill, fennel, and parsley that are known to attract some of these good guys. Have a birdbath nearby as a water source, and plant evergreens and other

shrubs to provide hiding places for these bugs. Place broken clay pots in the garden for frogs and toads to hide in. They will help you by feasting on a variety of insects. Although this book is all about growing your food organically, it's important to know that even organic pesticides can harm beneficial insects. In general, try not to spray any pesticides, and if you have to spray, use chemicals that won't harm beneficial insects. I'll discuss that more later when we talk about common organic insecticides.

You can also prevent many problems by growing insect- and disease-resistant varieties, cleaning up your garden well in fall, and destroying heavily infected plants during the growing season. Yes, sometimes you'll have to sacrifice a plant or two to save the rest. Many of these pests also overwinter in garden debris left from the summer, so if you remove the debris, you remove the pests that could be attacking your garden next year.

Some Bad Bugs

Before you start panicking about an insect on a damaged leaf, the first step is to know thy enemy. Properly identifying the insect will help you know if it's the culprit causing the damage. Sometimes the damage is caused by weather, animals, or other non-insect factors.

Once you know what the insect is, you'll need to control it. Here are fifteen of the most common insect pests that affect vegetables, herbs, and fruits and some control ideas. It's certainly not an all-inclusive list, but these are the ones most beginning gardeners will encounter at some time or another. More information about the sprays mentioned can be found later in the chapter.

> **Aphids:** These small, chubby insects can be black, white, green, or red, depending on the type. They love the young, succulent growth of many vegetables, herbs, and fruits. In fact, if you have had aphid

problems in the past, don't apply too much nitrogen fertilizer, because as you learned in the previous chapters, nitrogen stimulates lots of young, new growth. While a few aphids are no need for concern, unfortunately, aphids reproduce quickly and in a few days a whole congregation can be sucking on your leaves, flowers, and fruits. They cause problems in three ways. Their feeding sucks plant juices, weakening the plant. In addition, the juices aphids exude can grow a black sooty mold, which is unsightly. They also transmit diseases from one plant to another, especially among raspberries. Luckily, aphids are simple to control. I hose them down with a strong jet of water from my garden hose. Once off the plant, they're not likely to climb back up. You can also spray insecticidal soap or Neem oil to kill them. Also, watch for ladybugs. They love aphids and if they find your colony, don't spray—just let the ladybugs gorge themselves.

➤ **Cabbageworms:** This green worm (caterpillar) is found on a whole host of cabbage-family plants such as kale, broccoli, cauliflower, Brussels sprouts, and kohlrabi. The problem with cabbageworms, and their relative the cabbage looper, is that their color matches the leaves. You may not know you have a problem until you see shredded leaves on your plant. Be on cabbageworm alert when you see a small white butterfly flitting around your plant (that's the adult laying eggs) and you see some black droppings in the leaf crotch of the plant. You can handpick and drop a few cabbageworms in soapy water, but a better defense is to spray *Bacillus thuringiensis* (B.t.).

➤ **Colorado Potato Beetles:** If you grow potatoes and eggplants, you probably know this beetle. The brown-and-yellow-striped, hard-shelled adults lay clusters of orange eggs on the undersides of primarily potato and eggplant leaves. The eggs hatch into soft, squishy red larvae, which munch away on the leaves. Although potatoes can withstand lots of leaf damage and still give you a crop, you need to stop these guys before they get out of hand. The key to defense is looking for and crushing the orange egg masses. If you only have a short row of potatoes or a few eggplants, this may be all you need to do to control this beetle. You can grow 'King Harry' potato. It has hairy leaves the beetles don't like to eat. You can also spray a type of *Bacillus thuringiensis* (B.t.) called San Diego, which is specifically formulated to control this insect.

➤ **Cucumber Beetles:** These yellow and black, spotted or striped, elongated beetles love cucumbers, squash, and melons. They feed on the leaves and flowers, causing the plants to become stunted and, like aphids, they transmit diseases from plant to plant. Cucumber beetles are a bugger to control. I've had success with yellow sticky traps hung over young plants. The beetles are attracted to the color yellow and get stuck and die on the trap. Covering young plants with a floating row cover can reduce their spread as well. Try applying spinosad and pyrethrum sprays to control heavy infestations.

➤ **Cutworms:** These underground caterpillars are frustrating pests. After you plant your pepper, broccoli, basil, and other seedlings in the garden you'll wake the next morning to see them cut to the ground by cutworms. They lurk in the upper levels of the soil and wrap themselves around young, tender seedlings at night and chew through the stem. They are only a problem in spring, so once the plants are big enough, you're okay. I've stopped cutworms simply by using a barrier. Place toilet paper rolls or paper cups with the bottoms removed around the seedlings. Or try wrapping newspaper around the stems. These methods prevent cutworms from finding your seedlings. Maker sure the barrier extends 1 inch below and 2 inches above the soil line.

➤ **Flea Beetles:** They're black and they hop. Yes, they're flea beetles. These little, hard-shelled insects make small shotgun-like holes in the plant leaves, devastating young pepper, eggplant, tomato, broccoli, and other plants. They emerge in spring soon after you plant, so watch out! Cover young plants with a floating row cover and spray with pyrethrum or insecticidal soap to control these pests.

➤ **Japanese Beetles:** If you've ever grown roses, you know the Japanese beetle. This metallic green-and-bronze-colored beetle loves the leaves and flowers of a whole host of plants, especially basil, grapes, and raspberries. These beetles come out in late June or early July in our region to feed until later in the summer. They not only feed voraciously, but mate like rabbits, laying eggs in lawn areas around their favorite foods. Handpick Japanese beetles in the morning while they're sluggish, and drop them into a pail of soapy water. Protect prized plants with a floating row cover. Hang Japanese beetle traps at least 30 feet upwind and away from your garden to lure the insects away. Some experts now recommend not using Japanese beetle traps at all. Turns out they attract far more beetles to an area than they kill. Spray beneficial nematodes on the lawn area near favored plants in June and early September to control the grub or young stage of the beetle in the ground. Long-term Japanese beetle grub control is also gained by several applications of milky spore bacterial powder to the ground. It infects the grubs with a fatal disease and hurts nothing else.

➤ **Maggots:** The two most common types of maggots for home gardeners are apple maggots and root maggots. Apple maggots attack the fruit of apple trees, causing deformed and wormy fruits. Root maggots attack vegetables such as onions, causing tunneling and rotting of the bulb. Control apple maggots by hanging round, red apple maggot traps coated with a sticky substance such as Tanglefoot on trees in June. The adult flies land on the trap thinking it's an apple and get stuck and die. Control root maggots on onions by placing a piece of cardboard or tar paper on the ground around the onion plant when the plant is young. This will prevent the adult fly from laying eggs.

➤ **Leafminers:** You mostly know leafminers from their damage. These insects are so small they literally tunnel their way between the layers of spinach, beet, Swiss chard, and lettuce leaves. Although the leaves are still edible, they can be severely damaged. Simply pick off and destroy infected leaves or cover plants with a floating row cover to prevent the damage.

➤ **Snails and Slugs:** There's only one word to describe these mollusks: *yuck!* They love cool, dark, moist hiding places, from which they venture at night to munch on the leaves and fruits of lettuce, herbs,

strawberries, and a host of other plants. They are more plentiful during cool, rainy periods. Remove slugs and snail hiding places such as boards, weeds, or old pots. You can use their love of dark places to catch a bunch of them. Lay a board near affected plants, and early in the morning lift the board and knock the clinging slugs into a pail of soapy water. You can also set up or buy beer traps. Slugs and snails are attracted to the yeast in beer and will drown themselves enjoying it. I hear they love the German imports best. Set tubs of beer (butter lids also work well) at ground level or position traps close to favorite plants. Clean out the traps in the morning and refill the traps. For containers affix a strip of copper flashing around the edge to prevent the slugs or snails from entering. Because of a chemical reaction they will get a slight shock when crossing copper. Mulch around favored plants with sheep's wool. Slugs and snails don't like crossing the raw wool to get to their meal. Try spreading iron phosphate baits around plants. This bait is safe for wildlife, pets, and the environment, but kills slugs.

➤ **Squash Bugs:** Now here's an insect that moves in a pack. Squash bugs are gray or brown bugs that congregate on the undersides of squash, pumpkin, and melon leaves. The young look like smaller versions of the adult bugs. Their feeding causes the leaves to brown and die. Worse yet, when you squish them they emit a foul odor. Control squash bugs by crushing the clusters of brown eggs on the underside of leaves, covering young plants with floating row covers until the squash plants flower, and spraying insecticidal soap, Neem oil, or pyrethrum on plants to kill them.

➤ **Squash Vine Borers:** The squash vine borer is a little different from the squash bug. The adult fly lays an egg on the squash stem near the soil. The egg hatches and the caterpillar tunnels into the squash vine to feed. The feeding causes the plant to wilt during the day and eventually die. You can stop the squash vine borer from damaging your plants by growing butternut squash (they don't seem to attack it as much), placing a floating row cover over plants until they flower, slitting the infected squash vine and physically removing the worm (bury the stem afterward so it will reroot), or injecting *Bacillus thuringiensis* (B.t.) into the vine with a syringe to kill it.

➤ **Spider Mites:** These tiny pests are only really evident when there are too many of them. Spider mites are small pests that you'll notice when they reach epic numbers and form a webbing on your leaves and plants. They are particularly fond of tomatoes and beans. By the time you spot the webbing, they have probably caused stippling (small, yellow dots) by feeding on the leaves. If the infestation is severe, they can kill the leaves. Spider mites like hot, dry conditions, so they are less prevalent during cool, rainy summers. To prevent their damage, keep plants misted and well watered, and spray insecticidal soap when you start seeing damage.

➤ **Tree Borers:** Many fruit trees and some berries, especially apple, raspberry, and peach, can be infected with boring insects. The borers lay eggs on the stems or trunks and the young larvae tunnel into the stem or trunk to feed. The tunneling results in holes with sticky sap exuding from them and weakened branches, stems, and trunks. The holes create an opening for disease to infect the tree or bush. Control borer damage by removing infected stems. Keep trees and berries healthy and growing strong to overcome the damage. If you notice a freshly dug borer hole, take a clothes hanger–sized wire and probe into the hole to kill the young borer.

➤ **Whiteflies:** If you pass by your tomatoes, squash, beans, melons, cucumbers, or other vegetables and notice tiny white bugs flying around, look on the underside of the leaves and you'll see many whiteflies. Whitefly adults hover and feed on plants, and their young are small white gnats that love to suck the juices from your leaves and flowers. They love warm weather, so you'll see them more in the middle and end of summer. They reproduce quickly so they can become a swarm in your garden in no time. Control them with sprays of insecticidal soap or Neem oil, or hang yellow sticky traps above the plants to trap them. Spinosad also works really well on whiteflies.

Getting Rid of Diseases

Unlike insects, which you can attack once you see damage or the pest, diseases are tricky. Once you see disease symptoms, it's often too late. Fungi, bacteria, and viruses are the most common diseases that can attack your plants. Their damage can be weather dependent. For example, during cool, wet springs we might see many more rotting diseases on roots and fungal diseases on leaves. As with insects, there are good organisms and bad. There are now some organic disease control products on the market that use this concept and pit one microorganism against another.

Being on your game for diseases means doing more work preventing them than trying to control them after they attack. Keep your plants healthy by providing optimum growing conditions. Here are some guidelines for stopping diseases before they start.

- **Plant resistant varieties:** A number of fruits and vegetables are resistant to some common diseases. For example, look for blight-resistant tomatoes and scab-resistant apples.
- **Clean up after yourself:** It's commonly called garden sanitation, but really it means cleaning up plant debris well in fall. Like insects, many disease spores overwinter on plant debris, waiting to reinfect your plants in spring.
- **Rotate your crops:** Crop rotation means not planting a crop in the same family in the same location for at least three years. Some common families of vegetables that should be rotated include cabbage (cabbage, broccoli, cauliflower, kale, kohlrabi), tomato (tomato, pepper, potato, eggplant), cucumber (cucumber, melon, squash, pumpkin), and bean (bean, pea, soybean). By not planting any of the same family of vegetables in the same location for three years, the diseases that infect that family won't build up in the soil.
- **Water early:** Water your gardens in the morning, allowing the leaves to dry by evening. Wet leaves at night are more susceptible to fungi attacks.
- **Mulch:** Placing a mulch under your plants will slow the progression of some diseases. For example, mulch under tomatoes blocks early blight disease spores in the soil from splashing up onto the leaves and infecting them.
- **Keep the soil drained:** Poorly drained soil can harbor more diseases than soil that drains water well. Use raised beds or plant trees on small mounds to encourage water drainage.

Even after taking all the right precautions, your plants may still get diseases. Fortunately, there are some ways to slow their spread. Here are some of the more common diseases in the fruit and vegetable garden and some control ideas.

- **Damping Off:** This fungal disease attacks young seedlings after they germinate, causing them to wilt and die seemingly overnight. To stop damping off fungus, don't overwater, keep the air circulating well around plants, and remove any infected plants as soon as you see them to prevent the fungus from spreading to other plants.
- **Leaf Blights:** There are a number of different diseases that cause spotting, curling, and yellowing of leaves. Some of the more common ones are apple scab, early blight on tomatoes, and leaf curl on peaches.

These can all reduce production on your plant. Control them by growing resistant varieties and spraying with sulfur, copper, or *Bacillus subtilis* organic fungicide.

➤ **Powdery Mildew:** This fungal disease thrives during warm days and cool nights. Come late summer, you'll see the white powdery growth and yellowing leaves on pumpkins, cucumbers, melons, tomatoes, and many other vegetables. Most fruit trees are susceptible as well. Spray *Bacillus subtilis* on leaves to prevent its spread, or mix 1 teaspoon of baking soda and a touch of liquid soap into 1 gallon of water and spray on the leaves. This solution will help prevent the disease from spreading.

➤ **Root Rots:** There are a number of soilborne fungal diseases that attack the roots of plants. Usually they proliferate due to poor water drainage and can be most troublesome during wet years. To prevent these diseases, plant in well-drained soil, use raised beds, and remove dead plants as soon as they are noticed.

➤ **Viruses:** Viruses attack many herbs, vegetables, and fruits, causing plant stunting and deformed growth. They are often spread by insects, so controlling the insects helps control the viruses. Growing certified disease-free plants and removing infected plants are the best ways to limit damage.

➤ **Wilts:** Wilt attacks the insides of vegetables and herbs, causing the plants to shrivel and die. Cucumbers, squash, tomatoes, peppers, and eggplants are some of the vegetables infected by wilt diseases. Look for disease-resistant varieties and remove infected plants to stop the disease's spread.

What Are You Spraying?

Spraying should always be your last line of defense. Before you reach for the sprayer, always ask yourself if spraying is really necessary. Decide whether the damage really warrants control. Sometimes you can just live with it. Make sure it is the insect in question that's causing the problem. Sometimes it will be another pest, weather, or some other factor that is causing the damage. Try techniques that will block the insects from attacking, such as floating row covers, or use traps, such as Japanese beetle traps. These techniques are less harmful to the environment. Finally, if you do have to spray, always use pesticides that target the specific insect, if possible, and ones that are least harmful to wildlife and the environment. Always use caution when spraying pesticides. Just because it's organic doesn't mean it's safe. It kills insects and diseases for a reason.

Throughout chapter 8, I suggest a number of organic sprays and pest solutions you can use to keep specific vegetables, herbs, and fruits healthy. Here is a more detailed description of the products you can purchase at your local garden center.

➤ ***Bacillus subtilis*** **(Serenade®):** This is a relatively new biological agent that attacks fungi such as powdery mildew and blight. This bacteria is harmless to wildlife, pets, and humans.

➤ ***Bacillus thuringiensis*** **(B.t.):** This naturally occurring bacteria attacks insects in the butterfly family only. It is very targeted and is often used on insects such as cabbageworms, potato beetles, and tomato hornworms. To work, the bacteria must be eaten by the insects, so spray B.t. as soon as you see signs of damage.

➤ **Floating Row Cover:** This white, spunbonded, cheesecloth-like material lets light, water, and air through but blocks insects and animals from entering. There are different weights of floating row covers on the market. Some are thicker and good for frost protection down to around 25°F. Others are lightweight and suited for blocking insects. You can place the row cover on the plants and let them grow through it, or use wire hoops to create a tunnel and lay the row cover over that. They can be reused for a number of years.

➤ **Horticultural Oil:** Horticultural or summer oil is a highly refined oil that is used to smoother insects such as aphids and mites. It can also be used as a spray in winter to cover and kill overwintering eggs and insects on fruit trees.

➤ **Insecticidal Soap:** This refined soap-based product is quick working and has low toxicity to wildlife and humans. It's mostly used on soft-bodied insects such as aphids, whiteflies, and spider mites.

➤ **Neem Oil:** Refined from the seeds of the Neem tree native to India, this pesticide repels and kills a wide variety of insects, such as aphids and whiteflies. Neem also has good fungicidal properties. If sprayed in heat over about 87°F or in direct sunlight, Neem can be seriously phytotoxic (burns the plant leaves). It is best to spray very early or very late in the day.

➤ **Pyrethrum:** This botanical spray is derived from the pyrethrum flower. It is highly toxic to a number of insects and is considered a broad-spectrum insecticide, meaning it kills both the good guys and bad guys, including honeybees. However, it is effective on hard-to-kill insects such as cucumber beetles and squash bugs. Use pyrethrum only as a last resort.

➤ **Spinosad:** These bacteria are like B.t. in that insects must eat them to die. They attack a broad range of insects, including caterpillars, spider mites, and whiteflies. The product is safe for beneficial insects, but toxic to honeybees. Spray spinosad on cloudy days or in the evening when bees are less active.

➤ **Sulfur and Copper Sprays:** These mineral sprays are effective at controlling many diseases such as blight, leaf curl, and scab. They must be used carefully because they can cause leaf damage if sprayed during high temperatures, on the wrong plants, or in conjunction with other sprays such as horticultural oil.

➤ **Traps:** There are a number of traps on the market for everything from apple maggots to Japanese beetles. These traps trick insects into landing where they can't escape. Many use color or pheromones (natural chemical lures) to attract the insects and a sticky substance such as Tanglefoot to hold them onto the trap.

Welcome to Animal House

More and more the pests that I get questions about are not slimy diseases or flying beetles, but animals. Unlike most insects and diseases, our four-legged friends can create a mess in a garden, literally overnight. If you've ever grown sweet corn, you know what I mean. You may never see any signs of raccoons in your area until the night before you're ready to start harvesting the sweet corn. Then they come out of the woods and decimate your corn patch. As we have built homes in woodlands and fields, we have moved into animal habitats. Many people want to live with our wild creatures and not harm them. But that often puts them at odds with growing their gardens.

In my experience the two most reliable ways to keep animals away from a garden are a fence and repellent sprays. Often you'll see lists of animal-resistant plants to grow. While these lists focus on plants that certain animals may avoid, when hungry enough, animals will eat just about anything. The best methods of control involve understanding your pests and anticipating their behaviors before there is damage.

Here are some of the most common Northeast wildlife that attack vegetables, herbs, berries, and fruit trees with some suggested methods of control.

➢ **Birds:** Birds can cause problems in two different ways. Crows love to follow you in the garden and dig up newly planted seeds. Robins and others will feast on ripening cherries, strawberries, and blueberries. To thwart crows and other birds from digging up seeds, lay a floating row cover or wire caging over small beds after planting. Once your seeds are up, birds tend not to bother them as much. For fruits, try using bird netting. Although it is cumbersome to install and makes harvesting the berries more difficult, bird netting prevents birds from reaching the ripening fruits. It's best to construct a wooden or PVC pipe tent to place the netting on to avoid damaging the bushes when removing the netting. Construct the netting structure before the fruits ripen, so the birds don't know there's something good to eat. As with fences, if animals don't know there's a meal on the other side, they will be less likely to try to get through the netting or fence.

You can also try to scare birds away with various sight and sound repellents. Balloons painted to look like a hawk's eye, shiny Mylar reflective tape, and plastic owls all can be used in the berry patch to confuse birds. You'll have to move these often so the birds don't get used to them. Playing the radio or timing periodic air horn blasts or gun blasts will scare birds out of the berries. It might also scare the neighbors into calling the police, so check with them before trying this technique.

➢ **Cats and Dogs:** Man's best friend sometimes is not. Dogs love to dig and cats like to use freshly tilled earth as a litter box. The best dog control is to fence the garden so they know where their run is and the garden is off limits. For cats, place a floating row cover over a newly tilled and planted bed, or place sharp, thorny canes of roses, raspberries, or blackberries on the bed. Cats don't like their paws touching sharp objects and will avoid the bed.

➢ **Deer:** This is the biggest pest of many Northeast gardens. Because man has built houses and developments in forests, deer habitat has shrunk. However, instead of moving deeper into the forests, deer have adapted by eating our beautifully planted gardens. Since hunting is outlawed in suburban areas, the deer have free range. The result is an exploding population of deer in the Northeast.

A good fence is the surest way to keep Bambi away. There are a couple of options when it comes to fencing. You can build an 8-foot-tall fence around the garden so deer can't jump over it. However, that creates an expensive and imposing fortress. You can always build two shorter (4-foot-tall) fences spaced 5 feet apart. Deer won't jump over a fence if they are unsure of the landing area. They don't want to get caught between fences. The best bet is an electric fence. Construct an electric fence so the two strands are 2 and 5 feet off the ground, and bait the strands with peanut butter early in the season. The deer will be drawn to the peanut butter, nibble on it, and get shocked. You can train the deer not to come in that area with this

method, and I know gardeners who swear they turn off their electric fence in summer because the deer are trained to stay away. If you're growing berry bushes or fruit trees, protect the young plants from deer browsing in winter by putting up a fence. They love eating the tender branches of blueberries, raspberries, and fruit trees.

If you can't or won't use fencing, then try repellent sprays. The key to using repellents is to rotate three or four different sprays so the deer don't get used to any one smell or taste. Also, continue spraying in spring and summer as new growth forms. I'll talk about some different repellent sprays later in this chapter. Some gardeners even use motion sensors attached to their water hose. When they detect a deer browsing at night, the hose goes on to scare away the intruder. However, you'll have to remember the sensor is there or you may be the next one getting wet.

➤ **Mice, Voles, and Chipmunks:** These small rodents sure have a healthy appetite. I watched one year as a chipmunk systematically removed gooseberries from my bush, sucked out the juices, and left the skins on a rock nearby. He must have eaten twenty gooseberries before I scared him away. These rodents will tunnel underground or use mole tunnels to eat roots, bulbs, and tubers of vegetables. Chipmunks have been known to steal small fruits too. Fence the garden well with hardware cloth standing 1 foot above the ground and buried 12 inches below the ground. Try repellent sprays of hot pepper, garlic, and Bitrex used before the plants mature or fruits ripen.

Mice and voles also girdle (strip the bark from) young fruit trees and berry bushes in winter under the protection of snow. Place plastic or wire mesh trunk protectors on your young trees in fall to prevent this damage. Place the tree wraps a few inches below the ground and up to the first set of branches

➤ **Rabbits:** Peter Rabbit is not the smartest critter on the block, but he loves greens, carrot tops, and young seedlings. Like mice and voles, rabbits can also girdle young fruit trees in winter. A good fence will keep them away. Use small-mesh (1½-inch) fencing so they don't slip through, and secure it well to the ground with tent stakes so they don't crawl underneath. Repellent sprays such as hot pepper spray and garlic can also deter their feeding.

➤ **Raccoons:** Not only do these critters love corn, as I mentioned, but they will also feed on melons and ripening fruits. Protect small corn patches by taping shut the individual corn ears with packing tape or covering ears with bags right before they are ready to harvest. Construct an electric fence to keep raccoons out of larger patches or build a woodchuck fence as described below.

➤ **Squirrels:** For such a small animal, I get an awful lot of calls about squirrel damage. Squirrels have adapted too well to human activity. They nest in nearby trees and love to raid bird feeders, newly planted bulbs, fruits, and vegetables. I even saw a squirrel running away with a ripe tomato once. They are cheeky little guys and pretty fearless. To prevent squirrel damage, plant trees and berry bushes away from the house or other trees and structures from which squirrels can launch themselves onto your plants. Use squirrel baffles (metal cones around the trunk) on trees to prevent them from climbing up from the ground. Try repellent sprays on prized fruits and vegetables. Some gardeners have had success setting up squirrel feeding stations with dried corn on the opposite end of their property from the gardens. My fear is that you'll just attract that many more squirrels to your yard, but if you're at wits' end, it might be worth a try.

➤ **Woodchucks:** The whistling pig loves to munch through a bean patch or lettuce greens. Woodchucks will often dig holes near a house or garage foundation and become part of the family. The best control is a 3-foot-tall wire fence that is bent to an L shape at the bottom and buried 1 foot underground. As woodchucks approach the fence, their natural instinct is to dig under it. They will soon hit the bent wire underground and get frustrated. Young woodchucks will try to climb the fence. Don't attach the top 12 inches of the fence to the post so the weight of the woodchuck will bend the fence back to the ground outside the garden, preventing the animal from entering.

While fencing is surely the best way to keep out animals, there is a plethora of repellent sprays on the market as well. Here is a rundown of some home remedies and commercial products you might try. Many commercial products will have some of these items as ingredients, plus other materials such as natural oils and soaps. Remember to rotate three or four different sprays for the best results. I don't guarantee they will all work all the time, but they are worth a shot.

➤ **Animal Urine:** Sold as coyote, bobcat, or fox urine, this spray gives woodchucks, deer, rabbits, and other critters the sense that a predator is around and they should flee. It doesn't smell great, but seems to work for a time. Predator urine comes in granular form now, so it is much easier to apply and not so aromatic.

- **Bitrex:** This taste-based repellent is a bitter natural compound that I remember moms using to place on their kids' thumbs to stop them from thumb sucking. It lasts a long time in the environment, making it a good choice for tree fruits, especially in winter.
- **Dried Blood:** Although when used as a fertilizer it can attract animals such as dogs, when formulated as a repellent, dried blood seems to have the opposite effect on other animals such as deer. A number of deer and animal repellents feature dried blood as an active ingredient.
- **Garlic:** Sold as garlic clips or in baskets that you can hang from trees, garlic has an odor that will repel some animals.
- **Hot Pepper (Capsaicin):** Whether you use a commercial spray or flakes of dried chili peppers, this hot compound will discourage lots of animals. However, it will need to be reapplied often.
- **Human Hair:** Collecting human hair and placing it in bags around the garden will give animals the idea you're around. Well, maybe for a few days, but they soon get used to it.
- **Rotten Eggs:** Often used as an ingredient in deer and animal repellents, rotten eggs have a putrid smell that discourages critters, and probably you, from visiting the garden.
- **Soap:** Certain types of heavily perfumed soap, such as Irish Spring, are known to repel deer. Then again, I talked to a gardener recently who said the deer ate the soap hanging in his tree. You'll have to experiment.

A Word on Trapping Animals

While it seems humane to live trap an errant woodchuck, rabbit, or squirrel, you have to be careful. Some animals carry rabies. If you notice a wild animal acting strangely or aggressively in your garden, call the local game warden. Do not approach the animal. Using a live trap to move animals to another habitat isn't always the most humane thing to do. Depending on the time of year, the animal may have babies left behind who will die without their mother. Also, animals may get disoriented if moved to a new location and come into conflict with other animals already there. It's best to consult your state fish and game department about rules and regulations on relocating wildlife.

CHAPTER 7

STORING & PRESERVING THE HARVEST

I hope you've been anxiously awaiting this chapter on storing and preserving your harvest. That would tell me you did a great job growing your vegetables, fruits, and herbs and now don't know what to do with all the bounty. Surely you can get in the good graces of your family, friends, neighbors, and local authorities by giving away your harvest. It's always a satisfying feeling walking down the road and delivering a basket of vegetables to an unsuspecting neighbor. While it's usually a surprise, I have neighbors who now anticipate their summer deliveries.

But you should also think about what's next. We all know fall and winter comes with a crash to gardens in the Northeast, and soon we have only memories of green leaves, ripe tomatoes, and red strawberries. Storing and preserving your harvest is a way to extend that memory and reality into winter. Plus, it will help you save money on food, and you'll have the satisfaction of making a holiday meal from your own vegetables and fruits.

You can grow fresh produce late into fall by following the techniques described in chapter 5 for succession planting and growing a fall garden. Vegetables such as leeks, kale, carrots, and spinach can withstand freezing temperatures and still be tasty. However, there are many fruits and vegetables that won't survive outdoors after a freeze. Whether you just want to preserve a little extra harvest of beans or blueberries, or you want to go hog wild and plant extra rows of basil for pesto, tomatoes for canning, and strawberries for jam, the techniques for storing and preserving the bounty are the same.

Storing Fresh Vegetables & Fruits

Many vegetables and fruits can be stored fresh indoors in winter for months if you match the plant with the conditions. The first step is to harvest bruise- and blemish-free veggies and fruits at the peak of maturity. Fruits that are insect-ridden, disease-ridden, or overmature will rot in storage before you can use them. Many vegetables and fruits, such as greens, soft berries, cucumbers, summer squash, tomatoes, and corn, are better processed than stored fresh for winter use.

Most vegetables and fruits need cool conditions to last a long time. The degree of coolness varies, depending on the crop. Also, the humidity will influence how long a crop lasts in storage. There are four combinations of cool, cold, dry, and moist that are used to store your fruits and vegetables. Find the right conditions in your house and garage and you'll know what veggies and fruits you can store. If you want to get really advanced, you can create root cellars and other storage areas that provide the perfect storage conditions.

➤ **Cool and Dry:** The temperature should be between 50°F and 60°F and the humidity should be about 60 percent. Luckily, most home basements fit this bill. Pumpkins and winter squash can be stored under these conditions for up to four or five months. I've even stored potatoes and garlic under these conditions, and although they don't last as long as under colder or moister conditions, they still are fine into late fall.

➤ **Cool and Moist:** Again, the temperature should be between 50°F and 60°F, but with 90 percent humidity. A simple way to increase the humidity around your vegetables in a typical basement is to store the fruits in perforated plastic bags. Cucumbers, eggplants, peppers, summer squash, tomatoes, and watermelons can be stored in these conditions, but probably for only a week or two. The exception is sweet potatoes, which can be stored under these conditions for four months.

- ➤ **Cold and Dry:** Temperatures here must be approaching freezing with highs only around 40°F and the humidity should be 60 percent. Some houses may have cold basements or garages that fit these conditions. Garlic, onions, and shallots store well under these conditions.
- ➤ **Cold and Moist:** Again, temperatures need to be just above freezing, but the humidity should be closer to 90 percent. Your handy refrigerator works well for these vegetables if you place the produce in perforated plastic bags. Apples, asparagus, beets, Brussels sprouts, cabbage, carrots, cauliflower, kohlrabi, melons, parsnips, pears, potatoes, and turnips can be stored for one to six months, depending on the fruit or vegetable.

Another way to store your vegetables is in the ground. Leave root crops, such as carrots, parsnips, and turnips, in the ground in winter. The key is to mulch the beds with a 6-inch layer of straw or hay and cover the hay with plastic secured to the ground with stones or boards. The mulch will prevent the soil from freezing, so you can go out even on the coldest winter day to harvest your roots. Wait until late fall to protect your winter roots, because mice and voles would love the hay as a winter home, complete with food.

Preserving the Bounty

While storage in the ground, basement, garage, or refrigerator is great for many types of fruits and vegetables, other types are best processed to last more than a few weeks after harvest. Soft fruits, such as blueberries, currants, grapes, peaches, plums, strawberries, and raspberries, are all best processed, then stored. Vegetables such as beans, cucumbers, peas, peppers, squash, and tomatoes don't last long stored fresh. While herbs such as basil and parsley can make nice houseplants for a little while in fall and winter, they are best stored in another form.

There are three main ways to preserve your vegetables, fruits, and herbs: canning, drying, and freezing. Let's look at each one. As with storing produce fresh, always select damage-free fruits and leaves picked at the peak of ripeness to process.

Canning

One of my fondest childhood memories is sitting in the garage with my mother and cleaning tomatoes to can. Canning tomatoes is an Italian and Nardozzi family tradition. I've carried it on by teaching my daughter how to can tomatoes. There's nothing like opening a jar of home-canned tomatoes on a cold winter's day to add to soups or sauces.

Canning is a bit involved for the beginning gardener, so if you want to delve into the world of canning vegetables and fruits, I recommend that you find a friend or family member who has the equipment and knowledge to do it correctly. However, once you are set up, canning can become an event. It's nice to can communally with friends and family. The work goes faster and the time quicker when chatting about the day's events while peeling fruits, sterilizing jars, cooking, boiling, and sealing the canning jars. Throw a canning party and invite your friends to bring their produce to add to the mix.

Drying

Drying, like canning, takes time, but you won't be as involved on a minute-by-minute basis. I have to admit I haven't done a lot of drying of vegetables and fruits. Our variable Northeast climate isn't conducive to drying anything outdoors. Ideally, you should have two to four hot days with low humidity to dry fruits and vegetables. That's rare in our humid climate.

So that leaves you indoors using your oven or dehydrator. A dehydrator is the perfect tool for drying batches of berries, cherries, summer squash, and tomatoes. It's a money investment for sure, but if you get into it you'll be amazed at how easy it is and how much you can dry and store.

Beginners are more likely to use the oven. A convection oven is ideal because of the air circulation, but a regular oven will do. Set it on 140°F, keep the door ajar, slice the vegetables about ¼ inch thick, and lay them on trays, not touching. Place the tray in the oven. Depending on what you're drying, it can take six to thirty-six hours. Some of the easiest vegetables and fruits to dry for first-timers are apples, cherry tomatoes, hot peppers, and pears.

You can also make your own fruit leathers easily. Blend together your extra fruits, pour the slurry onto parchment paper, and dry in a dehydrator or oven. It's a great snack for kids. You can store dried fruits and vegetables for months. Heat your oven to 140°F and leave the doof slightly ajar. You might even turn on a small fan right outside the door to aid in air circulation. Use a thermometer in the oven to make sure the heat stays around 140°F.

Freezing

Freezing is probably the easiest way for newbie gardeners to preserve some of their harvest. Most everyone has a freezer and, unlike canning and drying, the process doesn't require lots of equipment and time. Some of my favorite fruits to freeze are blueberries, cherries, raspberries, and strawberries. While the consistency is not the same as fresh fruits, when you thaw these fruits in winter, they still impart their flavor in cooking and fruit smoothies. My winter ritual is making a banana and berry smoothie almost every morning.

Many vegetables freeze well too. I freeze beans, corn, peas, and batches of pesto made from basil. The key to freezing is to blanch your vegetables before popping them in freezer bags. Blanching means submerging the vegetables in boiling water for only a few minutes. The process stops enzyme activity in the vegetables, so they retain their color and flavor in the freezer. Follow the directions as to how long to blanch for each vegetable from the resources section. Underblanching may not stop all the enzyme activity, while overblanching makes for tasteless food. After the vegetables have been blanched, cool them off, tuck the produce in freezer bags, store in the freezer, and, voilà, you're done.

There's certainly more information available for storing and preserving fruits and vegetables than I can provide in this brief chapter, so check out these two excellent resources on how to can, dry, and freeze your produce safely.

➤ National Center for Home Food Preservation (www.uga.edu/nchfp/)
➤ Pick-Your-Own (www.pickyourown.org)

CHAPTER 8

VEGETABLES, HERBS & FRUITS

Now that you understand *how* to garden in the Northeast, it's time to talk about *what* to plant. This chapter includes vegetables, fruits, and herbs that are some of the most well known and easiest to grow in the Northeast.

For each edible, there is an easy-to-follow guide that includes When to Plant, Where to Plant, How to Plant, Care and Maintenance, Harvesting, and Additional Information. This takes the guesswork out of planting your favorite variety or trying something new. After all, starting with the right plant is the best way to get your garden off on the right foot. So, all that's left to do is decide what to grow, select your seeds or plants, and get started growing a garden that will reward you with delicious vegetables, fruits, and herbs all season long. Refer to chapter 6 for more details on pest control.

ARTICHOKE

Most people think of globe artichoke (*Cynara scolymus*) as a specialty vegetable from California. When I used to visit the Central California coast each winter, I enjoyed wandering the artichoke fields and eating "chokes" right from the farm. But now I can grow artichokes right here in the Northeast too.

With new varieties adapted to our climate, globe artichokes are no longer a specialty item, but a regular vegetable at farmers' markets and stands in summer. This thistle-family perennial vegetable produces a large, attractive, gray-green-foliaged plant with edible flower buds. You're actually eating the flowers before they open. Steaming is the best way to prepare this Italian delicacy. Pull off the leaf bracts (petals) and work your way down to the artichoke heart, dipping each part in butter. It's a tasty adventure in eating. You can also eat the cooked hearts in salads or tossed in pasta dishes.

■ *When to Plant*

In California artichokes are planted in fall, are overwintered, and produce buds in spring. They need the cold period to induce bud formation. Since they're not hardy in the Northeast without extensive winter protection, we have to plant them as annuals in spring for a late-summer crop. The key is to select varieties adapted to our growing season. These will produce buds without having to be exposed to winter's chill. Sow seeds indoors six to eight weeks before your last frost date. Plant in late April to late May, after the threat of frost has passed.

■ *Where to Plant*

Plant artichokes in full sun on well-drained, fertile soil. The plant grows quickly to 4 feet tall, so it needs lots of nutrients and water. Artichokes don't like cold, wet soil, so if your garden has heavy clay soil, consider building and planting in a raised bed.

■ *How to Plant*

The key to getting artichokes to set buds without going through a winter is to expose the seedlings to temperatures between 32°F and 50°F for ten days in spring. You can purchase seedlings from a greenhouse that has already had this cold treatment or set them outside yourself in late spring.

Amend the soil with a 2-inch layer of compost prior to planting and set plants 2 to 3 feet apart in rows spaced 4 feet apart.

■ *Care and Maintenance*

Artichokes need constant soil moisture and good fertility to grow their best. Keep plants watered and well weeded. Once established, mulch with a 2- to 3-inch layer of straw mulch. Dry soils result in small and fewer flower buds. Fertilize monthly with a high-nitrogen organic fertilizer such as soybean meal or fish emulsion.

Artichokes don't have many pest problems. Poor soil drainage will result in root rot. Keep the soil well drained to avoid this disease. Slugs and snails may attack young plants during periods of wet weather. Control these pests with traps and organic baits.

■ *Harvesting*

Spring-planted artichokes begin setting flower buds in midsummer, about eighty to ninety days after planting. Buds should be harvested when they're still firm, but full sized. The first bud is the largest. Cut the bud a few inches below the flower. Smaller side buds will continue to form and can be harvested until frost. A large, healthy plant can yield up to twenty buds.

■ *Additional Information*

'Imperial Star' and 'Tavor' were specifically bred for growing in the Northeast. They produce 3- to 4-inch-diameter buds. 'Tempo' is a new purple variety that can produce up to twenty buds in one season. Cardoon (*Cynara cardunculus*) is an attractive artichoke relative that doesn't form flower buds. It's grown for its edible stems that are best grown blanched (sunlight is blocked from reaching the stems), cooked, and eaten.

ARUGULA

Arugula (*Eruca vesicaria* ssp. *sativa*), or rocket, is an easy-to-grow, quick-maturing Italian green that has rocketed in popularity over the last twenty years. I love growing it in cold frames early in spring for the first taste of fresh greens. Because of its cold tolerance, it can withstand freezing temperatures and still survive. I've even seen a fall crop overwinter with a little winter protection. It's best eaten while the weather is cool. The dark green, tender leaves have a nutty, spicy flavor. If it is grown in the heat, overcrowded, or water stressed, the leaves turn chewy and the flavor becomes spicy hot.

While you can grow and eat arugula all by itself in salads or sautés, I like making a nutty, spicy pesto from it. However, most people use it mixed in salads with milder-tasting lettuces and spinach.

◼ *When to Plant*

Direct sow arugula seeds as soon as the soil has dried out enough to plant—as early as the beginning of April. Sow small patches of seeds every two weeks to extend the harvest season. Stop sowing seeds when hot weather arrives in early summer, but start again in late summer for a fall harvest.

◼ *Where to Plant*

Arugula grows best in loose, well-drained soil amended with compost. Unlike many other vegetables, arugula can be grown in part sun and still yield a good crop. I've even successfully planted it in a container on my

deck for a continuous crop of greens all summer. It can be planted in its own bed or grown between slower-to-mature vegetables, such as broccoli and cabbage. Since arugula will be harvested within forty days of sowing, you'll get a quick green crop before the larger plants get too big to shade it out.

■ *How to Plant*

Sow seeds ¼ inch deep and about 1 inch apart in rows, or broadcast evenly over a raised bed. Thin plants to 6 to 8 inches apart once they germinate. Eat the thinnings as baby greens in salads.

■ *Care and Maintenance*

Arugula seeds germinate and grow quickly. Keep the soil evenly moist and well weeded. Fertilize them with fish emulsion if the leaves are yellow. Protect young leaves from flea beetles by growing arugula under a floating row cover. Flea beetles are small black insects that eat shotgun-like holes in leaves. These row covers let air, light, and water in, but keep the flea beetles away from the leaves.

■ *Harvesting*

Arugula can be harvested as baby greens about twenty days after seeding or allowed to mature to full size in about forty days. Cut baby greens with scissors, snipping the plants an inch or so above their base. They will regrow for a second harvest. You can also pull out individual large plants.

■ *Additional Information*

There are some varieties of arugula with special characteristics. 'Astro' is a heat-tolerant variety with long, straplike leaves. 'Sylvetta' is also called "Wild Italian Arugula." It has smaller, more serrated leaves and a stronger flavor. It's also known as Rucola selvatica. A very fast-growing arugula variety is 'Surrey'. Its leaves are similar in shape to those of 'Astro'.

ASIAN GREENS

Asian greens (*Brassica rapa, B. juncea*) used to be thought of as just bok choy. However, with the popularity of Asian cuisine, people are growing a wide variety of Asian greens with flavors from mild to spicy. Leaf colors range from purple-leaved mustards to the white-ribbed komatsuna. The leaf shapes can be flat and spoon-shaped, long and round, or thin and serrated.

I like mixing young or baby Asian greens with milder-flavored greens to add a little zip to salads. Try using them in soups and sautés too. I love stir-frying some bok choy with garlic and soy sauce and tossing it over soba noodles. These greens are easy to grow, love the cool weather, and grow in small spaces. They're perfect for a Northeast gardener.

◼ *When to Plant*

Direct sow seeds in early spring (April to early May), two weeks before your last frost. Plant small patches of greens every two weeks until early summer for a succession of harvests. Sow another crop in late summer for a fall harvest. Greens maturing during cool weather will be tender and mild flavored. Greens maturing in the heat can turn spicy and tough textured.

◼ *Where to Plant*

Asian greens grow best in well-drained soil. They don't need full sun to thrive. Quick-maturing greens, such as mizuna, can grow with as little as two to three hours of direct sun a day. Slower-maturing greens, such as bok choy, need more light. Plant in raised beds or containers.

■ *How to Plant*

Sow seeds ¼ inch deep and about 1 inch apart in rows, or broadcast evenly over a raised bed. Thin plants to 6 to 12 inches apart once they germinate if growing them to full size. Keep the spacing closer for smaller greens, such as shungiku, and farther apart for larger greens, such as mustard. Eat the thinnings as baby greens in salads.

■ *Care and Maintenance*

Asian greens grow best on evenly moist and well-weeded soil. Fertilize young seedlings once they germinate with fish emulsion to encourage more growth. Mulch plants with straw or untreated grass clippings after the plants are established to prevent weed growth and keep the soil cool and moist.

Protect young leaves from flea beetles by growing Asian greens under a floating row cover. Flea beetles are small black insects that eat shotgun-like holes in leaves. These row covers let air, light, and water in, but keep the flea beetles away from the leaves.

■ *Harvesting*

Start harvesting baby Asian greens for salads twenty days after sowing seeds. Allow larger-sized Asian greens, such as tatsoi and bok choy, to mature in forty days to full size for use in cooking. Cut tender greens with scissors just above the ground and allow them to regrow. Pull to harvest large mature plants.

■ *Additional Information*

There are a number of different Asian greens to grow in the garden. Mizuna features pencil-thin stalks on deeply serrated light green leaves. There is also a purple-leafed version available. This mild-flavored green is often mixed in salads. Komatsuna is a heat-tolerant green with juicy, white-leaf ribs. There is also a purple version available. Shungiku, or edible chrysanthemum, has serrated 4- to 8-inch-long leaves and edible yellow or orange flowers. 'Osaka Purple' mustard grows up to 2 feet tall with large, purple, spicy leaves. It's great picked as a baby green for salads. Tatsoi forms a pretty rosette of spoon-shaped, dark green leaves.

There are a number of bok choy varieties available to choose from, many with thick, white, juicy stems. I like the baby bok choy varieties, such as 'Mei Qing Choi', since they're a good size for individual servings. There is also 'Red Choi' that has a hint of red coloring on the leaves.

ASPARAGUS

While most vegetables we grow are annuals, asparagus (*Asparagus officinalis*) is a delightful exception. This long-lived perennial is one of the first vegetables harvested in spring. It's native to the Mediterranean coast, which explains its love of well-drained, sandy soils.

The spears, or new shoots, are harvested for two months in spring. I like them oven-roasted with balsamic vinegar. You can also sauté them in butter or oil, add them to casseroles and salads, or even use them to make soup. After the harvest season, the spears grow into attractive ferns. I've even seen them grown as a ferny hedge to block an unsightly view.

■ *When to Plant*

Plant asparagus crowns in spring as soon as the soil dries out. These spider-like, bare-root plants are available online or at your local garden center.

■ *Where to Plant*

Plant asparagus in well-drained, loose soil. Choose a location that will stay in full sun for years to come. Avoid places with trees that may eventually grow, shading your asparagus bed and reducing production.

■ *How to Plant*

Amend the soil with lime to raise the pH to between 6.5 to 7.5. Dig a trench 6 to 10 inches deep (deeper in sandy soil, shallower in clay soil). At the bottom of the trench, make small mounds of soil, spaced 12 inches apart, and drape the asparagus crown over each one. Amend the native soil with compost and backfill the trench so the crowns are 3 inches deep. Water well. After six weeks, fill the remainder of the trench with compost and native soil.

■ *Care and Maintenance*

Based on a soil test, add phosphorus or potassium fertilizer to keep your asparagus growing well. Keep the bed well weeded, since asparagus doesn't compete well with other plants. Add a 2-inch layer of straw or bark mulch around the ferns to help keep weeds at bay and keep the soil cool and moist. Keep the bed moist for the first few years. Older asparagus beds are more tolerant of drought.

Watch for the asparagus beetle. This red beetle lays eggs on the asparagus ferns. The young, sluglike larvae feed on the ferns and can defoliate the plant. Handpick the larvae and the adults, or spray pyrethrum in the evening to control adult beetles and apply Neem oil in the evening to control the larvae. Neem oil isn't toxic to bees.

Fusarium wilt and rust disease may attack and kill asparagus, especially on poorly drained soils. Select your planting site wisely and purchase disease-resistant varieties to avoid these problems.

Cut back old ferns in fall after they have yellowed and you've had a frost. Asparagus is winter hardy throughout the Northeast, so it requires little winter protection.

■ *Harvesting*

Allow the spears to grow into ferns for the first two years without harvesting. This will strengthen the roots, and ultimately the plant, for the long haul. In the third year, harvest for four to eight weeks. Harvest spears when they are ½-inch in diameter or larger spears when they're 6 inches long. Leave thinner spears to grow into ferns.

To get white asparagus, blanch (block the light) the spears once they emerge from the ground by mounding soil over them or covering them with a pot. White asparagus has a more tender texture and a milder flavor.

■ *Additional Information*

The best varieties for our region are the Jersey hybrids. These Rutgers University–bred varieties are more productive and disease resistant than older varieties. They also produce mostly male spears and ferns. This means there are few female shoots producing red berries. The berries take energy away from production, and when the seeds in the berries sprout, the new plants can become weeds in the garden. 'Jersey Knight' grows well in heavier soils. 'Jersey Supreme' is a high-yielding variety with good disease resistance. While not part of the all-male Jersey series, 'Purple Passion' is unique for its purple spears and ferns. The spears turn green when cooked.

BEAN

If you're looking for an easy vegetable to grow, try beans. Whether bush or pole beans, they are the perfect vegetable for a beginner's or kids' garden. They're one of the first vegetables I taught my daughter to grow. The large seeds make this vegetable easy to plant. They need little extra fertilizer, and, with only a small amount of attention, you're almost guaranteed to get a harvest.

There's a wide variety of beans available to grow. Snap beans (*Phaseolus vulgaris*) are harvested while the pods are young and before the seeds form inside. There are green, yellow, and purple snap bean varieties. Shelling beans have green pods, but their seeds have formed. You eat the seeds. Lima beans, fava beans (*Vicia faba*), and soybeans (*Glycine max*) are popular selections of shelling bean. A dried bean has mature seeds (which you eat) and dried pods. 'Vermont Cranberry' and 'French Horticultural' are some varieties of dried beans. Most of these bean types have both bush and pole (climbing) varieties. Bush beans (shown below) grow about 2 feet tall, while pole beans can grow to 10 feet tall.

Beans are good for you. They're loaded with protein, fiber, calcium, and B vitamins. They can be used in almost any cuisine and can be pickled, canned, sautéed, cooked in soups and stews, or served raw in salads.

■ *When to Plant*

Although there's a wide variety of beans to grow, most of them like the same growing conditions. With the exception of favas, beans like growing in the heat. So plant in spring after all danger of frost has passed, when the soil is at least 60°F. This is usually in mid- to late May and even June. Plant fava beans two weeks before your last frost date (as early as the end of April) and again in late summer for a fall crop. Fava beans can survive temperatures in the 20s°F, making them great fall and early-winter plants.

■ *Where to Plant*

Beans are widely adapted plants. They grow well in clay and sandy soil and fruit best in full sun. Most also grow best with temperatures between 70°F to 85°F. If it gets warmer than that, they may not set fruit well.

■ *How to Plant*

Amend the soil with compost before planting. Bush beans are grown differently than pole beans. Sow bush bean seeds 1 inch deep, spaced 2 to 3 inches apart in rows, 2 feet apart. It's a good practice to inoculate beans just prior to sowing to provide the sprouting roots with the right rhizobia to support nitrogen fixing, especially if you have poor soil. Some studies indicate inoculation increases yield significantly, as much as 50 percent. Thin to 4 to 6 inches apart after the true leaves form. Pole beans are planted on 8-foot-tall poles arranged in a row or a tepee. Plant two to three seeds spaced evenly around each pole. Pole beans naturally want to twine up the poles. You can also grow bush and pole varieties in containers in smaller spaces. Trellis pole beans with wire or twine hung from a porch ceiling or roof.

Fava beans are the exception in the bean family, but are well adapted to our cool spring and fall growing conditions. Plant these as you would bush beans, but since the plants can grow 3 to 4 feet tall, trellis or stake the rows to keep the plants from flopping over.

If planting pole beans in the teepee shape, consider planting lettuce, mesclun mix, or radishes under the teepee. These quick-maturing veggies will grow and mature before the pole beans grow up to shade them. It's a great space-saving strategy in a small garden.

Consider planting successive crops of bush beans until early July, spaced two weeks apart. This will ensure a continuous harvest throughout the summer.

■ *Care and Maintenance*

Beans have the ability to fix nitrogen from the atmosphere through their roots, so they don't require much extra fertilization. Keep the plants evenly watered and well weeded. Beans are shallow rooted, so carefully cultivate around plants to remove weeds. Once the plants are 4 to 6 inches tall, mulch between rows or under the pole beans with a 2- to 3-inch layer of straw or untreated grass clippings.

Beans have a few major pests. Mexican bean beetles can become plentiful in summer and feed on bean leaves. This brown beetle with yellow spots looks like a ladybug, but can cause extensive damage. Handpick adults, crush the eggs, and spray the yellow larvae with Neem oil or spinosad to control it. Rust fungal disease causes orange spots on leaves that can eventually turn them yellow. Grow resistant varieties and don't walk in your bean patch while the leaves are still wet to avoid spreading the disease.

Rabbits and woodchucks love to feed on bean plants. Fence your garden to keep these critters away.

■ *Harvesting*

Snap beans are quick to mature and usually ready to harvest fifty to sixty days after seeding. They tend to mature all at once, so they're good for canning or freezing. Pole snap beans take a little longer to start producing, but tend to produce smaller amounts over time. Harvest snap beans when they're about 6 to 8 inches long, but before the seeds inside have formed. If harvested at a later stage, they tend to be tough and chewy.

Harvest shelling beans, such as limas, soybeans, and favas, when the pods are plump and the beans inside have formed. Depending on the bean, this can be from 60 to 80 days after seeding. Harvest dried beans once the pods and beans have dried on the plant, but before the pods open and drop the bean seeds on the ground. This is usually 100 to 120 days after seeding. Harvest whole plants and hang them to dry in an airy garage or shade out of direct sun. Remove the seeds from the pods when they're fully dry and naturally pop open.

■ *Additional Information*

Many green snap beans such as 'Provider' grow well in our region. However, I like growing the French filet snap beans such as 'Maxibel'. They

stay thin and slender and are more tender than other green snap beans. 'Concador' is a yellow filet bean and 'Velour' is a purple filet bean. Purple beans lose their color when cooked.

There are pole bean versions of many snap beans such as 'Kentucky Wonder' and 'Blue Lake'. I like the flat Italian pole bean 'Jumbo' for its meaty texture and flavor. 'Scarlet Runner' beans feature bright orange flowers, large green pods, and pink and black speckled bean seeds. They can be eaten as a snap, shell, or dried bean, depending on when you harvest. For something different try an asparagus bean. These grow like pole beans but produce 18-inch-long round beans. Harvest them young while the pods are still tender. I like the 'Red Noodle' asparagus bean for its burgundy color that stays red even after cooking.

Lima beans can be marginal in our climate, but 'Fordhook 242' is a good quick-maturing one to try. However, fava beans thrive. I like the heirloom 'Crimson' fava bean for its bright red flowers. 'Windsor' is another good variety.

Edamame or edible soybeans are varieties harvested in the shell stage. 'Envy' and 'Midori Giant' are two quick-maturing varieties that are ready to harvest in seventy to eighty days from planting. I like steaming these in salty water and squeezing the pods to make the seeds pop into my mouth. They're fun for kids to eat.

I couldn't write about our region without mentioning some of our traditional dried bean varieties, made famous by the classic baked bean church supper. 'Vermont Cranberry' features a brown bean with a mild flavor. 'Jacob's Cattle' yields beans with red and white speckles and a kidney-bean shape. They hold up well in cooking.

BEET

If your image of beets (*Beta vulgaris*) is small red balls in cans with a bland, earthy taste, you should give them another try. Beets fresh out of the garden are *delicious*. They're not only healthy for you—they're loaded with vitamins A, B, and C; iron; and potassium—but new varieties expand the color range of the roots to include pink, yellow, white, and candy striped. Beet leaves are now common in baby salad greens mixes. Shred raw beets in garden salads, make borscht soup, roast beets with other root crops (one of my favorite recipes), and, yes, pickle or can beets for winter usage. If you don't like the bleeding and staining from the juice of red beets, choose yellow varieties.

■ *When to Plant*

Beets are a cool-season crop that matures best in spring or fall. In fact, mature plants can withstand a light frost. If grown in the heat of summer, beets tend to be woody textured and less sweet. Plant beets whenever the soil can be worked, from early April to the end of May. Consider planting a fall crop in July or August so they can mature during the cool days of autumn.

■ *Where to Plant*

Plant beets on raised beds, in a neutral pH soil amended with compost. To grow well, beets need a loose, organic soil without many stones, sticks, or soil clumps to inhibit root formation. Beets grow well in light conditions ranging from full sun to only four hours of sun a day. Smaller-rooted varieties, and those grown mostly for their greens, perform well in containers.

■ *How to Plant*

To enhance seed germination, soak beet seeds in warm water the night before planting. Mix potting soil into the top layers of a raised bed to reduce the amount of soil crusting, which seeds may find hard to penetrate.

Sow seeds ½ inch deep and 1 inch apart in rows spaced 15 inches apart. Beets seeds are actually dried "fruits." Each fruit contains three to four seeds. So don't be surprised to see three or more seedlings emerge from each seed. Once seeds germinate and true leaves have formed, thin the seedlings to 4 inches apart. Don't toss them! You can eat the thinnings in salads. If you don't thin early enough, the roots may not develop properly.

■ *Care and Maintenance*

Keep beets well weeded and watered. This root crop doesn't compete well against weeds, so mulch around established plants with an organic mulch, such as straw or untreated grass clippings. Prevent leafminer insects from tunneling in beet roots and flea beetles from eating leaves by placing floating row covers over a crop as soon as it germinates. You can also spray Neem oil or pyrethrum to control these pests.

■ *Harvesting*

The roots of most beet varieties mature forty to sixty days after sowing seeds. Harvest beets at any size for eating, but young beets (with a diameter less than 2 inches) are the most tender. As you harvest individual beets, you'll provide more space for other plants to keep growing bigger roots. Greens can be harvested a few weeks after germination, depending on the leaf size you prefer.

■ *Additional Information*

'Red Ace' is a widely adapted, hybrid red beet selection. 'Chioggia Guardsman' and 'Bull's Blood' have roots with a candy-stripe appearance. 'Bull's Blood' also has burgundy-colored leaves. 'Touchstone' is a good yellow beet variety that holds its golden color when cooked and has a sweeter and milder flavor than red beets. 'Cylindra' features red cylindrically shaped roots that are easier to clean than round roots. 'Lutz Winter Keeper' is a red variety that can grow large, but doesn't turn tough and woody.

BROCCOLI

Whether it's sprouts or large heads, this Italian delicacy has become popular over the last twenty years, showing up in salad bars, casseroles, soups, and steamed side dishes. Broccoli (*Brassica oleracea* Italica Group) is loaded with vitamins A and C and contains the antioxidant sulforaphane, which is a known cancer fighter. Cooking largely removes the cancer fighting ingredient, however, so the benefit is largely gained from eating raw broccoli.

In my Italian family, we love the broccoli relatives, such as broccoli raab or gai lan, for which you eat the whole plant. They have small flower heads and tender stems and leaves.

■ *When to Plant*

Broccoli grows and matures best in cool weather. Sow seeds or plant transplants from late April to late May for an early-summer crop, and again from late July to August for a fall crop. Direct sow seeds in the garden two weeks before the last expected spring frost date, or start transplants indoors four weeks before you intend to plant them outside. Although broccoli is frost tolerant, if it's grown for several weeks with temperatures below 50°F, it will flower prematurely and form small heads. Similarly, if the plants are maturing during hot weather, the flower heads will also be small.

■ *Where to Plant*

Broccoli grows best in full sun in fertile, well-drained soil. It is a heavy feeder, so amend the soil generously with compost before planting. Consider planting quick-maturing crops of mesclun mix and radishes around broccoli plants, since broccoli will take up to sixty days to mature. These veggies will mature before the broccoli plants get large enough to shade them out, and you'll get a quick crop of greens from otherwise wasted space.

■ *How to Plant*

Broccoli germinates and grows quickly from seed. Sow seeds 6 inches apart in rows spaced 36 inches apart. Thin the seedlings to 18 inches apart once they have four leaves. Plant purchased or started seedlings 18 inches apart. Smaller-headed varieties may be spaced closer together to save some room—perfect if you have a small urban lot.

■ *Care and Maintenance*

Weed the broccoli patch well once plants are established, and then mulch with an organic material, such as untreated grass clippings or straw. To get the largest heads, side-dress your broccoli crop with a balanced organic

fertilizer, such as 5-5-5, three weeks after transplanting.

Protect young seedlings from cutworms by wrapping a 3-inch-thick strip of newspaper around the stem, keeping it 2 inches above the ground and 1 inch below. Spray plants with Neem oil to control flea beetles. If you want to avoid the notorious floating green worms when you cook your broccoli (my wife hates these), check the leaves and heads for signs of green cabbageworms and cabbage looper insects. They're easy to control with sprays of *Bacillus thuringiensis* (B.t.) or spinosad.

■ *Harvesting*

Once the broccoli heads form, but before the flower buds open, cut the heads off the stem about 6 inches below the head. Most varieties mature about sixty days after transplanting. Head size can range from 3 to 9 inches in diameter, depending on the variety. It's important to harvest broccoli before the flowers open or the flavor will be bitter. The exceptions are broccoli raab and gai lan; these can be allowed to flower and still taste good.

Most broccoli varieties will form side shoots off the main stem after the head is harvested. Continue harvesting these shoots as they form by cutting the entire side shoot back to the main trunk. This side shoot formation can continue into fall as long as the plant stays healthy.

■ *Additional Information*

'Arcadia', 'Bellstar', and 'Marathon' are widely adapted hybrid varieties with good disease resistance. 'Bellstar' is especially adapted to spring and summer growing, while 'Marathon' does especially well in fall. 'DeCicco' is an Italian heirloom with small, flavorful heads and prolific side shoots. 'Santee' is a hybrid sprouting variety that features small purple heads and abundant side shoots. It's best grown as a spring or fall harvest. The purple color turns green when cooked.

BRUSSELS SPROUTS

Brussels sprouts (*Brassica oleracea* Gemmifera Group) have gotten a bad rap. These mini-cabbages on a stalk may look weird, but they taste great if you harvest and prepare them correctly. I've learned the key to enjoying this cabbage relative is to let it get touched by light frost in fall before harvesting. Then the sweetness comes out. I like to roast "sprouts" with balsamic vinegar and root crops such as beets and carrots. Don't be afraid to sweeten them up with some of our good ol' maple syrup when cooking too.

■ *When to Plant*

Brussels sprouts are a slow-growing vegetable that prefers cool temperatures. Start seeds indoors in March or April, four to six weeks before your last frost. Plant seedlings, or purchased transplants from the garden center, in the garden four weeks later.

■ *Where to Plant*

Brussels sprouts grow best in full sun on well-drained, fertile soil. Amend the soil generously with compost prior to planting to support their long growth period.

■ *How to Plant*

Plant seedlings 18 to 24 inches apart in rows 2 feet apart. Plant them a little deeper in the garden than they were growing in the pot to help the stalk stand upright. Even if they flop over, the stalks will still grow upright and yield a great crop.

■ Care and Maintenance

Since Brussels sprouts take all summer to grow and mature, they need a little feeding to keep them strong. Add a small handful of organic fertilizer, such as 5-5-5, monthly through summer. This will help produce a bigger plant and more sprouts. Keep the row well weeded and apply an organic mulch, such as straw or untreated grass clippings, to keep weeds away and the soil moist. The mulch also keeps the soil cool, which all cabbage-family crops love. You can stake individual plants in late summer to prevent them from falling over during a thunderstorm. This will keep the sprouts cleaner.

Young seedling may fall victim to cutworms in spring. Protect transplants by wrapping a 3-inch-thick strip of newspaper around the stem, keeping it 2 inches above the ground and 1 inch below. The other major Brussels sprouts pest is cabbageworms and cabbage loopers. Check in early summer for green worms eating the leaves and spray an organic pesticide containing *Bacillus thuringiensis* (B.t.) on plants to control them.

■ Harvesting

Brussels sprouts are fun to watch grow and to harvest. The sprouts start maturing from the bottom of the stalk upward. New sprouts will continue to mature as long as the plants are healthy and the weather is warm enough. Pick individual sprouts as needed when they're about 1 inch in diameter. Larger sprouts are tough and woody. Remove the leaf just above the sprout first to enable you to see the sprout better and with a sharp knife cut it off the stalk. If my sprouts are slow to form, in early autumn I like to top the plant. Removing the top 6 inches of the plant makes more energy available to the sprouts forming below.

■ Additional Information

All Brussels sprout varieties take ninety to one hundred days to mature, from transplanting in the garden. 'Diablo' and 'Jade Cross E' are two popular varieties. 'Red Rubine' features purplish sprouts that hold their color even after cooking.

CABBAGE

I have to admit I'm not a big cabbage (*Brassica oleracea* Capitata Group) fan. I've grown and eaten it for years and certainly it's one of the easiest, most tried-and-true vegetables to grow. The cabbage types that do attract my attention are the red and Savoy (wavy leaves) varieties. They're beautiful in the garden, have a sweeter flavor, and add color and texture to salads and sautés. Whether you're growing green or red, smooth leaved or savoy leaved, cabbages are a good way to get a lot of vegetable in a small space. Varieties range in size from single-serving 1 pounders to whopping 8-pound heads. That's a lotta slaw and kraut! Select early-, mid-, and late-season varieties to extend your cabbage season from spring to fall.

■ *When to Plant*

Cabbages love it cool, so aim for a spring and fall crop. Unless you're growing cabbage for making lots of cole slaw or kraut, there's no need to plant lots of cabbages. It's best to stagger the planting in spring to have a few cabbages maturing each week. Sow seeds indoors five to seven weeks before your last frost and transplant these seedlings, or ones purchased at the garden center, three weeks later. For fall, plant seedlings in late summer. Cabbage can withstand a frost and still grow.

In general, cabbages grow best with temperatures below 80°F. If cabbage is trying to mature during the heat of summer, it may bolt (go to flower and not form a head).

■ *Where to Plant*

Cabbages grow best in full sun and well-drained, fertile soil. Amend the soil generously with compost prior to planting.

■ *How to Plant*

Plant seedlings 24 inches apart in rows 3 feet apart. Smaller varieties such as 'Dynamo' can be planted closer together. Consider planting fast-maturing radishes, mesclun mix, or lettuce around cabbages in spring. These will mature before the cabbages get too big to crowd them out. It's a great way to save space in a small garden.

■ *Care and Maintenance*

Cabbages love constant water and little competition from weeds. After plants are established, mulch with an organic material, such as straw or untreated grass clippings. This will help control weeds and maintain the soil moisture. Add a small handful of high-nitrogen fertilizer, such as soybean meal or fish emulsion, per plant about 1 month after planting. Don't fertilize

after that, because it may cause the heads to grow too fast and crack open. Cracked heads are an open invitation to disease.

Diseases, such as fusarium wilt and black rot, can stunt and kill cabbages and are especially prevalent on heavy soils and during rainy periods. Select resistant varieties if this is a problem. Young seedlings may fall victim to cutworms in spring. Protect transplants by wrapping a 3-inch-thick strip of newspaper around the stem, keeping it 2 inches above the ground and 1 inch below. As with other cabbage-family crops, cabbage-worms and cabbage loopers are major pests. Check in early summer for green worms eating the leaves and spray an organic pesticide containing *Bacillus thuringiensis* (B.t.) on plants to control them.

■ *Harvesting*

Harvest cabbage by the "feel" method. This is fun. Squeeze a head once it's full sized. If it's firm, cut it off just below the head with a sharp knife. Remove the outer "wrapper" leaves to reveal the main head. Don't pull up the plant. For spring-planted cabbages, you may get two smaller heads forming later in the summer. Try to harvest before a heavy rain. A quick influx of water can cause a head to crack open.

■ *Additional Information*

'Gonzales' (a miniature variety with softball-sized heads) and 'Farao' are two good green, smooth-headed varieties. 'Red Express' is a nice red variety. 'Caraflex' is an unusual cone-shaped green variety that has small, 2-pound heads and tender leaves. 'Famosa' is a good savoy variety. If you aren't keen on starting your own plants, these tried-and-true varieties are commonly available: 'Early Jersey Wakefield', 'Danish Ballhead', 'Copenhagen Market', and 'Mammoth Red Rock'.

CARROT

When I first traveled to northern India twenty years ago, I was amazed to see red, yellow, white, and purple carrots (*Daucus carota*), but no orange carrots. In fact, those are the native colors of carrots and it was the Dutch in the 1700s who popularized the color orange (after their national flag) as the modern color of carrots. We've been eating orange carrots ever since, but now those old colors have returned.

Carrots may be a little finicky for a beginning gardener, but the rewards are plenty. The sweet, crunchy roots are perfect raw, roasted, sautéed, made into soup, juiced, or used in dips. Plus, kids love them. It's like a treasure hunt when it's time to harvest carrots.

If you've never tasted a fresh carrot picked right out of the garden, you'll be amazed at the sweetness. Carrots grow well in small spaces and containers too. There are even diminutive varieties that fit perfectly in a pot.

If you're looking for a healthy vegetable, go no further than the carrot. It's loaded with vitamin A and beta-carotene, both known antioxidants and cancer fighters.

■ *When to Plant*

Although they grow best with temperatures in the 60s°F, carrots can remain in the ground all summer. That's the beauty of this vegetable. Spring-planted carrots can be enjoyed in midsummer through fall. Simply pull and eat the carrots as you need them. Sow seeds in April or early May, two to four weeks before your last frost date. In warmer parts of our region, sow again in midsummer for an additional fall harvest.

▪ *Where to Plant*

Carrots are root crops and need a loose, sandy, well-drained garden bed to grow in. I think raised beds are best. Although they'll grow best in full sun, they can produce even with only three to four hours of sun a day. Carrots also grow well in containers and even window boxes.

▪ *How to Plant*

Proper soil preparation is key to growing great carrots. If the soil is too heavy, has too many sticks, stones, and pieces of debris in it, the carrots will not grow to full size or will be deformed. Build a raised bed 8 inches tall, 3 feet wide, and as long as you wish. Remove any debris and smooth the top of the bed flat. Either sow seeds in rows spaced 18 inches apart, or broadcast seeds over the whole raised bed. Since carrot seeds are so small, you'll probably overplant. That's okay, because by thinning, you achieve the proper spacing of the carrot plants. I like to sprinkle the seeds on top of the bed and cover them with a ¼-inch layer of potting soil or sand. This protects the seeds from drying out, but offers an easy medium for them to grow through. If planted too deep, the carrot seeds may not have the strength to break through the soil. You can also buy pelleted carrot seeds that are coated with clay, and these larger seeds are easier to space properly. They are great for kids and gardeners with a small planting.

▪ *Care and Maintenance*

Be patient with your carrots. They may take up to two to three weeks to germinate. Keep the bed consistently moist during that time. I like to cover it with a floating row cover to help maintain the soil moisture. Once the seeds have germinated, just remove the cover.

The biggest reason carrots are spindly is gardeners don't thin early and often enough. Once carrots germinate, thin to 1 to 2 inches apart. Thin

again three weeks later to 3 to 4 inches apart. It will look like you pulled all your plants, but don't fear. The remaining carrots will fill in the voids and mature to full size.

Keep the bed consistently moist by watering regularly. Carrots don't compete well with weeds, so pull the weeds while you're thinning. Mulch the pathways between beds with straw. Cover any carrot root tops that are exposed with soil so they don't turn green. Although the green on carrots isn't harmful, it doesn't taste good.

Carrots can have a number of different problems, all solvable. Forked or spindly roots are due to debris in the soil, improper thinning, or too much nitrogen fertilizer. Unless your soil is very poor, avoid adding much nitrogen fertilizer in the form of compost or bagged fertilizer. The carrot rust fly can lay eggs on carrot tops and the larvae will tunnel in the upper portions of carrot roots. Cover the carrot bed with a floating row cover to avoid this pest.

Rabbits and woodchucks love carrot tops almost as much as beans. Fence the carrot bed well, burying the fence about 1 foot in the soil so these critters can't tunnel under it.

■ Harvesting

You can begin harvesting carrots as soon as the roots show color—as early as right after the second thinning. Harvest while the soil is moist so the carrots are easier to pull out. If you break the top when pulling, don't worry. Gently dig with a hand trowel around the root to pry it out.

Dig as many carrots as you need to eat. Carrots will take a frost and the flavor actually gets sweeter with cool weather in fall. If you really want to store your carrots in the ground, bury the carrot bed in November under a 6- to 8-inch layer of hay. You'll be able to dig through the hay and snow in winter and harvest carrots still fresh in the soil. They'll be as sweet as candy.

■ Additional Information

'Napoli', 'Yaya', 'Scarlet Nantes', and 'Danvers' are all good orange varieties to try in our region. 'Yellowstone' is a good golden variety, and 'Cosmic Purple' and 'Deep Purple' are good purple varieties. 'Atomic Red' is a good red variety, and 'White Satin' is a good white variety. For small spaces and containers, try 'Thumbelina', which grows in the shape of a half-dollar coin, and 'Kinko', which produces tasty, 4-inch-long orange roots.

CAULIFLOWER

I love the taste of cauliflower (*Brassica oleracea* Botrytis Group) but now I love the look of it too. I grew a purple-headed variety, 'Graffiti', a few years ago and the neon colors in the garden blew me away. There are now green and orange varieties as well.

What used to be a boring, white, cool-season vegetable has gotten a fashion overhaul. The colors also mean a nuttier flavor and higher nutrition. Serve cauliflower raw in salads. I like to steam it with other vegetables. Unfortunately, the purple varieties lose their color when cooked, but not the orange or green varieties.

■ When to Plant

Cauliflower, like all cabbage family plants, mature best under cool spring or fall conditions with temperatures under 70°F. Knowing that our spring can be very short and heat up quickly, I've found that growing cauliflower as a fall crop is more successful.

Sow seeds in the summer garden ninety days before the first frost for a fall crop. Look for spots where spring vegetables, such as peas and spinach, have finished producing. Yank out those crops and plant some cauliflower. For an early-summer crop, purchase and transplant seedlings from the garden center three weeks before your last frost.

■ Where to Plant

Cauliflower grows best in full sun and well-drained, fertile soil. As with cabbage, planting quick-maturing crops of radishes, mesclun mix, and lettuce around newly planted cauliflower allows you to harvest these crops before the cauliflower gets too large to shade it out.

■ How to Plant

Cauliflower loves lots of fertility, so amend the soil well with compost before planting. Sow the small seeds, or transplant seedlings, 18 to 24 inches apart in rows spaced 3 feet apart.

■ Care and Maintenance

Cauliflower needs a consistently moist soil and good fertility to form large heads. Add a small handful of organic fertilizer, such as 5-5-5, monthly to stimulate growth. Keep the soil moist with regular watering, and mulch established plants with a layer of organic mulch, such as straw or untreated grass clippings. When pulling weeds or hoeing, be careful not to damage the shallow roots.

To get a pure white color in older varieties of cauliflower, you need to blanch them (block the light) by placing a bag over the developing head or wrapping the leaves together. If not blanched, the heads develop a strong flavor. Newer varieties are called self-blanching, meaning the leaves automatically grow over the head and blanch it. Colored varieties don't require blanching.

Cauliflower is plagued with similar problems as other cabbage family plants. Seedlings may fall victim to cutworms in spring. Protect transplants by wrapping a 3-inch-thick strip of newspaper around the stem, keeping it 2 inches above the ground and 1 inch below. Cabbageworms and cabbage loopers are common pests, but less of a problem on fall-planted cauliflower. Check for green worms eating the leaves and spray an organic pesticide containing *Bacillus thuringiensis* (B.t.) on plants to control them. Grow disease-resistant varieties and rotate crops to avoid fusarium wilt and black rot.

■ Harvesting

With a sharp knife, cut under the head when they are about 6 to 8 inches in diameter, but before curds (small flower buds) have started to separate and have a ricelike appearance. Most varieties mature in about sixty days. Remove entire plants after harvest because they're unlikely to sprout another cauliflower.

■ Additional Information

The best white cauliflower varieties to grow are the self-blanching 'Fremont' and 'Cassius'. 'Cheddar' is an orange variety loaded with beta-carotene. 'Graffiti' is a purple variety and 'Panther' is a green variety. For something really wild, try 'Veronica'. This green-colored cauliflower is a Romanesco type, meaning it has small spires on its head. It looks like it's from another world.

CELERIAC

I love the taste of celery, but not the fussing required to grow it. That's why I was excited to discover celeriac (*Apium graveolens rapaceum*) a number of year ago. Celeriac, or celery root, is grown not for the leaves, but for its brown, round, knobby root. Inside the root is a moist white flesh that tastes just like celery. Celeriac is great mashed, sautéed, roasted with other root vegetables, added to soups, or shredded raw in salads. Celeriac is much more tolerant of the vagaries of the weather than celery and much easier for the novice to grow. Like celery, it needs a full summer of cool, moist soil conditions to grow best.

■ *When to Plant*

Celeriac is a slow-maturing, cool-weather-loving crop. Start seeds indoors eight to twelve weeks before your last spring frost. Transplant into the garden two weeks before the last frost.

■ *Where to Plant*

Celeriac grows best in full sun in well-drained, fertile soil. Like other root crops, celeriac can grow with three to four hours of sun a day, but the roots will take longer to develop. Plant celeriac in raised beds 8 inches tall and 3 feet wide. Root crops grow better in raised beds because the soil isn't as compacted as in regular beds and the roots can grow to the proper size more easily.

■ *How to Plant*

Amend the raised bed with compost before planting. Space transplants 4 to 6 inches apart in rows 2 feet apart in the bed. If the plants are spaced too closely together, the roots will be small and hairy.

■ Care and Maintenance

Keep the young transplants well watered. Once established, mulch with an organic material, such as straw or untreated grass clippings. The mulch keeps the soil cool and moist, which celeriac loves, and less weedy. If the soil dries out, your roots can develop hollow heart, a condition where the inside of the root has hollow spaces. To produce the largest-sized roots, add a small handful of organic fertilizer, such as 5-5-5, to the bed monthly. However, if your soil is already rich, don't add more fertilizer or you'll get hairy roots with a smaller edible portion.

Slugs can sometimes feast on the young transplants. Control these slimy pests with beer traps or organic baits, or by spreading sharp sand, diatomaceous earth, or crushed seashells or oyster shells around the plants. These sharp objects prevent slugs from getting to the plants.

Carrot rust fly larvae sometimes attack celeriac, causing holes in the tops of the roots. Prevent damage from this pest by placing a floating row cover over the planting. This will prevent the adult rust fly from laying eggs on the roots.

■ Harvesting

Celeriac roots actually grow on top of the ground, rather than underground. Once the roots reach 2 to 3 inches in diameter, you can start harvesting, usually about ninety days after seeding. Celeriac is tolerant of a few frosts. I like to leave the plants in the ground until after a few frosts have sweetened the roots. Pull the whole plant, cut off and discard the top and roots, and peel the knobby exterior to reveal the sweet white flesh.

■ Additional Information

The one downside of celeriac is sometimes the root is so knobby it's almost too much work to clean and prepare it for use. The solution is to choose varieties that have a smoother skin. 'Brilliant' produces small, softball-sized roots with a relatively smooth skin. 'Mars' is a newer variety that features an even larger root than 'Brilliant', but one that stays firm and solid throughout.

CELERY

If you're up for a challenge, try growing celery (*Apium graveolens dulce*). It's worth the effort. Homegrown celery has a stronger, fuller flavor and each crunch is loaded with juiciness. Although not the easiest of vegetables to grow at home, you just need a long (up to four months) growing season, cool temperatures, and moist soil. That sounds like a lot of places in the Northeast to me.

Besides eating celery raw in salads and with dips, you can enjoy it in soups, stews, and sauces. Since it's mostly water and fiber, it's low in calories too.

■ *When to Plant*

Plant celery seeds indoors three months before your last spring frost. Transplant purchased seedlings or homegrown ones into the garden around your last frost date, in May. Ideal temperatures for celery growing are between 55°F and 70°F. If celery transplants experience temperatures below 55°F for more than one week, they may bolt (produce a flower stalk). Protect young transplants by placing a floating row cover over them during cool spring nights.

■ *Where to Plant*

Celery needs full sun and well-drained, fertile soil to grow to maturity. Plant it in the garden where these 2-foot-tall plants won't be shaded by other taller vegetables as the summer winds on.

■ *How to Plant*

Soak seeds overnight in warm water to hasten germination. Amend the soil well with compost before planting. Plant individual seedlings 1 foot apart in rows spaced 18 inches apart.

■ *Care and Maintenance*

Celery needs regular feeding and watering to grow its best. Add a small handful of granular organic fertilizer, such as 5-5-5, monthly around plants to stimulate growth. Keep plants well watered. If the soil dries out, the celery stalks will turn tough and stringy. Add an organic mulch, such as straw or untreated grass clippings, around established plants to keep the soil moist and weeds at bay.

Prevent slugs from feasting on young transplants with organic slug baits such as Sluggo; beer traps placed around beds; or diatomaceous earth, sharp sand, or crushed oyster shells sprinkled around plants. Watch for aphids on leaves and spray with insecticidal soap to control them.

■ *Harvesting*

Harvest celery plants when the stalks are 10 inches tall. Cut the entire plant at the base with a sharp knife. If you're not growing self-blanching varieties and want a milder-tasting and more tender celery stalk, mound up the soil 6 inches high around plants to blanch them (block the light) a few weeks before harvest.

■ *Additional Information*

There are only a few varieties commonly grown by home gardeners. 'Tango' matures in only eighty-five days, produces nonstringy stalks, and is self-blanching. 'Tall Utah' is an old-fashioned variety still popular. 'Giant Red' has unique red-tinged stalks.

An easier-to-grow alternative to traditional celery is cutting celery (*Apium graveolens* var. *secalinum*). These plants are grown the same way as stalk celery, but they form 18-inch-tall plants without the traditional celery stalks, but mostly just celery-flavored leaves that can be used in cooking.

COLLARDS

When I talk about growing collards (*Brassica oleracea* Acephala Group) in Vermont, people think I'm a transplanted Southerner. While collards are known as a Southern green, there's no reason you can't grow them in the North. You might win over some Southern friends if you invite them over for dinner and serve collard greens and bacon.

Think of collards as a headless cabbage. You grow them the same way, but instead of waiting for a head to form, you eat the large, flat, green leaves. Unlike other greens, though, this one needs to be cooked to taste its best. The leaves are tough and chewy raw. But like our more familiar kale, collards are loaded with nutrition. Collard greens are high in vitamins A and C, potassium, and iron. And they're easy to grow in our Northeast climate, mature quickly (sixty to seventy days), and can take our erratic summer weather.

■ *When to Plant*

Collards grow equally well in cool and warm weather. As soon as the ground can be worked, sow seeds in April for an early-summer crop. Sow every few weeks into summer to have a continuous supply of collard greens to eat. Greens grown in the heat of summer may be tougher than those grown in the cooler spring and fall.

■ *Where to Plant*

Collards don't need full sun to produce. Locate the bed where it gets at least two to three hours of sun a day. The soil should be well drained and fertile.

■ *How to Plant*

Amend the soil with compost before planting. Sow seeds 1 inch apart in rows 2 feet apart. You can start seedlings indoors four weeks before planting or purchase transplants from the local garden center. Space transplants, thin the young seedlings to 6 inches apart, and eat the the thinnings in stir-fries.

◼ Care and Maintenance

Any green crop loves to have adequate nitrogen. Apply a high-nitrogen fertilizer, such as fish emulsion and alfalfa meal, when the plants are 6 inches tall to stimulate more growth. Although collard greens are tough, they do grow best when the soil is consistently moist. Mulching with an organic material such as untreated grass clippings or straw allows the soil to stay weed free and moist throughout the growing season.

The same pests that attack cabbages love collards as well. Watch for aphids on the leaves and spray insecticidal soap to control them. Although the thick, waxy leaves are less inviting for cabbageworms and cabbage loopers compared to broccoli and cabbage, they still may attack. Look for white butterflies in early summer. These lay eggs on the collard leaves that turn into green caterpillars: cabbageworms and cabbage loopers. Control these caterpillars with sprays of *Bacillus thuringiensis* (B.t.).

◼ Harvesting

Harvest collard greens by either handpicking selected outer leaves as needed or pulling the whole plant. Picking the outer leaves causes new leaves to form from the center and keeps production going. You can start harvesting individual leaves when they are large enough to cook. You can also harvest the entire 2- to 3-foot-tall plant when mature, about sixty days after seeding. Since the leaves are tough, chop them up well before sautéing and cooking.

◼ Additional Information

'Champion' features blue-green leaves on a compact plant that's slow to bolt. 'Flash' has dark green leaves on a productive plant.

CUCUMBER

There's nothing more refreshing than biting into a freshly picked cucumber (*Cucumis sativus*) on a hot summer day. It's cool, juicy, and thirst quenching. I've been known to stand in the garden munching a freshly picked cuke for lunch. Just pass the salt shaker. Traditionally there have been two types of cucumbers you can grow: short, spiny picklers and long, smooth slicers. Now, with more gardeners growing cucumbers in plastic hoop houses, there is a new group called greenhouse cucumbers that are long, thin, and seedless and don't require bees to pollinate them. They can grow indoors or outdoors, but should be spaced away from other cucumbers outdoors so they don't unintentionally get pollinated.

Cucumbers are heat and water lovers. Provide them with both and they will reward you with plenty of fruits for salads, soups, and pickling if you like. There are even varieties you can grow that are short vined, making them perfect for containers and small spaces.

■ *When to Plant*

Because cukes like the heat, direct sow seeds into the garden two weeks after the last frost date in your area. That would be May or early June. You can get a jump on the season by starting seedlings indoors four weeks before transplanting into the garden or just purchasing transplants at the garden center.

■ *Where to Plant*

Cucumbers grow best in full sun and fertile, compost-amended, well-drained soil. Since these are trailing plants, plant cucumbers in the front of a garden or on the south side where they won't be shaded by taller plants, such as corn and tomatoes. They also are great container plants.

■ *How to Plant*

Cucumbers love soil temperatures of at least 70°F. Because that can be a challenge in our cool climate, grow cucumbers in raised beds covered with black or dark green plastic. Build a bed 8 inches tall and 3 feet wide. To heat up the soil, place the plastic over the bed two weeks before you'll be planting. Poke holes in the plastic and plant seeds 2 inches apart in rows spaced 4 feet apart. Another way to plant is to create a raised circle or hill and plant four to six seeds. Thin to the strongest three seedlings after they germinate.

In containers, plant short-vined varieties such as 'Salad Bush' and 'Bush Pickle', planting two plants in a 12-inch-diameter pot.

■ *Care and Maintenance*

Protect your young cucumber plants from cold temperatures in spring by placing a floating row cover over them. Not only will the row cover keep the plants warm, but it will prevent insects, such as cucumber beetles, from gaining access to them. Remove the row cover once the flowers form so bees can pollinate your crop. To save space when growing regular 5-foot-long vining varieties, consider trellising them. Construct or buy a 45 degree angled wire-and-wooden cucumber trellis. Plant the cucumbers at the base and let them vine up the trellis. The fruits will hang through the trellis holes, staying straight, and will be less affected by diseases. You can also grow them straight up a string like a pole bean. However, the tendrils (curlicues) aren't strong enough to hold up the plants, so you'll need to tie the plants to the string to keep them growing upright.

Cucumbers need a consistent supply of water to grow their best. Water stress results in bitter-tasting fruits. Make sure they have at least 1 inch of water a week, more during dry or windy periods. If you haven't used plastic mulch, add a layer of straw or untreated grass clippings around plants once they start to run (vine). Keep cucumbers producing fruits by adding a small handful of 5-5-5 organic fertilizer around plants once young fruits form, and again one month later.

Most cucumber varieties have separate male and female flowers on their plants or they have all female flowers and need plants with male flowers to pollinate them. They need bees to pollinate the flowers and get fruits. If you have trouble getting fruits due to poor pollination, consider planting varieties that don't need pollination to fruit such as 'H-19 Little Leaf' and 'Diva'. You can also pollinate the fruits yourself in the morning by swishing a cotton swab around a male flower (no little cucumber behind it) and then in a female flower (a little cucumber behind it). Voilà, pollination!

This biggest pest of cucumbers is the notorious cucumber beetle. These insects come in black-and-yellow striped or spotted versions. Not only do they attack cucumbers, but they like squash and melons too. The adult beetles feed on young plants, flowers, and even fruits. Their feeding causes the leaves to die and spread diseases, such as bacterial wilt and virus. To control them, cover young plants with a floating row cover, place yellow sticky traps above the plants to trap and kill the beetles, and spray plants with Neem oil or pyrethrum. Remove the row cover when flowering begins.

There are a number of diseases that infect cucumbers as well. Bacterial wilt causes the plant to wilt suddenly even if well watered. Snip the vines to check for milky white sap, an indication of this disease. Control the cucumber beetles that transmit this disease. Powdery mildew is a white fungus that kills the leaves and can limit production. Spray Serenade® organic fungicide to control this disease. In general, look for disease-resistant varieties to avoid these problems.

■ Harvesting

The more cucumbers you harvest, they more they will keep setting fruits. Oversized cucumbers tend to be seedy and bitter flavored, so pick them young and keep picking. With a sharp knife, pick slicing varieties when they are 6 to 8 inches long. Harvest pickling varieties when they are 2 to 4 inches long. Some of the newer greenhouse cucumber varieties are harvested when they are up to 1 foot long.

■ Additional Information

Some good disease-resistant slicing varieties to grow include 'Olympian' and 'Marketmore 76'. Some good pickling varieties include 'National Pickling' and 'H-19 Little Leaf'. Some newer greenhouse types include 'Suyo Long' and 'Tyria'. For something different, try some of the yellow cucumbers such as 'Boothby's Blonde' and 'Lemon'. They're a conversation piece in the garden and have a crunchy texture and mild flavor.

EGGPLANT

I grew up in an Italian-American family, so eggplant parmigiana was a part of life. I didn't realize until I was older how many other uses and types of eggplant (*Solanum melongena*) there are. You can grow tiny green eggplants the size of a cherry tomato or oval-shaped, purple fruits the size of a melon. I love the long thin varieties available now that come in green, white, or purple-striped colors. Eggplants are great for grilling, sautéing, and making baba ghanoush, soups, stews, and, of course, eggplant parmigiana.

■ When to Plant

Eggplants are in the tomato family and enjoy the warmth just like their cousins. Transplant seedlings into the garden two weeks after the last frost date. The soil needs to be at least 60°F for best growth, so plant in May or June. You can start your own seedlings indoors six to eight weeks earlier or purchase ones from the local garden center.

■ Where to Plant

Eggplants love the sun and heat. Plant them on raised beds in well-drained, fertile soil. The beds warm up faster and dry out sooner in spring. Eggplants are beautiful plants as well. The purple flowers and attractive fruits make this the perfect edible landscape plant among your perennial or annual flowers. If you're having trouble getting eggplants to mature, plant them in a container. They'll grow faster than in the ground.

■ How to Plant

Amend the raised bed with compost before planting and place black plastic mulch over the bed two weeks before setting out seedlings. The black plastic mulch will warm up the soil, stimulating the eggplants to grow quickly. Space plants 18 to 24 inches apart on the bed.

■ Care and Maintenance

Eggplants grow best with temperatures above 70°F. During cool springs, protect young eggplants by placing a floating row cover over the plants during chilly nights. In fact, eggplants won't set fruits when temperatures are consistently below 65°F.

Eggplants need consistent fertility and water to grow best. Add a small handful of organic fertilizer, such as 5-5-5, around plants once a month during the growing season. Keep plants well watered with at least 1 to 2 inches of water a week. Water-stressed plants will produce bitter-tasting fruits.

I like to use small tomato cages to keep eggplants upright during summer thunderstorms and keeps the fruits off the ground and clean.

Eggplants can be attacked by a number of different insects. Flea beetles will eat shotgun-like holes in the leaves of young seedlings. Cover plants with row covers to prevent damage, and remove the row covers when the plants begin to get fruits; Neem or pyrethrum sprays are the remedy at this point. Colorado potato beetles love eggplants almost as much as potatoes. Handpick adult beetles, crush the orange eggs on the undersides of leaves, and spray larvae with *Bacillus thuringiensis* var. San Diego to control them.

The main disease that attacks eggplants is verticillium wilt. It can stunt and deform the plant. Avoid this disease by rotating crops or growing eggplants in containers filled with sterilized potting soil.

■ Harvesting

Harvest eggplants when the fruits reach full size, the skin is glossy, and the flesh is firm. Press the skin gently with your thumb. If it bounces back without cracking, the fruits are ready to harvest. If you dent the skin with your thumb, the fruits are overmature. It's better to err on the underripe than the overripe side when harvesting, since overripe fruits tend to be bitter tasting. Use a sharp knife and gloves, because some varieties have thorns.

■ Additional Information

Some good, large, oval-sized varieties to grow include 'Traviata' (purple skin) and 'Beatrice' (violet skin). Some long, thin varieties to try include 'Fairy Tale' (purple striped), 'Louisiana Long Green' (green skin), and 'Gretel' (white skin). Some really unusual small round varieties include 'Kermit' (green skin) and 'Turkish Orange' (orange skin).

ENDIVE

It looks like lettuce, but sure doesn't taste like lettuce. Endive (*Cichorium endivia*) and its cousin escarole are distinct-tasting greens popular in Europe and now gaining favor in our country. Endive has deeply cut, curly leaves, while escarole has broad, smooth leaves. Then there's Belgian endive, which also has smooth leaves. Endive and escarole form loose heads with tender white leaves and stems in the center.

I grew up eating my mother's escarole soup, so I love these slightly bitter greens, which stay somewhat crunchy even after cooking. The greens can be used like lettuce in salads or cooked in soups and stews.

■ When to Plant

Like lettuce, endive is a cool-season crop and grows best with temperatures in the 60s°F. Warm temperatures can make the greens not only bolt (form a flower stalk), but also taste more bitter. It's best to plant endive three weeks before your last frost date, in April or May. Grow a fall crop by sowing seeds or transplants in late summer for an autumn harvest. To get a jump on the season, you can also start seedlings indoors three to four weeks before your planting date.

■ Where to Plant

Endive grows best in full sun. If it receives only two to three hours of sun a day, it will still produce an edible plant, but the heads won't be as well

formed. It needs a well-drained, moist soil. If growing in heavy soils, consider planting in an 8-inch-tall and 3-foot-wide raised bed.

■ *How to Plant*

Amend the soil with compost and sow seeds 1 inch apart in rows spaced 18 inches apart. I like to cover the small seeds with sand or potting soil to keep them consistently moist so they germinate well.

■ *Care and Maintenance*

Once the seeds germinate, thin. Use the thinnings in salads. Keep thinning until the heads are spaced 7 inches apart in the rows. Keep the beds well watered. If the bed dries out, the heads will become more bitter flavored. Hand weed and then mulch with a layer of straw or untreated grass clippings. Fertilize the young seedlings with fish emulsion after thinning and again three weeks later.

To create an even milder-flavored head, you can help blanch (block the light) the heads by placing a pot over the heads two weeks before harvest. Although not as attractive to pests as lettuce, endive still has its share of problems. Rabbits and woodchucks love the young greens, so fence to keep these critters out. Aphids will feed on the tender leaves. Spray insecticidal soap to ward them off. Slugs and snails will also munch on the leaves. Use beer traps to catch and kill them; copper flashing, sharp sand, or crushed seashells or oyster shells to ward them off; and iron phosphate bait to lure and kill them. Space plants properly to avoid rot diseases.

■ *Harvesting*

Pick young leaves as baby greens when they're at least 2 inches long. Pick young heads about forty to fifty days after planting by harvesting the young outer leaves. Allow some heads to mature to full size in about sixty to eighty days, and cut the whole head to the ground for cooking.

■ *Additional Information*

Some good endive varieties to try in your garden include 'Frisee', which has finely cut leaves that are naturally blanched at the base. 'Rhodos' has lobe-shaped, blue-green leaves and a looser head. 'Batavian' escarole is less bitter than most endives. It has densely packed broad leaves with a tender center. This is the one my mom cooks into escarole soup.

GARLIC

Being an Italian-American who likes to cook, I eat a lot of garlic (*Allium tuberosum*). Lucky for me, growing garlic is almost as easy as eating it. Growing your own garlic offers some distinct advantages. You can try unusual varieties with spicy hot to almost nutty flavor. You can grow softneck garlic, which is great for braiding, or hardneck varieties, which produce scapes (green curlicue flower stalks) in early summer that can be eaten for a mild garlic flavor.

You can grow garlic in a small space. You can produce more than twenty-five bulbs in a 3 × 5 foot bed. That's a lot of garlic, even by my standards. Plus, the flavor of fresh garlic is much better than anything you buy in stores.

■ *When to Plant*

Garlic is planted in October, at the same time you'll be planting daffodils and tulips. This gives the garlic clove's roots a chance to get established before winter sets in.

■ *Where to Plant*

Garlic grows best in full sun. Well-drained soils are a must. Since the cloves will be sitting in the soil all winter, poorly drained soils lead to rotting cloves. Plant in raised beds to ensure that the soil stays well drained all winter and your garlic will be viable.

■ *How to Plant*

Create raised beds 8 inches tall, no more than 3 feet wide, and as long as you like. Amend the bed with compost. Purchase garlic bulbs online or at your local garden center, and break them apart into individual cloves. Select varieties adapted to our climate. Set cloves, pointy side up, 2 inches deep in the raised bed, spaced 6 inches apart in rows 1 foot apart.

■ *Care and Maintenance*

Garlic is a very easy vegetable to grow. Keep the soil moist in fall and protect the bed with a 4- to 6-inch layer of hay or straw added in November. Your garlic should be fine until spring. If we have a warm fall, sometimes the garlic cloves sprout green shoots. Don't worry, they will stop growing once the cold weather and shorter days set in.

In spring, remove the mulch once the garlic starts growing, usually in April or early May. Once three garlic leaves have formed, add a small handful of organic fertilizer, such as 5-5-5, per row. Keep the bed well weeded and watered.

If the soil conditions are right, garlic has few problems. Pest and animals don't really like them. In fact, some gardeners swear by planting garlic among other vegetables to ward off pests. Diseases are avoided by rotating crops annually.

■ *Harvesting*

Harvest the scapes of hardneck garlic varieties in early summer once they form their curlicues. The scapes have a mild garlic flavor, which is great in cooking. Removing the scapes causes the garlic plant to direct more energy into producing larger-sized bulbs.

Harvest garlic bulbs when the bottom third of the leaves yellow. Pull them out of the ground, knock off any extra soil on the bulbs, and store them in a cool, airy, shady, dry location for about two weeks, until the tops dry. With a pruner or sharp knife, cut off the tops ½ inch above the bulb and trim the roots. If you're growing softneck varieties, leave the tops for braiding.

Store bulbs in mesh bags in a dark, 40°F to 50°F room for winter. Garlic can keep for more than six months under the right conditions. I'm often still eating last year's garlic when harvesting this year's garlic scapes.

■ *Additional Information*

Some of my favorite hardneck varieties include 'Russian Red', 'Chesnok Red', and 'German Extra Hardy'. Some good softneck varieties to try include 'Inchelium Red' and 'New York White'. Elephant garlic features fewer, but larger, cloves and a milder flavor than other garlics.

JERUSALEM ARTICHOKE

This vegetable always puzzled me. It's not from Jerusalem and not an artichoke. But what is great about Jerusalem artichokes (*Helianthus tuberosus*), or sunchokes as they are now commonly called, is they're actually tall sunflowers that produce tasty edible tubers that look like knobby potatoes. The tall stalks and small yellow sunflowers make this a great edible background plant in the back of the garden or against a wall or fence.

The tubers have a sweet, almost nutty flavor. I like peeling and shredding Jerusalem artichokes raw into salads. You can also slice them like water chestnuts and add them to salads or stir-fries for a crunchy texture. They can be cooked like potatoes in soups or stews, or even mashed. They are smaller than potatoes and require more cleaning around the knobs, but they do have an interesting taste and texture.

It's easy to grow this perennial vegetable, native to North America. In fact, once you have Jerusalem artichokes in your garden, they sprout every year from leftover tubers in the ground, so you never have to plant again. Just be sure you want them in that section of your garden because they're tough to get rid of once established.

■ When to Plant

Jerusalem artichokes need all season to produce their tubers, so plant two weeks before your last frost date, which is usually in late April or May.

■ Where to Plant

Jerusalem artichokes grow in almost any kind of soil and grow best in full sun. They can tolerate dry and wet soils once they get growing. Since the stalks can grow up to 8 feet tall, plant them on the north side of your garden so they don't shade other vegetables. They also look good against a building or fence and can be used to screen an unsightly view.

■ How to Plant

Plant tubers 4 inches deep and 12 to 18 inches apart. Keep the newly planted tubers well watered. Each tuber will send up multiple stalks.

■ Care and Maintenance

Taking care of Jerusalem artichokes couldn't be easier. Keep the soil moist and weeded until the plants are up, and then leave them alone. They grow so fast they will crowd and shade out any weeds. To encourage a larger crop, you can remove the flowers, but I like the sweet-looking sunflowers to decorate my garden in summer. Jerusalem artichokes have few pests.

■ Harvesting

You can start harvesting the 6-inch-diameter, red- or brown-skinned tubers in fall once the plants start to yellow. For the best flavor, wait until a few light frosts have turned the stalks brown and then harvest. The tubers will have a sweeter flavor. If you want to have a crop next year, leave a few of the smaller tubers in the ground. Chances are when harvesting you'll probably not be able to find them all, so this usually isn't a problem.

■ Additional Information

The knobby tubers have a crisp, white flesh. The skin can be tedious to remove, so I like growing 'Fuseau', which has a smooth red skin, or 'Stampede', which has large brown-skinned tubers that are easier to clean.

KALE

I never used to be a big kale (*Brassica oleracea* Acephala Group) fan, but that has changed. I woke up to kale when I started seeing some interesting-looking varieties and started eating it in fall after the cool weather set in. That's the key with kale. Eat mature leaves in the summer and it's like chewing cardboard. Eat kale in spring or fall and it has a crisp texture and sweet flavor. Now it's one of my favorite "plant it and forget about it" crops. I let it grow to full size (sometimes 5 feet tall!) all summer, but I don't begin to eat it until fall. It's worth the wait. My kale "trees" remain into winter, providing great fresh greens during the dark, cold months.

Kale is also one of the most nutritious crops you can grow. It's loaded with vitamins A and C, potassium, iron, and calcium. I love kale steamed, or cooked in soups or stir-fries, and baby kale leaves are tasty in salads. You can even make kale "chips" roasted in the oven. Kale is often included in mesclun and lettuce mixes to add a deep green color and crunchy texture.

■ When to Plant

While kale is a cool-weather-loving crop, it can grow all summer. The key is sowing seeds when the ground is cool and harvesting either young greens or mature plants in spring or fall. Plant as soon as the ground can be worked, usually April, four weeks before your last frost date. You can also plant a fall crop in August or September, six weeks before the first frost date, to enjoy in autumn.

■ Where to Plant

Kale is one green that doesn't need lots of sun to thrive. If it gets two to three hours of direct sun a day, it will grow fine. The more sun, the bigger and fuller the plant. Like all greens, it grows best in fertile, well-drained soil.

■ How to Plant

Amend the soil before planting with compost, plant on raised beds if you have heavy clay soil, and sow seeds 1 inch apart in rows spaced 2 feet apart. Cover the small seeds with ½ inch of fine soil or potting soil. Thin young seedlings to 6 inches apart when they're 4 inches tall. Use the kale thinnings in salads.

■ Care and Maintenance

Kale loves nitrogen fertilizer. Give new seedlings a dose of fish emulsion or soybean meal when they are 4 inches tall. Keep the kale bed well weeded and watered. Consider mulching with an organic mulch, such as straw or untreated grass clippings, once plants are established.

Kale has some of the same pest problems as other cabbage-family crops. Control aphids on the leaves with sprays of insecticidal soap. Look for adult cabbageworm and white butterflies in early summer. The butterflies lay eggs on kale leaves that hatch into green caterpillars that eat holes in the leaves. Control this caterpillar with sprays of *Bacillus thuringiensis* (B.t.).

◼ *Harvesting*

Harvest baby kale plants twenty days after seeding for use as greens in salads. Wait until sixty to seventy days after seeding for the plants to mature to full size for larger leaves. In fall, pick the outer leaves first, allowing the inner leaves to continue to develop. In this way, your kale plant will keep producing until the cold eventually kills it. Since it can withstand temperatures in the low 20s°F, you may still be eating kale into December.

◼ *Additional Information*

'Toscano' or dinosaur kale is one of my favorite varieties. The long, thin, puckered, blue-green leaves are beautiful to look at. This Italian variety stays crunchy even when cooked, making it great in soups and stews. 'Red Bor' features curly, burgundy-colored stems and leaves that turn a deeper purple in fall. 'Red Russian' has flat green leaves with red veins. It's more tender and is good chopped in salads. 'Ripbor' has frilly green leaves on a compact plant.

KOHLRABI

Now here's one weird-looking vegetable. When I show kids a kohlrabi (*Brassica oleracea* Gongylodes Group), they say it looks like a satellite or spaceship. It's always a conversation piece when people visit my garden. In spite of its looks, kohlrabi is an easy cabbage family vegetable to grow. It's wildly popular in Eastern Europe, but just catching on in this country. While you can eat the leaves, it's the round, swollen stem at the base that's mostly used. When you peel kohlrabi, a crisp, crunchy, white-fleshed vegetable is revealed that's great shredded and used raw in salads or in "kohl" slaw. The flavor is like a cross between a cabbage and a turnip, but milder. You can also cook it in soups and stews.

■ *When to Plant*

Grow kohlrabi as you would cabbage. Sow seeds directly into the garden two to four weeks before your last frost date, usually April or May. You can also start plants indoors four weeks earlier or purchase them at the local garden center. Since they mature in only forty to fifty days, grow some kohlrabi as a fall crop planted in late summer.

■ *Where to Plant*

Kohlrabi like full sun and well-drained soil amended with compost. This cool-season crop is the least hardy of the cabbage family, so plant where they can be protected from late-spring frosts.

■ *How to Plant*

Sow seeds 1 inch apart in rows 18 inches apart. Thin plants to 8 inches apart once the true leaves (second set of leaves) form. Transplant seedlings to 8 inches apart as well.

■ *Care and Maintenance*

Kohlrabi grows best during cool weather, but temperatures below 40°F can cause the young plant to bolt (form a flower stalk) before forming a ball. Also, if the weather gets too hot, kohlrabi stems will be tough and woody textured. The key is to get plants off to a good start and maturing before the heat of midsummer. Fall is a good time to grow them for that reason. They will mature more slowly, but have a more tender texture and a sweeter flavor.

Once plants are growing, add a small handful of organic fertilizer, such as 5-5-5, per row. Keep the young plants weed free and well watered. Once they're established, mulch around plants with untreated grass clippings or straw. This will help keep weeds away and keep the soil cool and moist. Kohlrabi is attacked by similar pests as cabbages and broccoli. Rotate crops, not planting cabbage family plants in the same location for three years, to avoid diseases. Spray plants with Neem oil to control flea beetles or place floating row covers over plants when young. Once plants are established, flea beetles are usually not a problem. Check leaves for signs of green cabbageworms and cabbage loopers. Spray *Bacillus thuringiensis* (B.t.) on plants to control these pests.

■ Harvesting

Once the swollen stem is at least 1 inch in diameter, it's time to harvest. Pull up the entire plant and cut off the leaves and roots. You'll get one swollen stem per plant. You can safely harvest until the stems are about 3 inches in diameter. If you let most varieties grow any bigger than that, the stem becomes woody. You can eat kohlrabi fresh or peel and dice the stems to freeze for winter use.

■ Additional Information

'Korridor' produces green, sweet-tasting roots in only forty-two days from transplanting. 'Kolibri' has a unique purple skin and fiberless flesh. 'Kossack' is a large green variety that's harvested when it's 8 inches in diameter. It can be stored in a cool, dark room for several months.

LEEK

I'm surprised more gardeners don't grow leeks (*Allium porrum*). They are the quintessential "plant it and forget about it" crop. Leek stalks have a mild onion flavor, and I've harvested leeks that were frozen in fall and they still tasted good. I like to shred raw leeks in salads or sauté them in butter. But for the best treat, make potato leek soup. It's one of my daughter's favorite garden dishes.

Leek plants are attractive too. They stand 2 to 3 feet tall, and some varieties have stunning blue-green leaves. I've planted them among annual flowers to provide a nice color contrast.

■ *When to Plant*

Leeks can take well over one hundred days to mature from transplanting, so you have to start early. It's the first vegetable I seed indoors in late winter (eight to twelve weeks before the last frost date) for transplanting into the garden around the last frost date, which is sometime in May. You can also purchase them as seedlings from your local garden center.

■ *Where to Plant*

Leeks grow best in full sun and well-drained, fertile soil. Plant them where they won't be shaded by other taller vegetables, such as corn.

■ *How to Plant*

Keep seedlings indoors clipped to 3 inches tall and fertilized with fish emulsion to create a strong root system. In the garden, amend the soil with compost and build a raised bed if the soil is poorly drained. Dig shallow trenches (4 inches deep) in the raised bed spaced 1 foot apart. Plant the leek seedlings spaced 6 inches apart in the trench. Cover the roots with soil. As the leek grows, slowly fill in the trench. This will help create a strong root system and a white stalk that is mild tasting.

■ *Care and Maintenance*

Keep the leek plants well watered and weeded. Leeks need a constant supply of water to keep growing all summer. Leeks don't tolerate weeds, but once they get established, their leaves will shade any weeds out. Once the trench is filled in, mound more soil up around the stalks to blanch them further. When watering, try not to let dirt splash into the leaves. The dirt will lodge there and be hard to remove when cleaning in the kitchen. Mulch with straw or untreated grass clippings to prevent the dirt from splashing and keep the soil moist.

Add a small handful of organic fertilizer, such as 5-5-5, per row once a month to form large leek stalks. Leeks have few insect or pest problems. Rotate crops, not planting any onion family crops in the same location for three years, to avoid diseases.

■ *Harvesting*

You can start harvesting leeks when they are only ½ inch in diameter. However, I think they taste best and have a sweeter flavor after a few light frosts. You can eat the whole plant, but most people trim off the top green leaves and roots and use the white stalks, which are the most tender parts. However, I often use the green tops in soups, letting them cook down to become tender. The strong flavor is particularly good when making vegetable stock.

■ *Additional Information*

'Tadorna' is a good disease-resistant variety. 'King Richard' is a favorite quick-maturing variety, but isn't as cold tolerant as other varieties. 'Lancelot' has blue-green leaves and good cold tolerance.

LETTUCE

I must admit I've been seduced by all the new, colorful, unusual greens on the market these days. But for old-fashioned flavor and utility, you can't beat lettuce (*Lactuca sativa*). Even lettuce has had a facelift in recent years. There are new varieties with red- and green-speckled leaves, lime green leaves, and burgundy-colored leaves. I grow them among the flowers because they're so beautiful. They also are a great window box, hanging basket, and container plant. I even grew lettuce in an old shoe once.

You can grow crunchy romaine heads, frilly looseleaf heads, or creamy butterheads. But before you get overwhelmed with all the lettuce variety choices, it's good to know the four basic lettuce groups and characteristics.

Crispheads form tight heads and crunchy leaves. Iceberg lettuce falls into this category and needs a long, cool growing season to be its best. Butterheads produce a smaller, looser head. They're easier to grow than crispheads. 'Bibb' and 'Buttercrunch' are two common varieties of this type. Romaine, or cos, forms tall cylindrical heads and have the sweetest flavor. 'Rouge D' Hiver' and 'Winter Density' are two popular varieties. Looseleaf doesn't form a head. It is the quickest to mature and easiest to grow. 'Black Seeded Simpson' and 'Red Sails' are two classic looseleaf varieties.

When making salads, get creative with your lettuces. Use them as a mild base and mix them with more dramatic greens, such as arugula, Asian greens, beet greens, and Swiss chard. Crunchier romaines and crisphead

varieties are great as a bed under summer salads, such as potato salad and couscous salad. I even have a friend who will make a meal out of a stack of romaine lettuce leaves and salad dressing.

When to Plant

Lettuce is a cool-weather-loving crop and grows best with temperatures in the 60s°F. Although there are varieties such as 'Summertime' that are more resistant to the heat, it's best to plan on growing lettuce starting in late April or early May, a few weeks before your last frost date, and again in late summer for a fall harvest.

The best way to grow lettuce is to sow small batches or rows every two to three weeks in spring and again in late summer. In this way, you'll avoid the notorious lettuce glut (all the lettuce is ready to eat at once) that can happen when you plant a large row only once.

To get a jump on the season, you can also start seedlings indoors three to four weeks before your planting date or buy seedlings from the local garden center.

Where to Plant

Lettuce is a part-shade-tolerant vegetable. You need only two to three hours of direct sun a day to get a crop. This is especially true if you're harvesting your lettuce as baby greens (picked when they're only 2 inches tall) or growing looseleaf varieties. They need water, but don't like wet, heavy soils. They grow best in beds raised 8 inches tall and no wider than 3 feet.

■ *How to Plant*

Amend the soil with compost and remove any rocks and debris from the bed. Sows seeds 1 inch apart in rows spaced 18 inches apart. You can also broadcast seeds on the top of the bed instead of planting in rows. I like to cover the small seeds with sand or potting soil so they can germinate more easily. Keep the bed consistently moist.

■ *Care and Maintenance*

If you'll be growing your lettuce into mature heads, once the seeds germinate and the true leaves (second set of leaves) form, thin the looseleaf varieties to 4 to 6 inches apart; thin romaine, crisphead, and butterhead varieties to 8 to 10 inches apart. If you're just growing lettuce to harvest as young greens, you won't have to thin. Protect tender seedlings from cold weather by placing a floating row cover over the plants. This also discourages rabbits and insects from eating your crop.

Lettuce is shallow rooted, so keep the plants well watered. Hand weed the rows so as not to disturb the plant roots. Mulch after weeding with a layer of straw or untreated grass clippings. Since you're growing lettuce for the leaves, make sure they have enough nitrogen fertilizer. I like to spray fish emulsion on the young plants and then spray again a few weeks later to keep them growing strong. Fish emulsion is a readily available form of nitrogen fertilizer that's gentle on plants.

Young lettuce seedlings can be subject to a fungus disease called damping off. You'll notice seedlings rotting *en masse* indoors or in the garden. Avoid overwatering to prevent this disease from getting started. If it does occur, replant. Slugs and snails are one of lettuce's biggest foes. Use beer traps to catch and kill them; copper flashing, sharp sand, or crushed seashells or oyster shells to ward them off; and iron phosphate bait to lure and kill them. Slugs and snails are more of a problem during wet springs. To avoid eating a slug that hitched a ride into your kitchen, soak the lettuce in salted water. The slugs will rise to the top. Yum.

Rabbits and woodchucks love lettuce. Fence your garden area before the seedlings emerge to prevent damage. Once a four-legged critter knows there's something good to eat, it will try extra hard to get in the garden.

◼ *Harvesting*

If growing any type of lettuce for baby greens, start harvesting when the leaves are about 2 inches long. Looseleaf varieties are also known as "cut and come again" varieties. This means you can cut the leaves at ground level and they will resprout. You can cut a number of times before a lettuce plant gets too woody to harvest.

If growing butterhead or romaine types of lettuce, about sixty days after seeding, when the leaves are 4 to 6 inches long and heads are formed, cut the whole plant at its ground level. These plants may grow more leaves after harvest, but won't be as prolific as looseleaf types. If growing crispheads, wait until the head is firm when it's squeezed before harvesting.

◼ *Additional Information*

Beside the varieties mentioned earlier, there are some unusual lettuces to try as well. 'Green Ice' is a looseleaf variety with lime green leaves. 'Dark Lollo Rossa' has very frilly, burgundy red leaves. 'Oakleaf' comes in red and green types and features, you guessed it, oak-shaped leaves. 'Freckles' is a red-spotted romaine variety. 'Deer Tongue' is an heirloom butterhead variety that features long, thin green or red leaves.

MELON

My wife, Wendy, grows a big patch of melons (*Cucumis melo*) each year. Come late summer, we vigilantly watch for the first melon to ripen. There's good reason to be so interested. Fresh melons picked warm from the garden are sweet, juicy, and certainly a decadent treat, much better than anything bought in the grocery store.

While melons love the heat, you can still grow these sweet treats in the Northeast if you select the right varieties and have the right growing conditions. And don't limit yourself to the traditional cantaloupe (technically a muskmelon). Exotic melons are all the rage in the gardening world. Charentais, honeydews, crenshaw, and Galia (a cantaloupe-honeydew cross) are some of the unusual melons available to grow that feature different-colored flesh, unique flavors, and sweet aromas.

Melons do take up space and need hot conditions, abundant water, and the right level of fertility to mature. But once you find the right spot for your melons and have had success, they will undoubtedly become a regular member of your garden each year.

■ *When to Plant*

You can plant melons directly from seed into the garden. Start transplants four weeks before your last frost date or purchase transplants. Whatever way you choose, plant seeds or plants when the soil is warm (ideally at least 60°F). This usually is two weeks after the last frost date—May or June.

■ *Where to Plant*

Don't skimp on sun and heat for your melons. Find the sunniest, warmest spot in your garden to plant. Consider planting near a south-facing wall or fence to protect young seedlings from cold spring breezes. Since melon plants like to vine, or "run," plant on the garden edge or in a location where they will have room to ramble.

How to Plant

Plant in raised beds that are covered with black or dark green plastic mulch. Create the beds and cover with the plastic mulch two weeks before planting to allow the soil to heat up. Amend the soil with compost before planting and forming beds. Poke holes in the plastic 12 to 18 inches apart in rows 3 feet apart, and sow two to three seeds or plant one seedling per hole. You can also plant in circles, or "hills," with four to six seeds per hill. Space hills 4 feet apart.

I like to plant melons on the edge of the garden near the lawn, so the vines can grow into the grass. I stop mowing where the vines are growing in midsummer. Although it might look a little messy, it's a good way to save space in the garden.

Care and Maintenance

Once the seeds germinate and the true leaves (second set of leaves) form, thin so there's only three seedlings per hill or two seedlings per hole in the row. Melons are slow growing in early summer, so cover young seedlings and transplants with a floating row cover until the soil and air warm. This will encourage plants to continue growing during cool days and night. Once the flowers form and the plants start to run, remove the row cover. The row cover also prevents some insects from attacking the plants.

Keep melons well weeded, especially during the first few weeks. Melons also need a consistent supply of water. Apply at least 1 to 2 inches of water a week, more during hot, dry, windy periods. Reduce watering a few weeks before harvest so the fruits taste sweeter.

Weed the plants well, especially during the first month of growth. Mulch the areas between hills or rows with a layer of straw, newspaper, or untreated grass clippings to keep the soil moist, prevent weeds from growing, and give the melon fruits a soft place to grow. Besides heat and water, melons love food. Fertilize with a small handful of an organic product, such as 5-5-5, per plant when vines begin to run and again when the first fruits form.

To save space, consider growing melons up a trellis or fence. You'll have to support the heavy fruits with pantyhose or mesh attached to the fence, but it's a way to grow these delicious gems in a space-starved garden.

You're not the only one who likes melons in the garden. These plants have a number of insects, animals, and diseases to watch out for. Aphids

and flea beetles will attack young plants. Spray insecticidal soap for aphids and cover plants with a floating row cover to control the flea beetles. Cucumber beetles and squash bugs are two major pests. Not only do cucumber beetles feed on melon leaves and flowers, but they transmit disease to plants. Control these beetles by spraying pyrethrum in early evening, using traps, and covering young plants with a row cover. Squash bugs love congregating on the undersides of melon leaves. Handpick and kill these pests in the morning when they're sluggish or spray pyrethrum.

Rotate crops, clean up plant debris in fall, and select disease-resistant varieties to reduce problems with diseases such as powdery mildew and leaf blight.

Animals can sometimes be the biggest problem in the melon patch. Raccoons and mice love these sweet jewels. Protect individual fruits by wrapping them in a wire cage before they ripen. As soon as the fruits are ripe, pick. Leaving them in the garden may entice these critters to come have a look.

■ *Harvesting*

Speaking of harvest, you'll know when your melons are ripe when they have a sweet smell, the fruits "slip" off the vine when lifted, and the skin changes to the mature color for that type. Some melons, such as crenshaw and honeydew, can be harvested early and matured indoors. The best flavor is from a melon harvested at the peak of maturity in the garden and eaten immediately. There are hot summer days when a melon gets eaten right in my garden and never makes it to the kitchen.

■ *Additional Information*

It's important to choose melon varieties adapted to our sometimes-cool summers. 'Halona', 'Delicious', 'Minnesota Midget', and 'Sweet Granite' cantaloupes produce 2- to 3-pound, orange-fleshed fruits and are well adapted to our cool weather. 'Athena' is a disease-resistant cantaloupe with a good shelf life. 'Rocky Ford' is a 2-pound, disease-resistant, green-fleshed heirloom cantaloupe. 'Savor' is a unique French Charentais melon (sweet, small variety of cantaloupe) that produces 2-pound, orange-fleshed fruits with a gray-green skin. 'Arava' is a 4-pound Galia type that has light green flesh and a very sweet flavor. 'Honey Orange' is a salmon-orange-fleshed honeydew that grows well in the Northeast.

MESCLUN MIX

It used to be that salad was made of lettuce and, maybe, spinach greens. Then Americans discovered mesclun mixes. I remember first eating a mesclun mix salad and being amazed at the flavors, colors, and textures. Mesclun mix is a European invention. Gardeners there would traditionally gather wild and cultivated greens and herbs and mix them together in a salad with a homemade dressing. (My European friends scoff at our bottled dressings.) By mixing various greens, you can create a number of different colorful and flavorful salads. Some mixes are mild and mostly lettuce based, while others feature greens such as arugula, mustard, and endive and have a strong, spicy flavor.

You can certainly grow a host of greens, pick the leaves when young, and make your own blends, or buy some blends growers have created. Since the greens are harvested when very young, growing mesclun mixes is a no-brainer. Seed, water, and harvest. What could be easier?

■ *When to Plant*

Most of the greens in mesclun mixes are cool weather loving, so sow seeds three weeks before your last frost date—April or May. Continue sowing seeds every few weeks until early summer. Sow another crop in late summer for an autumn harvest.

■ *Where to Plant*

Mesclun mixes are quick-growing greens that are harvested young. Plant them in raised beds or among slower-growing vegetables such as tomatoes and broccoli for a quick crop before these other vegetables shade them out. These greens only need two to three hours of direct sun a day to produce, so they also work well in small yards and containers.

■ *How to Plant*

Build raised beds 8 inches tall and 3 feet wide. Amend the soil with compost and broadcast seeds ½ inch apart across the top of the beds. The seeds are small, so cover them lightly with potting soil or sand. Water and place a floating row cover over the bed until the seeds germinate. The row cover will keep the bed moist.

■ *Care and Maintenance*

Since mesclun mix matures in less than one month and the seeds are grown so close together, weeding usually isn't necessary. Fertilize with fish emulsion only if the greens appear yellow. Keep the beds evenly moist and control pests, such as aphids and flea beetles. Spray insecticidal soap to control aphids and use the floating row cover to stop flea beetle damage.

■ *Harvesting*

Start harvesting your mesclun greens when they're 4 to 6 inches long. This can be as soon as two weeks after planting. Cut the greens with a scissors to 1 inch above the ground. Water and fertilize the cut greens with fish emulsion and they will regrow for a second harvest. Harvest only as much as you'll need for a meal because mesclun greens don't last long in the refrigerator.

■ *Additional Information*

There are many greens mixes on the market; some are advertised as mesclun mix, while others are called greens or salad mix. They all are a blend of various greens. 'Provencal' mesclun mix features arugula, lettuce, endive, and herbs for a mildly piquant flavor. 'Tangy' mesclun mix has stronger-flavored mustards, arugula, and endive to add a zip to salads. 'Mild' mesclun mix features lettuce, mizuna, and kale, and has a quieter flavor. 'Micro Greens' mix features mild-flavored greens, such as chard, beets, kale, and spinach, which should be picked at the seedling stage when leaves are only a few inches long.

OKRA

Now, here's a vegetable that you don't normally think of as a Northern crop. However, it grows well here, if you have a taste for it. My family isn't big on okra (*Abelmoschus esculentus*), calling it "too slimy." The one way my daughter will eat it is roasted until crisp like a French fry. Then all the slime is gone. I also like it in stir-fries and soups, but that meal usually happens when I'm home alone.

If you have a sunny, hot spot in your garden, you can grow okra. The plants are beautiful, so they make an ideal edible landscape plant. Some varieties have colorful red leaves and pods. You can grow them in the flower garden or along a south-facing garage wall or fence to maximize the amount of sun and heat.

Most okra varieties are tall growing (6 feet), start producing fruits about two months after planting, and keep producing hibiscus-like yellow flowers and fruits until frost. I actually have to remember to keep picking my okra, because the fruits can get large and woody quickly, especially during hot weather. The young fruits are tender and easy to harvest, and I've even slipped a few by my family at dinnertime disguised with other vegetables.

■ *When to Plant*

Since okra is a heat lover, start seedlings indoors six weeks before the last frost date to transplant outdoors in late May or early June. Okra doesn't like its roots disturbed, so start okra seedlings in peat, cow, or coir (coconut fiber) pots. These pots are planted, container and all, in the ground. You can also sow seeds at that time, but the plants will take longer to mature.

■ *Where to Plant*

Plant this tall, thin vegetable in full sun and well-drained soil on the north side of your garden so it doesn't shade other plants. Consider planting along a south-facing garage, barn, or house to add some beauty and produce a faster crop.

■ *How to Plant*

Besides heat, okra likes water. Plant in compost-amended soil. To get a jump on the season, consider placing black plastic mulch on the bed two weeks before planting to preheat the soil. Poke holes 2 feet apart in the plastic to transplant your seedlings or sow seeds. If your soil is consistently wet, consider growing okra in an 8-inch-tall raised bed. Okra can withstand a drought, but not a flood.

■ Care and Maintenance

Keep okra plants well watered, but allow the soil to dry out between waterings. Add a small handful of organic fertilizer, such as 5-5-5, monthly around plants to keep them growing strong. Okra doesn't have any significant pests.

■ Harvesting

The secret to getting someone to love okra is to pick the pods before they reach 3 inches long. There's no surer way to turn off a potential okra fan than to serve thick, woody, chewy pods. This may mean harvesting daily, since the pods grow so fast. If you miss a few pods, cut them off with a sharp knife and compost them. If you allow pods to stay on the plant and form seeds, the plant will slow its production of new pods. The flowers are edible, too, and tasty stuffed. Wear gloves to protect your hands from the spines on some varieties.

■ Additional Information

'Clemson Spineless 80' is a new, improved version of the Southern classic that grows only 3 to 4 feet tall and doesn't have sharp spines. 'Millionaire' is a fast-maturing variety. 'Red Burgundy' features red leaves and fruits.

ONION

One vegetable I use regularly in the kitchen is the onion (*Allium cepa*). That's why growing onions is so important to me. You can grow a wide variety of onions in our cool climate, from sweet red onions to pungent yellow onions. The flavor of fresh onions is incomparable. Give them well-drained soil, water, sun, and cool temperatures and they will reward you with an abundant crop for salads and cooking. They're a garden staple.

The key to growing onions is to start with the right variety. Onion varieties can be confusing because they are grouped as long-day, intermediate, or short-day varieties. Short-day varieties are planted in the fall in the South to mature in early summer. The famous 'Vidalia' onion is one of these. We usually don't grow these around here. Long-day varieties are planted in spring in the North to mature in midsummer. There are also intermediate, or day-neutral, varieties that mature in summer from a spring planting regardless of where you grow them. You can also grow sweet or pungent varieties. Pungent varieties last longer in storage and are best for cooking. Sweet varieties should be eaten soon after harvest and are great raw in salads and in sandwiches.

If you love the taste of onions but are intimidated by growing bulb onions, there are other easier *Allium* choices. Scallions, or green onions, are grown for their mild-flavored green tops. You can even grow varieties with purple stems. Shallots are small bulbs that produce more side bulbs around the main one over time. They're simpler to grow and produce a mild-flavored bulb that's less pungent than an onion.

■ *When to Plant*

Onions like growing in cool weather, so start seeds indoors six to eight weeks before your last frost date. You can also buy onion starts (small green plants) or sets (small bulbs). Whether you're planting onion plants or sets, plant three weeks before your last frost date—late April or May.

■ *Where to Plant*

Onions grow and size up best when planted in well-drained soil in full sun. They don't like growing in wet soils, so build a raised bed 8 inches tall and 3 feet wide. Remove rocks and debris from the beds before planting. Since onions are low-growing plants, build your bed away from taller plants that may shade them later in the season.

■ *How to Plant*

The easiest way to grow bulb onions is by starting with sets. Sets are young bulbs the size of a quarter that you buy. You'll have a limited number of varieties to grow, but they're simple. Plant the sets, pointy side up, 2 inches deep in the soil. Space them 6 inches apart in rows 1 foot apart. Shallot bulbs have a similar look and feel as sets and are planted the same distance apart. Scallions are planted from transplants or seed and are spaced 2 inches apart.

If you grow your own bulb onion seedlings or purchase ones at the garden center, plant them 2 inches apart in rows and thin, once they're big enough to eat, so they're ultimately spaced 6 inches apart.

■ *Care and Maintenance*

Onions don't compete well with weeds, so it's imperative to keep the bed hand weeded. They also need a constant supply of water, especially when the bulbs are getting larger, to make the biggest bulbs. Keep the beds well watered and mulch with a layer of straw to help prevent weeds from growing and to keep the soil moist. Apply a high-phosphorus plant food that also contains nitrogen, such as bonemeal, to beds monthly to ensure the onions grow large.

Onions only have a few pests that are cause for concern. Onion maggots are small worms that attack the bulbs by tunneling holes in them. Spread sharp sand or diatomaceous earth around the bulbs to kill them. Onion thrips are small aphid-like insects that feed on leaves. Spray insecticidal soap or spinosad to kill these pests. Most disease problems are related to

poor water drainage in the soil, so make sure the beds are loose and drain well. Also, rotate crops and grow disease-resistant varieties to prevent disease problems.

■ *Harvesting*

Scallions are easy to harvest. As soon as they grow 6 to 8 inches tall (about two months after planting), pull them out and enjoy in salads and stir-fries. Shallots are harvested when the side bulbs that form around the planted bulb begin to separate and the leaves yellow. Pull the entire plant, separate out the side bulbs, and store. You can grow specific varieties of scallions or just grow any onion and harvest the tops once they form. Of course, if you cut the tops of a bulbing onion repeatedly, you won't get much of a bulb to form.

Bulbing onions should be harvested about three to four months after planting, when one-half of the onion tops naturally fall over. Bend the remaining tops and leave them for one week to cure in the garden. Then pull the onions out of the ground and dry them in a shady, airy, well-ventilated room. Once the onions are dry, cut off the tops and store in a cool basement in mesh bags. Some varieties will last for up to six months in storage.

■ *Additional Information*

Some good scallion varieties to grow include 'Evergreen Hardy' with white stems and 'Deep Purple' with purple-tinged stems. 'Ambition' is a good shallot variety for our region.

For a great sweet onion, you can't beat 'Walla Walla'. This yellow-skinned white onion from Washington State features juicy, sweet bulbs. 'Ailsa Craig Exhibition' is a sweet variety hailing from Britain. 'Candy' is a day-neutral variety that produces sweet, white-fleshed bulbs. For a red sweet onion, try 'Redwing Hybrid'.

For storage onions with a naturally pungent flavor, 'Copra' and 'Cortland' are longtime-favorite yellow-skinned and white-fleshed varieties. 'Red Zeppelin' is a new red-skinned and red-fleshed storage onion that will last up to six months in storage. 'Purplette' is a small onion that forms golf-ball-sized bulbs within two months of planting.

If you're looking for onion sets, you'll find varieties such as 'Sweet Sandwich', 'Yellow Spanish', 'Yellow Stuttgarter', and 'Red Wethersfield' in garden centers and online. All are long-day and grow well in our climate.

PARSNIP

When I first started growing parsnips (*Pastinaca sativa*), I wasn't impressed. They seemed to take forever to germinate, they grew slowly, and the carrot-shaped roots looked fine but didn't have any special flavor. Then I learned to allow them to be exposed to the cold and even overwinter in the garden before picking them. The difference in flavor made it all worthwhile. These white roots turned sweet and flavorful, making them perfect to mash, toss in soups or stews, or add to roasted root-crop casseroles.

Although parsnips are widely grown in England and Europe, American gardeners have been slow to warm up to them. I grow them because they fit in my "plant it and forget about it" category of vegetables. Once growing, they require little work and reward you with sweet roots in fall and winter.

■ *When to Plant*

As with carrots, sow parsnip seeds two weeks before the last frost date in your area. That would be April or May.

■ *Where to Plant*

Parsnips grow best in full sun, but can receive only three to four hours of direct sun and still produce a crop. They do, however, need a well-drained, loose soil, so grow them in a raised bed 8 inches off the ground, 3 feet wide, and as long as you like. Plant so these roots don't get shaded by other crops during the summer.

■ *How to Plant*

Amend the raised bed with compost before planting. Remove rocks and debris from the bed, which can block the growth of the roots. Sow the flat seeds ½ inch deep and ½ inch apart in rows spaced 18 inches apart. The seeds are large enough so that you can easily space them properly. Parsnips do take up to three weeks to germinate, so I like to cover the seeds with sand or potting soil, water, and then place a floating row cover over the bed to keep it moist. Once the seeds germinate, remove the row cover. Another method I've used is to poke 6-inch-deep holes in the soil with a trowel handle, fill the hole with potting soil, and plant the seeds ½ inch deep. This allows the parsnip roots to grow straight and long into the potting soil.

■ *Care and Maintenance*

Once the seeds germinate, thin so there is at least 4 inches between plants. Parsnips need room to expand, so if they aren't properly thinned, you'll

get thin and spindly roots. Because they take so long to germinate, it's important to keep your parsnip bed weeded well early in the season. Keep the bed well watered. Water deeply so the water soaks at least 6 inches into the soil. Mulch between the parsnip rows with straw to help keep the soil moist and weed free.

Parsnips have few pests. A floating row cover kept on young plants will help ward off leafhoppers and rabbits.

■ Harvesting

As I mentioned, don't rush to harvest parsnip roots. They taste best after a month of cool temperatures in fall. I've even had success mulching them with a 6-inch layer of hay in November and leaving the roots to overwinter in the soil. In March or April, once the ground thaws but before the roots sprout new shoots, dig up the parsnips and cook them. You'll be amazed at how sweet they taste.

■ Additional Information

There aren't many varieties of parsnips, but I've found some that produce well. 'Lancer', 'Harris Model', and 'Javelin' germinate well and produce clean, white, smooth roots about one hundred days after seeding.

PEAS

There are few vegetables more anticipated in spring than peas (*Pisum sativum*). Fresh peas are seldom found in grocery stores, even in season, making them even more essential in the garden. While I grew up eating English peas, which need to be shelled, now we have snow peas and snap peas, which can be eaten pods and all. It makes pea growing and eating even easier. Most of our pea crop ends up being eaten in the garden, because it's so easy to walk down the rows munching happily as you go. Besides being tasty raw, peas are great sautéed, steamed, or added to a soup or stew. You can also harvest the young tendrils (curly shoots) and add those to salads.

■ *When to Plant*

Pea seeds can germinate in soils as cool as 45°F, so as soon as the soil dries out enough to turn, plant your peas. Most likely it will be April or early May in our region. I've had success sowing a fall crop in late July or early August for harvest in October.

■ *Where to Plant*

Pea seeds can rot if sitting in cool, wet soil in spring. It's important to build an 8-inch-tall, 4-foot-wide raised bed before planting. The raised bed allows the soil to dry out and warm up faster. Peas need full sun to grow their best. Most varieties grow 4 to 7 feet tall and need a trellis or fence to grab on to grow up. Peas can be grown along an existing fence or building.

■ *How to Plant*

Amend the soil with compost before planting. To hasten germination and reduce the chance of seeds rotting in the ground, soak pea seeds overnight in warm water before planting. This starts the germination process, so they sprout faster. I construct my fence for tall varieties in the middle of my raised bed. I use a 6-foot-tall wire fence supported every 5 feet with a wooden or metal post. Sow seeds in rows on either side of the fence. I get more pea plants, and peas, that way. Sow seeds 2 inches apart and space the rows 1 foot apart. If you're growing dwarf pea varieties that only grow 2 feet tall, you won't need a fence. Like beans, treating seeds with inoculants is a good idea, especially if you have poor quality soil.

■ *Care and Maintenance*

Since peas are a legume and convert nitrogen from the air, they need little extra fertilizer. Keep the soil cool and weed free by hand weeding after germination and then mulching the rows with a layer of straw or untreated grass clippings.

In addition to pea seeds rotting in cool, wet soils, there are a few other problems you'll find with your pea plants. Diseases, such as fusarium wilt, pythium, and powdery mildew, can be avoided by growing disease-resistant varieties and by rotating your crops, not planting a pea-family crop in the same area for three years. Aphids will love the young pea shoots. Spray insecticidal soap to control them. Rabbits and woodchucks love the tender pea plants. Fence your garden before peas emerge to keep these critters away.

■ *Harvesting*

Peas start maturing a few months after planting. Harvest English peas when the pods are full and round. Pick daily, and don't allow the pods to become overmature or they will be tough and starchy tasting. Harvest snap peas when the peas inside start to form but don't fill the pod. Harvest snow peas (flat-podded peas) when the peas just begin to form.

■ *Additional Information*

Some good English pea varieties to grow include 'Green Arrow' and 'Premium', which both grow 30 inches tall. 'Tall Telephone' is an old-fashioned variety that grows 6 feet tall. For snap peas, 'Super Sugar Snap' is a disease-resistant version of the classic 'Sugar Snap' and grows 5 feet tall. 'Sugar Sprint' grows 2 feet tall and produces prolifically. 'Oregon Sugar Pod II' is a good snow pea variety, and 'Golden Sweet' is another snow pea that produces yellow pods on 4-foot-tall plants.

PEPPER

Peppers (*Capsicum annuum*) can be hot or sweet, but freshly picked from the garden, they are always delicious. Being Italian, I have fond memories of my mother making sausage and sweet peppers for summer dinners. The long, sweet, banana-shaped peppers are what I grew up with. As an adult I've grown sweet bell peppers, Italian frying peppers, and a whole range of hot peppers. With peppers, diversity is king. You can grow a pepper that looks like a Chinese lantern and is so hot it will strip paint, or a red banana pepper that's as sweet as candy. What's great is we can grow them all in our climate, with varying degrees of success.

Peppers can be used in a wide range of dishes, are loaded with vitamins, and are beautiful plants in the landscape. There are varieties of sweet peppers with red-, orange-, ivory-, purple-, yellow-, and even chocolate-colored fruits. There are hot varieties with purple foliage and fruits, and some whose fruits look like a rainbow of colors. If you don't think you have a lot of space, peppers can grow in containers on a deck or patio, or mixed in an annual garden with your flowers.

■ *When to Plant*

Peppers are in the tomato family, so they love the heat. Don't rush them into the garden or they will stay stunted and not yield well. Either start seedlings

indoors six to eight weeks before your last frost date, or buy transplants at the local garden center. Wait until the soil is at least 60°F, about two weeks after the last frost date in your area—usually mid-May or June. You can try planting earlier in containers, but protect the plants from cool nights.

■ *Where to Plant*

Peppers need full sun and well-drained, fertile soil to grow and produce their best. If you have heavy clay soil, consider building a raised bed and covering it with dark green or black plastic mulch. The mulch will heat up the soil before planting.

■ *How to Plant*

Amend the soil with compost before planting. Poke holes in the plastic and space plants 2 feet apart in rows 3 feet apart. I like to plant my peppers in a zigzag pattern in the bed to maximize the number that I can fit. Plant at the same depth as they were in their pots. To keep my peppers upright, I like to place small tomato cages around them or place individual stakes next to them. Assuming you'll get a big crop, the cages and stakes help keep the plants upright and keep the fruits cleaner during summer thunderstorms. A floppy plant tends to be less productive too.

■ *Care and Maintenance*

Peppers are finicky about temperatures. If it gets below 60°F or above 90°F, the pepper blossoms will drop off without setting fruit. We're mostly

concerned about cool temperatures in our region, so protect young plants with a floating row cover in spring until the air temperatures warm consistently into the 70s°F. Snip off the first flowers on small transplants so they send more energy into growing roots and shoots. This will lead to a higher overall production.

Peppers like consistent feeding. Add a small handful of organic fertilizer, such as 5-5-5, per plant once a month to keep them growing strong. I've also used 1 tablespoon of Epsom salts mixed into 1 gallon of water twice during the summer to grow a healthier plant too. Peppers like the magnesium in the Epsom salts. Don't use this treatment if a soil test indicates you already have high magnesium levels in your soil.

Keep plants well watered, and if you don't use plastic mulch, place a layer of straw or untreated grass clippings around the base of plants once the summer temperatures warm consistently above 70°F.

Protect pepper transplants from cutworms with newspaper wrapped around the stem 2 inches above and 1 inch below the soil line. Spray insecticidal soap for aphids. Pepper maggots are small worms that tunnel into fruits. Cover plants with a floating row cover to prevent them from laying eggs on fruits. Rotate crops, not planting any tomato-family vegetables in the same location for three years, to prevent any diseases from taking hold.

■ Harvesting

When Italian frying (banana-shaped) peppers or bell peppers are full sized for that variety, cut the fruits from the stem with a sharp knife. For an even sweeter-tasting pepper with more vitamins, you can also wait another two weeks for the fruits to ripen to their mature color (usually red). But don't let all the fruits go to this mature color, because your peppers will stop producing new fruits. They will think their job is done for the season.

Hot peppers can also be harvested in the green (immature) or red stage. I've found they're quicker to turn red than sweet peppers, and since the plants are generally smaller and you only need a few fruits to make an impact, they're perfect for container growing. Hot peppers vary in their degree of hotness, based on the type of hot pepper and the weather. The Scoville heat scale grades peppers as to their hotness. For example, Anaheim peppers are about 500 units, while habanero peppers can be over 100,000 units. The higher the number, the hotter the fruits. Also, the weather and growing conditions influence hotness. Cool, cloudy summers will make a hot pepper mild flavored. If you don't feed or water your hot peppers well, they will produce fewer, but hotter, fruits. For the hottest varieties, wear gloves to protect yourself when harvesting. More than once I have inadvertently rubbed my sweaty face with my hands after harvesting hot peppers, only to get a sensational burn in my eyes from the chemical capsaicin, which is prevalent in hot peppers.

■ *Additional Information*

There are hundreds of varieties of peppers to grow. Let me share a few of my favorites with you. For sweet peppers, go with varieties adapted to our sometimes-cool summers. 'King of the North' and 'Ace' are reliable short-season bell peppers, maturing fruits in seventy days from transplanting. 'Sweet Chocolate' has unique brown-colored skin and 'Islander' has lavender-colored skin. Both eventually turn red. For a productive Italian frying (banana-shaped) sweet pepper, I love 'Carmen'. It's so productive the plants fall over from the weight of the fruits. It's also quick to turn red. 'Italia' and 'Corno di Toro' are two classic banana-shaped peppers that are great for frying, grilling, and roasting.

For hot peppers, I like the mild 'Early Jalapeño' for its quick-maturing and tasty fruits. To add spice to cooking, try a 'Numex Joe E Parker', 'Anaheim', and 'Super Cayenne II Hybrid' chili pepper. To really get a kick out of your hot peppers, grow a habanero with red or orange fruits. These are so hot you can literally burn yourself if you're not careful handling them.

If you're looking for beauty in your hot peppers, try 'Black Pearl', which features jet black foliage and stems, and fruits that turn from purple to red. Also, 'Numex Twilight' has fruits that mature in different colors such as purple, yellow, orange, and red.

POTATO

I still remember helping pick potatoes (*Solanum tuberosum*) on my grandfather's farm. It was hard work, but the rewards were tasty spuds all winter long. Since potatoes are also readily available in stores and relatively inexpensive, you may wonder, why grow your own? Well, like all vegetables, fresh potatoes dug from your own soil taste better, and you can grow a wider variety of potatoes than you'll find in a grocery store. Some of these varieties have yellow, red, or even purple flesh. You don't need a farm to grow potatoes either. You can grow potatoes in a small bed or even a container.

■ *When to Plant*

Potatoes thrive in cool, moist conditions. Plant the seed potatoes (small tubers) two to four weeks before your last frost date—April or May.

■ *Where to Plant*

Potatoes grow best in full sun, but you can still get a crop if your garden gets only three to four hours of sun a day. Plant in well-drained, fertile soil in the garden or a container.

■ *How to Plant*

Potatoes grow best in soil rich in phosphorus and potassium. Based on a soil test, make sure your soil has plenty of both. Potatoes aren't planted from seed but from small tubers called seed potatoes. Buy these locally or through the mail. Don't use store-bought spuds as seed potatoes, because they are treated with a sprout inhibitor to slow growth and may have diseases on them.

Plant potatoes in a trench dug 6 inches deep. Place seed potatoes spaced 1 foot apart in rows spaced 2 feet apart. Fill the trench with just enough soil to cover the seed potatoes. Water well.

You can also plant four seed potatoes in the bottom of a 15-gallon tub, potato bag, or plastic barrel. Fill the tub with potting soil so it covers the seed potatoes. As they grow, continue to add more soil until you reach the top. Keep the containers well watered.

■ *Care and Maintenance*

Once the potatoes sprout and are 6 inches tall, mound soil over them with a hoe. Do this a second time two weeks later. Not only does hilling create more area for potatoes to develop in the soil, but it is a fast way to weed and it shades the developing tubers from the sun so they don't turn green. Green-skinned potatoes are off-flavored and mildly toxic.

After the second hilling, mulch the rows and hills with a layer of straw or untreated grass clippings. If you can keep the soil evenly moist, more tubers will form and they will be larger.

Colorado potato beetles love to eat potato leaves. Crush the orange eggs on the underside of the leaves, spray B.t. San Diego on the soft-bodied red larvae, and handpick the adults. Keep the pH around 6 to avoid potato scab disease, and plant disease-free seed potatoes to avoid late blight. Remove any leftover sprouting potatoes from the last harvest to reduce diseases.

■ Harvesting

Potatoes take about seventy to ninety days to mature, but you can harvest new potatoes six weeks after planting. New potatoes are baby spuds that you "steal" from the hill by lightly digging around by hand. Don't take too many or you'll reduce your yield later. Mature potatoes are harvested when the tops start to yellow and die. Pull up the entire plant and pick the potatoes attached to the vine and left in the surrounding soil. Turn over potato containers and pick through the soil for these spuds. Eat any damaged tubers first and cure the rest in a 70°F airy, shaded room for two weeks. Store in a cool, dark basement or garage for up to six months.

■ Additional Information

'Yukon Gold' is my favorite potato variety. It has moist yellow flesh and is great baked, boiled, or roasted. 'All Red' has red flesh and 'All Blue' has blue flesh. 'Burbank' is a good white-fleshed baker and 'Russian Banana' is a good fingerling potato, perfect for roasting.

PUMPKIN

Nothing says fall in the Northeast garden like orange pumpkins (*Cucurbita pepo*). I used to grow pumpkins for my daughter and I would carve her name in the young pumpkin's skin, pretending it was garden gnomes at work. As the pumpkins grew, so did her name. She was amazed.

Pumpkins are not just orange any longer. There are white-skinned, red-skinned, and even blue-skinned varieties available. Some fruits look like Cinderella's carriage, while others are as small as a tomato. Some varieties grow as large as a truck! You can carve pumpkins, make pies from the flesh, and roast and eat the seeds from many varieties. Yes, pumpkins love to run and take up room, but with some planning you can grow a pumpkin patch with satisfying results, even in a small yard.

■ *When to Plant*

Pumpkins, like all squash, grow best during warm weather. Sow seeds or transplant seedlings into the garden after all danger of frost has past. That's usually May or June.

■ *Where to Plant*

To get the most and biggest fruits, plant in full sun and fertile, well-drained soil. I like to plant pumpkins on the edge of my garden so they can trail off into the lawn. It makes for less lawn to mow and the vines don't take over the garden. I often lift and train the vines when they're small to make them grow in the direction I'd like them to.

■ How to Plant

Amend the soil with compost or composted manure. Pumpkins need lots of fertility to grow, especially the large-fruited types. In cool-summer areas, cover the pumpkin bed with black plastic mulch two weeks before planting to preheat the soil. Poke holes in the plastic and plant three seeds or one transplant 3 feet apart. Thin seed-grown plants to the healthiest seedling once they're all 4 inches tall.

■ Care and Maintenance

Once the pumpkin vines start to run, and again when the first fruits set, add a small handful of organic fertilizer, such as 5-5-5, around each plant. Keep plants well watered with at least 1 inch of water a week. Weed around young plants and then mulch, if you didn't use plastic, with a layer of straw or untreated grass clippings.

Watch for squash bugs, cucumber beetles, and squash vine borers in your pumpkin patch. Cover young plants with a floating row cover to prevent these pests from getting started. Remove the cover when flowers form so they can be pollinated by bees. If your pumpkins aren't setting fruits, it could be due to cloudy weather and few bees visiting the flowers. See the cucumber section to learn how you can pollinate your own crop. Rotate crops, not planting a squash family crop in that area for three years, and use resistant varieties to eliminate disease problems.

Pumpkins need a long season to mature. If you have fruits forming in late September, cut them off and compost them so the pumpkins put more energy into maturing the fruits already on the plant.

■ Harvesting

Wait to harvest pumpkins until their skin turns the mature color, but harvest before a hard frost. With a sharp knife, cut the stem 2 inches above the fruit and let the pumpkin cure in a warm room for a few weeks. Then let the kids have at it for carving, decorating, and seed roasting. Pumpkins can be stored for two to three months in a dark, 50°F basement.

■ Additional Information

For a classic carving pumpkin, you can't beat 'Connecticut Field'. It grows up to 25 pounds and has a perfect pumpkin shape. For little kids, try the 'Baby Bear' pumpkin, which only grows to 2 pounds. 'New England Pie' is a great pie and cooking pumpkin. 'Dill's Atlantic Giant' is the monster variety that can grow to hundreds of pounds. 'Lumina' has white skin, while 'Queensland Blue' has blue skin. 'Rouge Vif d'Etampes' is a flat-shaped French heirloom pumpkin that looks like Cinderella's carriage.

RADISH

If you're an impatient gardener, like me in the spring, you must grow radishes (*Raphanus sativus*). This root crop goes from seed to harvest in as little as twenty-five days. I'm always amazed at how fast radishes germinate and grow during our cool spring weather. They add crunch, color, and zip to any salad. As long as they're grown while the weather is cool, the flavor is pleasant and mild. However, with any kind of stress such as lack of water or hot temperatures, the flavors turns sharp and hot. I personally love a spicy radish, but others in my family don't.

These spring radishes grow in round or elongated shapes and are usually white, red, or purple skinned. There are also winter radishes, or daikons. These take longer to grow and are best eaten as a fall crop when the cool weather sweetens the roots. Some winter radish varieties have elongated white roots, round black-skinned roots, or green skin with red-fleshed roots. I like growing winter radishes to shred raw and add to salads, or use in Japanese cooking.

■ *When to Plant*

Plant spring radishes as soon as the soil can be worked, usually April or May. Plant again in late August or September for a fall crop. Since they mature so quickly, sow small batches every week in spring to extend the harvest into summer.

■ Where to Plant

Radishes are very forgiving plants. I once found a daikon growing underneath other vegetables, completely forgotten until I discovered this large root in fall. Since these are root crops, they grow best in raised beds. They need only three to four hours of direct sunlight to grow and mature. Tuck them in among slower-maturing crops, such as broccoli, tomatoes, and squash. By the time you pull the radishes, these other crops will have started to expand and fill in the open space.

■ How to Plant

Amend the raised bed with compost only if you have poor soil. Too much compost or nitrogen fertilizer inhibits roots formation. Sprinkle the small seeds 1 inch apart in rows spaced 1 foot apart, or broadcast the seeds over the top of the bed. Don't worry if you can't get the spacing down. You'll be thinning anyway. Cover the seeds with potting soil or sand and water well. They will germinate, literally, within a few days.

■ Care and Maintenance

When radish seedlings are 1 inch tall, thin them so they're spaced 2 inches apart. Thin winter radishes to 4 inches apart. Use the thinnings in salads. Some growers just grow radishes for the baby greens to add to salad mixes. Keep the bed well watered and weeded. Any stress from lack of water, poor thinning, or weed competition will prevent the roots from forming, or cause them to crack or be hot flavored. No extra fertilizer is necessary.

Watch for aphids and flea beetles on young radish leaves. These create shotgun-like holes in the leaves. Spray insecticidal soap to control them or cover the radishes with a floating row cover.

■ Harvesting

Keep a close eye on your spring radishes. They mature quickly. Gently remove the soil from the base, and as soon as you see a round (or elongated) root, pull it up. It you wait too long, the roots can become woody textured and hot flavored. Harvest winter radishes the same way, but they will take up to one month longer to mature.

■ Additional Information

'Easter Egg' is a mix of spring radishes with white, red, and purple skin colors. 'D'Avignon' is an elongated red-and-white-skinned variety. 'Red Meat' is a round winter radish with red flesh. 'Miyashige' is an elongated white-rooted daikon for fall growing.

SPINACH

After a long winter in the Northeast, spinach (*Spinacia oleracea*) is a welcome sight. It's one of the first greens to appear in spring, and I've actually overwintered it from a fall planting to have it available as early as April in my Vermont garden. Not only is spinach a great green for salads, but it's versatile too. You can steam it, toss it in stews and soups, and simply sauté it with garlic and olive oil.

This cool-weather-loving veggie will satisfy your cravings for fresh greens in early spring, and is loaded with nutrients such as vitamin A, iron, and calcium.

■ *When to Plant*

Spinach needs cool temperatures to grow and mature. It's best planted as a spring or fall crop. Plant in spring six weeks before your last frost date, usually April. Spinach seeds can germinate with temperatures around 40°F, so once the ground is dried out, start seeding. Continue planting small patches every two weeks until late spring to ensure a continuous harvest. Plant again in late summer for a fall crop. I like to plant in late August in a cold frame and let the spinach overwinter in this protected space for an early-spring harvest.

■ *Where to Plant*

Spinach will grow with as little as a few hours of full sun, but forms the biggest leaves and plants in full sun. Since you're planting so early, plant spinach on a raised bed 8 inches tall and 3 feet wide. The soil will dry out and warm up faster on the raised bed, allowing for faster germination and growth.

■ *How to Plant*

Amend the raised bed with compost before planting. Soak seeds overnight in warm water to start germination. The next day plant seeds 1 inch apart in rows spaced 12 inches apart. You can also broadcast seeds on top of the bed.

■ *Care and Maintenance*

Thin spinach seedlings to 6 inches apart when they're 3 inches tall. Thinning helps the plants grow large and reduces the risk of diseases such as rust by giving the plant more room to grow. Use the thinned seedlings in salads. Keep the soil cool and moist by watering regularly and mulching with a layer of organic mulch, such as straw or untreated grass clippings, after thinning. If the young leaves are pale green or yellow, spray the plants with fish emulsion fertilizer. This quick-reacting organic fertilizer will add nitrogen to help green up the leaves.

Watch for aphids, leafminers, and flea beetles on your spinach leaves. Wash off aphids with an insecticidal soap spray, and cover plants with a floating row cover to prevent flea beetle and leafminer damage.

If growing to overwinter, cover the fall-seeded spinach crop in November with a floating row cover and a 4- to 6-inch layer of straw. Check in early spring for signs of growth and remove the straw.

■ *Harvesting*

Start harvesting outer spinach leaves when there are six leaves on the plant—about thirty days after seeding. If you don't harvest the outer leaves, pull up and harvest full heads about two weeks later. Continue harvesting individual leaves until the weather warms and a seed stalk forms on the plants (called "bolting"). Then pull all plants and compost them.

■ *Additional Information*

'Tyee' is one of my favorite crinkled-leaf varieties. It has good bolt resistance, allowing you to harvest into early summer. 'Space' is a good smooth-leaf variety. If you want to grow a spinach-like green in summer, try 'Red Malabar' spinach. Although not botanically a spinach, this climbing vine has spinach-like leaves, a flavor like Swiss chard, and the ability to withstand heat. 'Winter Bloomsdale' is a good variety if you're trying to overwinter your spinach.

SUMMER SQUASH

You've got to watch out when growing summer squash (*Cucurbita pepo*) and zucchini. When it's ready to harvest, you'll get so many fruits so fast you'll be begging neighbors to take them away. I've even heard of people dropping extra zucchini through opened windows in unattended cars just to move the stuff. Yes, summer squash and zucchini have a reputation for being prolific. That's a good thing for a new gardener, because it's so satisfying to be able to offer extra produce to friends and family.

Summer squash and zucchini come in a variety of skin colors and sizes. The skin can be dark green, light green, or yellow, and the shape can be long, crooked necked, scalloped, or round. All have mild-tasting white flesh, making them perfect for baking in breads, sautéing with other vegetables, adding to stews or casseroles, or shredding raw and tossing in salads, I love to pick the flowers and sauté them with garlic and olive oil. Summer squash is as versatile as it is easy to grow.

■ *When to Plant*

Summer squash are warm-weather-loving crops, so don't rush them into the garden in spring. Either directly sow seeds or transplant seedlings after all danger of frost has passed—usually May. To get a jump on the season, buy transplants from local garden centers or start seedlings indoors four weeks before planting outside.

■ *Where to Plant*

Plant summer squash in full sun and well-drained, fertile soil. Unlike winter squash and pumpkins, these plants stay bushy, so they are great for smaller gardens. I like to place black plastic mulch over the bed two weeks before planting to warm the soil. I poke holes in the plastic to sow seeds or plant seedlings. This gives them a jump on the growing season, prevents weeds from growing, and keeps the soil moist.

■ *How to Plant*

Summer squash like a fertile soil, so amend the bed well with compost prior to planting. Plant seeds or seedlings 2 to 3 feet apart in rows spaced 4 feet apart. Summer squash do not like cool spring air temperatures, so consider covering the planting with a floating row cover during cool nights.

■ *Care and Maintenance*

Keep plants well watered and weeded, especially early in the season, until the plants get established. Once established, if not growing in black plastic mulch, spread a layer of organic mulch, such as straw or untreated grass clippings, around plants. When they start flowering, add a small handful of organic fertilizer, such as 5-5-5, around each plant.

Summer squash are susceptible to a number of insects, such as cucumber beetles, squash bugs, and squash vine borers. See the pumpkin section for more on controlling these pests.

■ *Harvesting*

The mantra for picking summer squash is "early and often." Start harvesting young squash when they are 6 inches long. Harvest pattypans, or scalloped squash, when they are 3 inches in diameter. The more you harvest, the more the plants will produce. If you make the mistake, like I do every year, of forgetting to harvest for just a few days, you'll discover some large squash "clubs" in the garden that are better used as bowling pins than food. They can actually be stuffed and baked, so even large summer squash have a use.

■ *Additional Information*

'Yellow Crookneck' is a classic yellow summer squash, while 'Partenon' and 'Raven' are high producers. The Italian heirloom 'Costata Romanesco' has green-and-white-striped and ribbed fruits and great flavor. I like the light green Lebanese, or cousa, summer squash, such as 'Magda'. It has a sweet, nutty flavor. If you like pattypans, or scalloped squash (kids call them "flying saucer squash"), try the yellow 'Sunburst'. For bowling (just kidding), try 'Eight Ball'. It has green skin and grows to the size of a bocci ball. Let's play!

SWEET CORN

There's is nothing more all-American than sweet corn (*Zea mays*). I remember working on an organic farm when I was younger and discovering just how sweet, sweet corn is. I would be harvesting ears for market and whenever I got hungry I would just peel (shuck) and eat the corn raw right in the field. The flavor was sweeter than any cooked corn I ever ate.

Most gardeners think they need a large field to grow corn. Actually, the key to growing sweet corn is to plant in small blocks or multiple short rows to maximize pollination. Also, grow different varieties. Early-, mid-, and late-season varieties extend the time you'll have sweet corn to eat. Traditional varieties lose their sweetness quickly after harvest. However, newer sugar-enhanced and supersweet varieties stay sweet longer, not requiring you to sprint from field to kitchen to cook it as fast as possible. However, they require warmer soils and are a little more demanding to grow.

While most gardeners think of eating sweet corn steamed, corn is also good roasted. I like to shred the kernels and freeze them for use in winter in soups, breads, and salads.

■ *When to Plant*

Sweet corn is a warm-season crop, so don't hurry to plant it in spring. Direct sow seeds in the garden two weeks after the last frost date in your area. That would be May or early June. The soil needs to be at least 60°F for germination, but the warmer the better.

■ *Where to Plant*

Sweet corn grows best in full sun and fertile, well-drained soil. Since corn grows so tall (up to 7 feet), plant it on the north side of your garden where it won't shade other vegetables.

■ *How to Plant*

Sweet corn is actually in the grass family. Like a lawn, it needs a rich soil high in nitrogen to grow its best. Amend the soil before planting with a thick layer of compost. Ideally, plant it in a location that had a legume, such as peas or beans, growing the previous season. Legumes add nitrogen to the soil, and corn is the perfect vegetable to take advantage of it the next year. Sow seeds 8 to 12 inches apart in rows spaced 2 to 3 feet apart. To ensure germination, soak seeds overnight in warm water to presprout them.

While the Northeast tribes of Native Americans perfected the practice of growing corn in hills, in the modern home garden, growing in blocks is best. A block is a "square" of at least four 10-foot-long rows. Make the walkway between blocks 3 to 4 feet wide, so they're easy to navigate. A block helps prevent the corn from blowing over during a thunderstorm and also facilitates better pollination. The tassels (tops) need to drop pollen on the silks (hairs) of ears in order for complete pollination to occur. Every kernel in an ear of corn needs a pollen grain in order to form. If you ever saw an ear that had some "teeth" missing, that's improper pollination. Plant blocks of all one variety, so they don't cross-pollinate with each other. If you're seeing yellow kernels in your white sweet corn, that's cross-pollination. This is particularly important for the supersweet varieties. If they cross-pollinate with traditional varieties, you'll lose some of the added sweetness. Plant supersweet varieties 250 feet away from other corn varieties to prevent cross-pollination.

If you only have a small space to garden and still want to grow sweet corn, try planting it in a raised bed. Select a quick-maturing dwarf variety such as 'Earlivee'. Fill the raised bed with a mix of topsoil and compost and plant at least twelve cornstalks spaced 8 inches apart. When the tassels form, shake them to ensure the pollen falls on the ears, so your ears fill in with kernels.

■ *Care and Maintenance*

Sweet corn needs a steady supply of nitrogen fertilizer to grow as fast as it does (yes, I swear I can actually see it grow during one of our hot, humid summer days) and produce a good crop. Besides adding compost at planting, add supplemental nitrogen fertilizer, such as alfalfa meal or

soybean meal, when corn is knee-high and again when it starts to form ears. If your corn leaves are yellow, it could be a sign of nitrogen deficiency.

When the plants are 8 inches tall, hill (mounding up soil) around the plants. Hilling kills weeds and helps support the corn plants, so they're less likely to blow over in a summer thunderstorm. After hilling, mulch with straw or untreated grass clippings to preserve soil moisture. Corn that is stressed from lack of water will have narrow leaves and ears missing kernels. Remove any small corn plants or suckers that form at the base of the main plant.

Unfortunately, lots of insects, diseases, and animals love corn too. Corn earworms are small worms that feed on the tips of ears. Simply cut off the end of the ear when harvesting to remove this insect. Corn borers tunnel into cornstalks, causing them to topple over. Spray with pyrethrum or spinosad early in the season to prevent this damage. Probably the biggest thief of corn is raccoons. They have an uncanny way of knowing just when your corn is ripe, and the night before you want to harvest, they come in and devastate a patch. String an electric fence around your corn or cover individual ears with paper bags after pollination to ward them off. Birds have been known to pull newly germinated corn seedlings out of the ground. Cover your patch with a floating row cover until the corn is at least a 3 to 4 inches tall and less appealing to birds. Control diseases such as bacterial wilt and leaf blight by growing disease-resistant varieties.

■ *Harvesting*

Most corn varieties produce one or three ears per stalk. Depending on the variety, your corn is ready to pick sixty to one hundred days after planting.

To determine when to harvest, watch the silks (hairs on the ears). When they turn a dark brown color, pull back the top of the husk a little bit and squeeze a kernel with your thumbnail. If the corn is ripe, a milky white liquid will squirt out. Immature kernels will be watery, while overmature kernels will be tough and have little liquid. With a sharp motion, pull down on the ear to harvest it without breaking the stalk.

■ *Additional Information*

The three most common types of sweet corn to grow are standard, sugar-enhanced, and supersweet. In seed catalogs, these categories are often indicated by (Su) for standard/normal sugary, (Se) for sugar-enhanced, and (Sh2) for supersweet. Some good standard varieties for our region include 'Earlivee' (yellow), 'Silver Queen' (white), and 'Sugar and Gold' (bicolor). Some good sugar-enhanced varieties are 'Sugar Buns' (yellow), 'Luscious' (bicolor), and 'Sugar Pearl' (white). Some good supersweet varieties are 'Northern Xtra Sweet' (yellow), 'X-tra Tender' (bicolor), and 'How Sweet It Is' (white). An old-fashioned variety for our region is 'Ashworth' (yellow).

SWEET POTATO

Now here's a vegetable you normally don't think of growing in the Northeast, but you actually can. Sweet potatoes (*Ipomoea batatas*) are a traditional Southern crop and need heat and a long season (up to four months) to form potatoes. However, with a few tricks, I've been able to grow good-sized sweet potatoes even in Vermont, so it is possible.

The keys to growing sweet potatoes in our sometimes-cool summer climate are to get them off to a good start, keep the plants well watered and fertilized, and keep the soil warm. Besides being tasty baked, mashed, or in soups and pies, sweet potatoes are high in vitamin A, and fresh tubers dug from your garden are much tastier than anything store-bought. Plus, they're an attractive ground cover. Some varieties are sold as ornamentals for their beautiful leaves, not their edible tubers.

■ When to Plant

Unlike most other vegetables, sweet potatoes are planted from little plants or "slips." While you can grow your own slips, it's much easier to buy them locally or order them through the mail, and they will be certified disease free. You need to wait to plant until the soil has warmed to 65°F, at least two weeks after your last frost date. That's late May or June in most areas.

■ Where to Plant

To get a good crop, sweet potatoes need lots of sun and warmth. Plant them in the hottest place in your garden. They also need well-drained soil, so

build an 8-inch-tall raised bed two weeks before planting and place black plastic mulch on it to preheat the soil.

How to Plant

Amend the soil with compost prior to building the raised bed. Plant slips in holes poked in the plastic 1 foot apart in rows 3 feet apart for bush varieties and 4 feet apart for vining varieties. Place a small handful of organic fertilizer, such as 5-5-5, in each planting hole.

Care and Maintenance

Cover the planted slips with a floating row cover during cool nights. Once the vines begin to grow, or "run," mulch the pathways with a layer of organic mulch, such as straw or untreated grass clippings. Although sweet potatoes are somewhat drought tolerant, keep the young plants well watered until they're established. Stop watering a few weeks before harvest to avoid rotting the roots.

Sweet potatoes don't have many pest problems, except deer, which will browse them heavily to the point where there is no foliage left. Rotate crops, not growing sweet potatoes in the same area for three years, to avoid diseases. Don't plant in an area that was recently lawn to avoid wireworms tunneling holes in the tubers.

Harvesting

Knowing when to harvest sweet potatoes can be a bit tricky. Start checking for tubers about three months after planting. Look for signs of leaves yellowing too. Gently lift the plants out of the ground before the cool weather of autumn begins. They won't grow much during cool temperatures, and the longer the tubers are in the ground, the more likely they are to be attacked by wireworms or other pests.

Don't eat sweet potatoes immediately or you'll be disappointed. Cure the tubers in a warm, high-humidity room for two weeks so the skins toughen. Store them in a dry, 60°F room for at least six weeks before eating. During that time the starches will turn into sugar, creating the sweet tubers we all love. They can be stored for up to six months.

Additional Information

'Beauregard' is a fast-maturing vining type with red skin and moist orange flesh. 'White Yam' is a white-skinned, dry-fleshed vining variety. 'Bush Porto Rico' has red flesh that turns yellow when ripe.

SWISS CHARD

One of the most attractive plants in my garden has nothing to do with flowers: it's 'Bright Lights' Swiss chard (*Beta vulgaris cicla* Cicla Group). 'Bright Lights' has multicolored stems and leaf ribs in yellow, pink, red, orange, and white, with dark green leaves. Because it's so attractive, I've started growing it among the flowers. Plus, it's an easy green to grow and versatile in the kitchen. The young leaves are good in salads. Older leaves can be sautéed in stir-fries or tossed in stews and soups. Unlike other spring greens, such as spinach, Swiss chard doesn't bolt (form a flower stalk) in the heat, so it makes a great summer green.

■ *When to Plant*

Sweet chard is a beet without the rootball. Like beets, it loves cool weather, so sow seeds a few weeks before your last frost date, usually May.

■ *Where to Plant*

Swiss chard can tolerate some shade and still produce edible greens. Give it at least two to three hours of direct sun. For bigger plants, plant in full sun. The plants grow best in fertile, well-drained soil. If you have heavy clay soil, consider building an 8-inch-tall, 3-foot-wide raised bed.

■ *How to Plant*

Soak seeds overnight in warm water before planting to start the germination process. Like beet seeds, Swiss chard seeds are actually dried fruits containing a number of seeds, so don't be surprised if you see two or three plants coming up from one seed. Amend the soil with compost before planting. Sow seeds 2 inches apart in rows spaced 2 feet apart. You can also mix in some Swiss chard seeds when sowing your salad mixes and harvest the chard as baby greens.

■ *Care and Maintenance*

Because you'll get multiple plants per seed, it's important to thin Swiss chard seedlings once they're 4 inches tall, leaving the healthiest seedlings spaced about 1 foot apart. Use the thinnings in salads.

Keep the soil moist and weed free by adding a layer of organic mulch, such as straw or untreated grass clippings, around plants. When the seedlings are 6 inches tall, fertilize with fish emulsion to help them grow faster. Fertilize again in midsummer.

Swiss chard plants are attacked by many of the same pests as spinach and beets, such as aphids, flea beetles, and leafminers. Spray insecticidal soap for aphids, and cover plants with a floating row cover to stop flea beetles and leafminers from attacking.

■ *Harvesting*

Start picking the outer Swiss chard leaves when they're 5 inches tall. If growing Swiss chard in salad mix, harvest greens when they are only a few inches tall. Keep harvesting outer leaves as needed and new leaves will keep growing from the center of the plant. Swiss chard can take a light frost and still keep growing, but before a killing freeze in fall, harvest the whole plant.

■ *Additional Information*

'Bright Lights' is the obvious choice for the most colorful variety, but you can also get varieties with single-colored stems and leaf veins, such as 'Bright Yellow' and 'Rhubarb'. 'Fordhook Giant' produces large leaves and white stems.

TOMATILLO

This tomato relative is an essential ingredient in Mexican cooking. It's also known as the husk tomato, because the 2- to 3-foot-tall bushy plants produce 2-inch-diameter green or purple fruits with a papery husk around them. They're cool to look at, easy to grow, and the fruits have a sweet, tart, citrusy flavor. Use tomatillos (*Physalis ixocarpa*) when making salsa, chili, kebabs, salads, and other Mexican dishes. Tomatillos are prolific, and unless you're making tons of salsa and Mexican food, you'll probably only need a few plants.

I grow a relative of the tomatillo called the ground cherry (*Physalis pruinosa*), too. This smaller plant has sweet-tasting, cherry-sized golden fruits inside papery husks that can be eaten raw. Kids love to "discover" the yellow fruits inside the husks and pop them in their mouths.

■ *When to Plant*

Like tomatoes, tomatillos need a long, warm growing season to produce the most fruits. Start transplants indoors six weeks before your last frost date or buy seedlings from a local garden center.

■ *Where to Plant*

Tomatillos need full sun and well-drained, fertile soil to grow their best. They are a bushier plant than most tomatoes. Plant tomatillos where they

won't get shaded by taller plants such as corn. They also can be grown in containers.

How to Plant

Amend the soil with compost before planting. You can plant directly into the garden soil or place black or red plastic mulch on the planting bed two weeks before transplanting to preheat the soil. Poke holes in the plastic and plant tomatillo seedlings 3 feet apart. As with tomatoes, you can plant the stems deeper in the hole if they are tall and leggy, and they will root along the stem.

Care and Maintenance

Keep the soil moist and weeded. If you're not growing in plastic mulch, add a layer of organic mulch, such as straw, around plants once established. Add a small handful of organic fertilizer, such as 5-5-5, around each plant monthly to keep it growing strong. Since these plants can get bushy, consider placing a small tomato cage around each one to keep the fruits off the ground and away from insects and diseases.

Tomatillos are attacked by many of the same pests that attack tomatoes. Use newspaper wrapped around the stems 2 inches above and 1 inch below the ground to ward off cutworms. Handpick hornworms and Japanese beetles. Select disease-resistant varieties; rotate crops, not planting any tomato family crops in that bed for three years; and remove any self-sown tomatillo seedlings from previous years to avoid diseases, such as blight and wilt.

Harvesting

When the husks turn a light brown color, the husks split, and the fruits are firm, cut the tomatillo fruits from plants. Check the plants often, since mature fruits will drop to the ground. Keep harvesting, and if frost is predicted, pick any fruits that are close to ripe, bring them indoors, and store in a warm, well-ventilated room. Like tomatoes, tomatillos will continue to ripen indoors.

Additional Information

Tomatillo varieties have either green or purple fruits. 'Toma Verde' is a green variety that matures a few months after planting. 'Purple' is sweeter flavored with purple skin and flesh and makes a unique-colored salsa.

TOMATO

It's hard to imagine a vegetable garden without tomatoes (*Lycopersicon esculentum*). They are the number-one vegetable grown in gardens, and there are hundreds of hybrid and heirloom varieties to choose from. There are white, black, green, red, pink, orange, yellow, purple, and striped varieties. Some grow as large as 7 pounds, while others are as small as a cherry. Some plants are as small as 1 foot tall, and others grow to 7 feet tall. Regardless of which variety you grow, homegrown tomatoes just taste better. The flavor is sweet and juicy, so different from a store-bought variety. Plus, they're loaded with vitamins, minerals, and antioxidants.

I like growing a mix of tried-and-true hybrids along with some special colored and flavored heirlooms. I'm always at a loss for space when it comes to tomatoes. I'm like a kid in a candy shop, looking at all these amazing varieties and only having room to grow a few. So every year I plant a few experimental heirloom varieties to see how they grow. This is important because heirloom varieties are very regionally adapted. What might grow well in Tennessee or Oklahoma may not thrive in my Vermont garden. I also check regional seed catalogs and see what they offer. If it can grow in their trial grounds in my climate, it's worth a shot in my garden.

When deciding what variety to grow, think of the usage. For kids, salads, and general snacking, grow a few cherry tomatoes. For sandwiches and cooking fresh, try some large-fruited varieties. For sauces and canning, think plum tomatoes.

■ *When to Plant*

Tomatoes love the heat, so don't rush them into the garden. They're more capable than their cousins, peppers and eggplants, of bouncing back from cool weather, but why strain them? Six to eight weeks before your last frost date, start tomato seedlings indoors. Harden off your plants, gradually getting them accustomed to the outdoors, and then move your transplants, or ones bought at the local garden center, outdoors after the last frost date.

■ *Where to Plant*

Tomatoes grow best in full sun and fertile, well-drained soil. You can also grow dwarf varieties in containers or even window boxes on a deck or patio.

■ *How to Plant*

In heavy clay soil, create 8-inch-tall raised beds before planting and amend the soil well with compost. Cover the bed or soil with red plastic mulch. The color red has been proven to stimulate more tomato production. It also preheats the soil, keeps it moist, and prevents weeds from growing. Poke

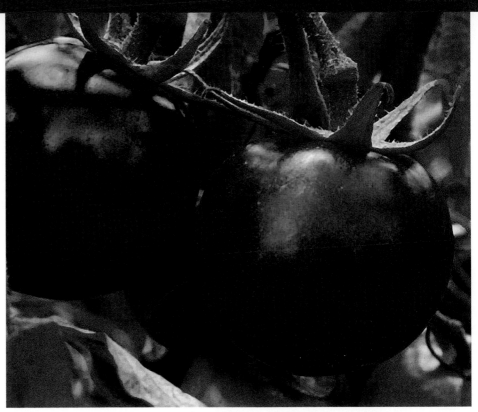

holes spaced 2 to 3 feet in the plastic. If the seedlings are tall and leggy, plant the stem deep in the soil, up to the first set of true leaves. If you can't plant deep, lay the stem horizontally on the soil in a trench and leave the top cluster of leaves pointing upward out of the soil. Either way, tomatoes can grow roots from the stems, creating a bigger root system and a stronger growing plant.

Use floating row covers or Wall-O-Waters (plastic sleeves in a cylinder that you fill with water) to protect the seedlings during cold weather in spring. I've used Wall-O-Waters for years. They release heat when the water chills, keeping the plants inside the cylinder warm. They can protect plants from temperatures down into the low 20s°F. Remove them once the weather warms and plants get large.

■ Care and Maintenance

Most tomato varieties need to be caged, staked, or supported in some way to keep the fruits off the ground. This will help prevent insects and diseases from attacking the fruits and make for easier harvesting. Dwarf varieties that grow only a few feet tall are good for containers and don't need supporting. After planting, decide on your support system. If you use stakes, drive a 7-foot-high stake 1 foot into the ground, a few inches from the tomato plant. Tie the main tomato stem to the stake with twine or

Velcro ties. Prune out any suckers (shoots that emerge from the junction of the main stem and side branch), so the plant doesn't get too big. Metal or wooden cages work best if they're at least 5 feet tall, anchored well to the ground, sturdy, and have large enough holes to harvest tomatoes through.

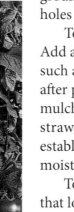

Tomatoes need food to grow strong. Add a small handful of organic fertilizer, such as 5-5-5, around each plant monthly after planting. If you haven't used plastic mulch, add an organic mulch, such as straw, around plants once they get established to keep the soil consistently moist and keep weeds away.

Tomatoes also have a number of pests that love to attack them. First, determine if it is a disease or insect attacking the plant. Blossom end rot, where the tip of the tomato fruit rots as it ripens, is caused by a calcium deficiency in the plant due to fluctuating soil moisture levels. Mulch and water regularly to address this problem.

Tomatoes are subject to many diseases. Look for disease-resistant varieties when buying plants. You'll see many letters after some varieties. These are abbreviations for various diseases. At the least, get a variety with resistance to fusarium wilt (FW), verticillium wilt (VW), and tobacco mosaic virus (TMV). Some diseases, such as late blight, can wipe out an entire crop and spread to others. Wilts, blights, and viruses can all cause so much damage that it will reduce your yields. Besides planting resistant varieties, space plants properly, mulch, clean up plant debris in fall, and rotate crops, not planting tomato family crops in the same location for three years, to slow down disease problems.

Certain insects can be problems too. Wrap newspaper around plant stems 2 inches above and 1 inch below the soil to ward off cutworms in spring. Whiteflies suck leaf juices and cause the leaves to yellow. Spray insecticidal soap to control them. Handpick hornworms (those big green worms munching on the leaves) before they defoliate the plant. Spray Neem oil to deter Japanese beetles from feeding on leaves or just handpick them and drop them into a pail of soapy water to kill them.

■ *Harvesting*

Anywhere from sixty to ninety days after transplanting, look for your tomatoes to start turning the mature color for that variety. Harvest when they're fully colored. In fall, harvest tomatoes before a frost even if they haven't fully matured. When stored in a warm, dark, airy room, the fruits will continue to ripen. If your tomatoes are slow to mature any fruits, a month before your first frost date, remove any new flowers or small fruits. They won't have time to mature before a frost and will take energy away from maturing the other fruits. Don't remove the foliage, though, because it protects the fruits from getting sunburned.

■ *Additional Information*

Some good main-season varieties include 'Big Beef' with its red fruits and good disease resistance. 'Defiant' has red fruits and resistance to the dreaded early and late blight diseases. 'Brandywine' is a classic heirloom that comes in pink, red, or yellow versions. It has unique potato-shaped leaves and outstanding flavor. 'Cherokee Purple' is a large-fruited purple heirloom. 'Green Zebra' is a tangy-tasting, green heirloom.

'Sungold' is a sweet-tasting yellow cherry tomato. 'Black Cherry' has dark brown fruits and an earthy taste. 'Yellow Pear' is a unique-shaped heirloom. 'San Marzano' is a classic Italian heirloom that's meaty and great for making sauces.

TURNIP

I got turned on to turnips (*Brassica rapa*) rather late in life. I was visiting a farm in New Hampshire when the farmer pulled a 'Hakurei' white turnip from the ground and bit into it like an apple. The only turnips I had known up to that point were the mashed ones at Thanksgiving dinner. I tried it and was hooked. The texture was juicy and crunchy and the flavor sweet and mild.

While Southerners have long enjoyed turnip greens as part of their traditional cooking, we Northerners are just getting turned on too. Turnips are an efficient crop. You can eat the roots, stems, and leaves, and they all taste great in the right dishes. Use baby greens in salads, or sauté mature greens and stems in stir-fries. The roots can be shredded and used raw in salads, or added to soups, stews, or roasted vegetables.

If you're wondering about the rutabaga (*Brassica napus*), it's a cross between a turnip and a cabbage. Rutabagas have large, yellow-fleshed roots with a sweet, nutty flavor and are used like potatoes; they can be mashed, boiled, or added to soups and stews. They are grown the same way as turnips.

■ *When to Plant*

Turnips like it cool, maturing with temperatures in the 60s°F. Sow seeds four weeks before your last frost date—April or early May. They'll take about fifty days to mature.

■ *Where to Plant*

Turnips grow best in raised beds and well-drained soil. Before planting in the bed, remove any sticks and debris, which can inhibit root growth. Turnips can produce a crop with as little as three to four hours of sun, but you'll get better roots if they're grown in full sun.

■ *How to Plant*

Amend the raised bed with compost before planting. Sow seeds 2 inches apart in rows spaced 1 foot apart. Cover the small seeds lightly with garden soil or potting soil and keep well watered. Like radishes, turnips germinate quickly and should be up in a few days.

■ *Care and Maintenance*

Thin turnips to 4 inches apart when they're 4 inches tall. Use the thinned greens in salads. Keep the soil evenly moist and well weeded. Mulch with a layer of organic mulch, such as straw, after weeding and thinning to keep the crop growing strong. If the plants are growing strong, additional fertilizer usually isn't necessary.

To avoid diseases, such as root rot, rotate crops, not planting another cabbage family crop in the bed for three years. Watch for aphids feeding on young turnip leaves, causing shotgun-like holes. Spray insecticidal soap to control them. Control flea beetles that feed on leaves and root maggots that feed on developing roots, by placing a floating row cover over the bed. This prevents the adult fly from laying eggs on the roots.

■ *Harvesting*

You can harvest turnips for weeks for a variety of uses. Harvest young greens when they are 4 inches tall for salads. Harvest the outer leaves, letting the inner leaves grow and feed the developing root. Harvest young turnip roots when they are 2 inches in diameter for shredding and using raw in salads. Harvest larger roots (3 to 4 inches wide) for cooking. If you let turnips get much larger than this, they will get woody. Let turnips mature during cool weather and you'll be treated with a sweet-tasting root.

■ *Additional Information*

'Hakurei' is the white-rooted Japanese variety my farmer friend shared with me. 'Purple Top White Globe' is a traditional cooking variety with white roots and a purple top. 'Scarlet Queen' has red stems and sweet-tasting red-skinned roots. 'American Purple Top' is a good rutabaga variety to try.

WATERMELON

Yes, you can grow watermelons (*Citrullus lanatus*) in our climate and they're worth the effort. I've grown the small, round, icebox types and kids and adults love to crack them open, munch on the sweet juicy flesh, and have seed-spitting contests.

While watermelons are mostly water, they do contain vitamins such as A, B, and C and high amounts of the cancer-fighting antioxidant lycopene. Varieties are either oval or round, and seeded or seedless, with pink, yellow, orange or red flesh.

■ When to Plant

Watermelons like the heat, so wait until two weeks after your last frost date (May or June) to plant seeds and seedlings.

■ Where to Plant

Watermelon plants need full sun to fruit. They also vine, or "run," like pumpkins and winter squash, so give them room to ramble. I like to grow watermelons on the edge of the garden and let the fruits vine into the lawn. I just mow around them, and it reduces the amount of lawn mowing and gives me more space in my garden to plant other vegetables. Plant flowers nearby to attract bees to pollinate the watermelon flowers.

■ How to Plant

Amend the soil with compost before planting. Get watermelons off to a good start by planting them on raised beds covered in black or dark green plastic. The raised beds warm up and dry out faster in spring, allowing you to plant sooner. The plastic placed on the bed two weeks before planting preheats the soil. Poke holes in the plastic every 12 inches and plant three seeds or one seedling per hole. Thin the seeds to the strongest per hole after germination.

■ Care and Maintenance

Watermelons need consistent water and fertility to produce fruits. Add at least 1 inch of water a week—more during hot, dry weather. If you aren't using plastic mulch, hand weed around plants. Add a small handful of organic fertilizer, such as 5-5-5, around each plant at transplant time, when the vines start to run, and at first flowering. Toward fall, as the nights dip into the 50s°F, help the existing fruits ripen by cutting off the tips of the vines, new flowers, and any young fruits. This will send more energy into the existing fruits. Place the existing watermelons on a piece of wood or upside-down pail to keep the fruits off the ground where diseases and critters might attack.

Watermelons are attacked by the same pests that love melons. See the melon section for tips on controlling these pests and diseases.

■ *Harvesting*

Knowing when to harvest watermelons can be tricky. If you pick them too early, they won't continue to ripen off the vine. If you wait too long, the flesh becomes mealy textured. Some of the techniques for determining when to pick require some experience. Do a little experimenting and take notes on what works.

Here are some techniques to try: Check the curly tendril (curlicue) on the stem closest to the ripening watermelon. When it turns brown, the watermelon is ripe. Check the underside of the watermelon. When the spot where it sits on the ground turns from white to yellow, the fruit is ripe. Finally, and this one takes some practice; thump the watermelon with your thumb. It's ripe when you hear a dull thumping sound rather than a tinny sound.

■ *Additional Information*

In general, the icebox-shaped watermelon varieties are better for our climate because most mature faster than the oblong-shaped ones. Icebox types average 4 to 8 pounds per fruit, whereas oval-shaped varieties can grow to 25 pounds per fruit. 'Sugar Baby' is a tried-and-true icebox type with sweet red flesh. 'Baby Doll' is an icebox type with yellow flesh. 'New Orchid' is an orange-fleshed icebox type. 'Moon and Stars' is a unique oval, red-fleshed heirloom with dark green skin and yellow markings that resemble a moon with stars.

WINTER SQUASH

It's tough to pigeonhole winter squash (*Cucurbita maxima*, *C. pepo*, and *C. moschata*). There are so many shapes, colors, and sizes, they can turn your garden into a cornucopia of fruits. They take all season to produce and most take up lots of space. I love going into my basement in December and pulling out a buttercup squash from storage to eat for dinner. The flesh is sweet and the flavor is satisfying on a cold winter day.

Pumpkins are a type of winter squash, but they're so special I talk about them in their own section. This is where I'll talk about buttercup, butternut, acorn, delicata, and spaghetti winter squash. If it's hard to know which to grow, buy a few from the local farmers' market to decide which you like best.

■ *When to Plant*

Winter squash seeds or transplants should be planted after all danger of frost has passed in your area. That's usually sometime in May or June. Start seedlings indoors four weeks before transplanting into the garden.

■ *Where to Plant*

Most winter squash varieties need room to vine, or "run." I like planting on the edge of the garden and letting plants run into the lawn area. It saves space in the garden and reduces the amount of mowing I do. Winter squash need full sun, so don't plant where they'll get shaded from taller crops. Like pumpkins, summer and winter squash plants have separate male and female flowers, so plant flowers nearby to attract pollinating insects or do a little hand pollinating yourself (see the cucumber section).

■ *How to Plant*

Amend the soil with compost before planting. To get a jump on the season, place black plastic over the bed two weeks prior to planting to preheat the soil. The plastic also acts as a weed barrier and conserves soil moisture. Poke holes in the plastic every 3 feet and plant three seeds or one seedling per hole. Space rows 5 feet apart. After the seedlings germinate, thin to the strongest plant per hole.

■ *Care and Maintenance*

Winter squash need a consistent supply of water and fertility to vine and set fruits. Water 1 to 2 inches per week during the growing season. Add a small handful of organic fertilizer, such as 5-5-5, per plant at transplanting or seeding and again when the vines begin to run. Keep beds well weeded until the vines fill the area and can shade out any young weeds.

To encourage fruits to mature before frost, snip off the flowers and any young fruits in fall. The flowers and young fruits are great tasting sautéed. These won't have enough time to mature before frost kills the vine, but the plant will redirect energy to mature the other fruits.

Winter squash are infected with the same pests and diseases as pumpkins. Check out the pumpkin section for details on these problems.

■ *Harvesting*

Let winter squash mature in the garden until they develop the mature skin color for that variety. The skin should be so thick that it feels hard when you press your thumbnail into it. Cut fruits so a 2-inch-long stem remains. Harvest before a killing frost to protect the fruits from rotting in storage. The cold will weaken the skin. Wipe the skins clean with a 10 percent chlorine bleach solution to kill disease spores, cure in a warm, 80°F room for two weeks, and then store for up to three to four months in a dark, airy, 50°F location.

■ *Additional Information*

'Waltham Butternut' has a moist, sweet orange flesh. 'Table Queen' acorn has a sweet, nutty flesh. My favorite kabocha, or buttercup, squash variety is 'Sunshine' with its bright orange skin and dry, sweet flesh. It's great for baking or making pies. Spaghetti squash is unique because the moist, yellow flesh is stringy when cooked, making it a fun pasta substitute.

While most varieties of winter squash can vine for 10 to 20 feet, 'Cornell Bush Delicata' produces 2-pound, sweet, yellow-fleshed fruits on a zucchini-sized plant.

BASIL

A good Italian boy like me has to grow basil (*Ocimum basilicum*). I grew up eating tomato, basil, and mozzarella cheese sandwiches. I freeze pesto cubes in summer so we can enjoy the flavor right through winter. If you can grow lettuce, you can grow basil. While I favor the Italian Genovese basil, there is a wide variety of basils with other flavors to grow. Cinnamon, Lemon, and Anise basil all make for great additions to soups, stews, sautés, and pesto. Some, like Thai basil, have beautiful purple stems and veins in the leaves, making it a striking ornamental plant. Basil grows equally well in containers. My eighty-seven-year old mother still grows basil in a pot on her deck each year.

■ *When to Plant*

Basil loves the heat. Either sow seeds or plant seedlings in pots or the soil after all danger of frost has passed. That's usually mid-May or June.

■ *Where to Plant*

Basil grows best and produces the biggest, best-tasting leaves if grow in full sun and well-drained soil. If you have clay soil, build 8-inch-tall raised beds. Basil grows well in a 12-inch or larger container. Since these are beautiful plants, consider tucking a few in among your annual flowers.

■ *How to Plant*

Amend the soil with compost prior to planting. In the garden, sow seeds 3 to 4 inches apart in rows 2 feet apart. Thin seedlings once the second set of leaves form, so plants are about 1 to 2 feet apart. Start seedlings indoors four weeks before setting into the garden. Transplant homegrown or store-bought seedlings so they're also spaced 1 to 2 feet apart.

■ *Care and Maintenance*

Cover young plants in spring with a floating row cover if nighttime temperatures are expected to dip below 50°F. The leaves may get discolored from cold temperatures. When the plants are 6 inches tall, pinch off the top to promote side branching. This will create a bushier, leafier plant. Fertilize with fish emulsion when transplanting and again one month later to promote leaf growth.

Keep the soil well weeded and watered. Pinch off the flower stalks as they form to encourage more leaf production.

Aphids, Japanese beetles, and fusarium wilt are common problems on basil. Grow wilt-resistant varieties, such as 'Nufar', to avoid this disease.

Aphids can be sprayed with insecticidal soap. Japanese beetles can be handpicked, trapped, or sprayed with Neem oil to thwart them.

Harvesting

Begin harvesting basil when at least four sets of leaves have formed and the plant is 1 foot tall. Snip the top just above the second set of leaves. As it bushes out over the summer, remove individual stems instead of just individual leaves. This will result in fewer, but larger leaves growing. Keep harvesting and removing the flower stalks until fall. Before a frost, remove the whole plant and pick it clean. Pick leaves as needed since they don't store well, or in batches to preserve as pesto or in olive oil.

Additional Information

'Genovese' is the classic Italian basil with large green leaves and a strong basil flavor. 'Purple Ruffles' has purple leaves. 'Sweet Dani' is a lemon-flavored variety. There's also a lime-flavored basil. 'Siam Queen' is a good anise-flavored Thai basil variety. 'Spicy Bush' is a small container variety with an attractive rounded shape. Holy basil (*Ocimum tenuiflorum*) has a mint and clove scent and is used for cooking and medicinally.

An easy way to make pesto is in ice cube trays. Fill the trays with pesto and freeze. Pop the pesto cubes out of the trays when frozen and store in freezer bags.

CILANTRO

My family is split on cilantro (*Coriander sativum*). I love it in Asian and Mexican foods, such as stir-fries, soups, salsa, and burritos. My wife, Wendy, hates the flavor of it. She will even pick it out of dishes at restaurants. I love my wife, but I think she's in the minority when it comes to cilantro. Cilantro is exploding in popularity due to the interest in Latin and Asian cuisines. It's easy to confuse the cilantro with Italian flat-leafed parsley because they are similar in appearance. However, while the leaves look alike, the taste is dramatically different. Cilantro leaves have a pungent tang. If the plant is allowed to flower and go to seed, the seeds are known as the spice coriander. Coriander is an essential ingredient in Middle Eastern, Indian, and other ethnic cuisines.

■ *When to Plant*

If you're growing cilantro for the leaves, it needs to grow while the weather is still cool. As soon as the air warms up, the plants send up a flower stalk. That might be fine if you're going to collect the seeds for coriander, but most people are interested in the leaves for cooking. Sow seeds around your last frost date—usually May in our region. Keep planting small batches in spring and summer as long as the air temperatures stay cool. Plant again in late summer for a fall crop.

■ *Where to Plant*

Plant cilantro in a full-sun or part-shaded location and in well-drained, slightly acidic soil. For clay soil consider building an 8-inch-tall raised bed to create a better-drained bed. Cilantro grows well in containers too.

■ *How to Plant*

Amend the soil with compost before planting. Sow seeds in the garden or a container, 1 inch apart in rows spaced 1 foot apart. Once the second set of leaves form, thin seedlings to 4 inches apart. Plants not thinned properly will bolt (produce a flower stalk) faster. Use the thinnings in salads. Cilantro plants have a taproot, so they don't transplant easily. It's best to plant seeds where the plants won't have to be moved or plant seeds indoors in peat, coir (coconut fiber), or cow pots that can be planted, pot and all, in the garden. Sow seeds every two to three weeks during the summer to harvest a continuous supply of leaves. The warmer and drier the conditions, the faster the plants will bolt.

■ *Care and Maintenance*

Keep plants well watered and weeded. Drought stress or overcrowding from weeds will cause the plants to bolt faster. Mulch around plants with an organic mulch, such as straw or untreated grass clippings, to keep the soil moist and weed free. Pull and compost plants as soon as they start flowering, unless you'll be collecting seeds for coriander.

Cilantro has the tendency to self-sow and reseeds itself readily. I haven't planted cilantro for years, but every spring I see seedlings popping up everywhere. I just select the ones I want to keep and thin out the rest. Cilantro has few pest and disease problems.

■ *Harvesting*

Begin harvesting leaves once at least two stems have formed. Pick the lower leaves first. These have more flavor than the thinner, upper leaves. Pick and use as needed fresh in salads and for cooking. Leaves from plants that are flowering have a milder flavor.

If growing cilantro to produce seeds (coriander), let the plants flower and harvest the seedheads once they turn brown. Hang the heads upside down in a well-ventilated room in paper bags. As they mature and dry, the seeds will drop into the bag. Grind the seeds to make ground coriander for cooking.

■ *Additional Information*

'Santo' and 'Slow Bolt' are two varieties that are slow to go to seed, making for a longer harvest time.

DILL

Most gardeners think of dill (*Anethum graveolens*) as that herb in pickles, but dill is much more. This easy-to-grow annual herb has ferny leaves (called dill weed) and a flat clusters of yellow flowers. If you let the flowers mature, you can collect the dill seeds in late summer. Beside using dill in pickles and beans, I also like it in potato salad, egg salad, bread, soups, and various dips and spreads. I even cut and use dill plants in flower arrangements indoors. They have a great airy feel to them.

Dill has an important role to play in the garden besides being a food for us. Beneficial insects love the flowers and I like to let a few plants go to seed, even if I'm not using the dill seeds, to attract the insects that will attack some of my pest insects. Also, dill leaves are a favored source of food for the caterpillars of the black swallowtail butterfly. Plant a little extra to share with this beautiful creature.

When to Plant

Dill loves to grow in cool weather. Sow seeds or plant seedlings in spring after all danger of frost has passed. That's usually May in our region. You can also plant in late August for a fall harvest.

Where to Plant

Dill grows best in full sun and well-drained, fertile soil. Since the dill stems are hollow and can grow up to 3 feet tall, plant where they will be protected from damaging winds. Plant shorter varieties in containers as well.

How to Plant

Amend the soil with compost before planting. Sow seeds 1 inch apart in rows spaced 2 feet apart. Once plants are 2 inches tall, thin seedlings to 12 inches apart. Plants not thinned properly will bolt (produce a flower stalk) faster. Use the thinnings in salads. Plant small patches of dill every two weeks until midsummer to have a continuous harvest of leaves and seeds in late summer and fall.

Care and Maintenance

Dill grows quickly, so keep plants well watered and weeded. As long as you have fertile soil, you shouldn't have to add fertilizer. If you want more dill leaves, pinch out flower stalks as they form. To get dill seeds, allow some plants to flower.

Dill also self-sows readily. If you don't want dill babies this summer and next year in the area where they are currently planted, pinch out the flowers before they mature. The larvae of the swallowtail butterfly love to feed on dill plants. Handpick them if they are taking over; otherwise share with them and you'll be rewarded with beautiful butterflies in your garden.

■ *Harvesting*

Snip off leaves as needed, starting about one month after planting. Pick leaves and flowers for use in pickling. You'll have to wait another six to eight weeks for the seeds to mature. To harvest dill seeds, cut the stalk 4 inches below the flower once the flowers have passed, but before the dill seeds drop to the ground. Place the heads upside down in a paper bag and hang in a warm airy location until the seeds naturally drop into the bag.

■ *Additional Information*

'Fernleaf' is a shorter, slow-to-bolt variety that's good if you're growing dill for the leaves. 'Superdukat' is a variety with high oil content and flavor. 'Bouquet' is an early-maturing variety with large, 6-inch-diameter flowers.

FLORENCE FENNEL

Although listed as an herb, I think of Florence, or bulbing, fennel (*Foeniculum vulgare* var. *azoricum*) as a vegetable. I've made a meal out of a fennel bulb. Once you get hooked on the licorice flavor of fennel and the juicy, crunchy texture, you'll be growing these 3-inch-wide bulbs for grilling, steaming, or roasting. No Easter meal would be complete in my mother's house without a marinated fennel salad.

There is also the perennial herb fennel (*F. vulgare* var. *dulce*) that is grown for its decorative and tasty leaves. But Florence fennel is grown for its swollen bulb at the base of the plant, and that's the one I'd like to talk about.

■ *When to Plant*

Plant fennel after all danger of frost has passed—May in our region. Fennel forms bulbs best during periods of cool weather. If the temperature gets too high the plant will bolt (send up a flower stalk) and the bulbs will be small and woody tasting. To get a jump on the season, start seeds indoors three weeks before the last frost. Fennel seedlings don't like to be transplanted, so grow seedlings in peat, coir (coconut fiber), or cow pots that can be planted directly in the soil with the seedling. These pots will decompose over time.

■ *Where to Plant*

Plant fennel in full sun and well-drained soil. Because of its taproot, plant on 8-inch-tall raised beds so the roots can grow deeply without obstruction. Fennel only grows 1 to 2 feet tall and wide, so it makes an excellent container herb and an attractive plant in the flower garden.

■ *How to Plant*

Amend the raised bed with compost before planting and remove any large sticks or debris. Sows seeds 4 inches apart in rows spaced 18 inches apart. Thin seeds, or transplant seedlings, to 8 inches apart when plants are 4 inches tall.

■ *Care and Maintenance*

The longer you can keep the soil and air cool and moist, the larger the bulb will grow. Fennel can take up to three months to be ready for harvest. Keep the bed weed free and watered regularly. Be careful not to disturb the roots, as this will stimulate the plant to bolt early. Once established, mulch the bed with a layer of straw or untreated grass clippings to preserve water and keep the soil cool. Cut off any flower stalks that form to encourage a larger bulb.

When the bulb is 2 inches in diameter, mulch around it with soil to blanch it (block the light). Blanched bulbs are white colored and more tender. Fennel has few pests other than the larvae form of the black swallowtail butterfly. Handpick these caterpillars if they become too plentiful in the garden; otherwise enjoy the butterflies once they form.

◼ *Harvesting*

Harvest bulbs when they're 3 inches in diameter, before they flower, by pulling the whole plant out of the ground. Cut off the roots, trim the stems and leaves 2 inches above the bulb, and either save the stems and leaves for eating or compost them. The stems and leaves can also be harvested anytime to be used in salads and soups, but they have a stronger licorice flavor.

◼ *Additional Information*

'Perfection' is an early-maturing variety that's slow to bolt. 'Orion' is a new high-yielding variety.

PARSLEY

One herb that grows easily in our climate is parsley (*Petroselinum crispum*). Whether you're growing the flat-leafed Italian varieties or curly-leafed parsley, the plants thrive during periods of cool weather but also survive the heat of summer. This biennial (plant that flowers the second year of growth) usually dies in winter, but I've dug them up in fall, potted the plants, and brought them indoors to enjoy for another few months before they stop growing.

Parsley is not just a dark green garnish. The leaves are high in vitamins and minerals. I use parsley in soups, salads, and a scrumptious green smoothie of parsley, bananas, maple syrup, and water. Yum. Parsley is also a good edible landscape plant. This low-growing herb makes a good dark green edging for annual and perennial flower gardens.

■ *When to Plant*

Plant parsley seeds or transplants directly in the garden after all danger of frost has passed. Like the seeds of its cousin the carrot, parsley seeds are notoriously slow to germinate. If you're growing just a few plants, it's easier to buy seedlings locally. For larger plantings, start seeds indoors six weeks before your last frost date to grow seedlings that will be transplanted into the garden or containers later.

■ *Where to Plant*

Parsley grows best in full sun and well-drained, compost-amended soil. If you have clay soil, consider growing parsley in an 8-inch-tall raised bed. Parsley does well in a container, window box, or hanging basket as well. Plant parsley along walkways with your flowers, or near the kitchen so it will be readily accessible when cooking.

■ *How to Plant*

Amend the soil with compost and space seedlings 12 inches apart in rows spaced 12 inches apart. If sowing seeds, thin the seedlings to the proper spacing when they're 2 inches tall. Since germination can take up to three weeks, keep the bed well watered. Consider covering the bed with a floating row cover to help keep it moist.

■ *Care and Maintenance*

Parsley likes a rich soil, so add a small handful of organic fertilizer, such as 5-5-5, monthly around each plant. Keep plants well watered and mulch after weeding with straw or untreated grass clippings to help keep the soil cool and moist and to keep soil out of the crevices of curly parsley's leaves.

Control for aphids with insecticidal soap sprays. Black swallowtail butterfly larvae love to feed on parsley. It's actually a great plant to grow in a butterfly garden for that reason. Unless there are many caterpillars on your plant, don't worry about controlling them. A few won't cause too much damage. Handpick and move those that are devouring a plant.

◼ *Harvesting*

Harvest parsley starting about one month after planting, removing the outer leaves first and snipping the leaf stem to the plant crown. Snipping the outer leaves allows the inner leaves to continue to grow. Harvest as needed during the summer. In fall before a hard frost, dig up plants in the ground and pot them. Place the pots in a shaded, protected area outdoors for one week. Gradually move it indoors near a sunny window. It will continue producing leaves until the light levels diminish in fall. Then harvest what's left and compost the plant.

◼ *Additional Information*

'Moss Curled' and 'Forest Green' are two curly-leaf varieties with good flavor and yields. 'Italian Flat Leaf' and 'Giant of Italy' are tall, big-leafed varieties good for soups and cooking. 'Par-cel' is like a cross between celery and parsley. It has a sweet celery flavor, but grows more like a parsley plant.

APPLE

Apples (*Malus domestica*) are one of the easiest fruit trees to grow in our climate. Don't believe me? Just look around. There are thousands of wild apple trees growing in abandoned fields and meadows, leftovers and offspring from cultivated varieties on old farms. Some actually taste pretty good and I love wandering fields in fall taste-testing these wild apples. While most heirloom or old-fashioned varieties grew on trees that could reach 40 feet tall, newer varieties grow on dwarf trees (as short as 8 feet tall), making apples much more accessible for a gardener with a small yard. Also, pests used to discourage home gardeners from growing apple trees. There's nothing worse than coddling your apple tree only to get wormy, scab-infested fruits. Now there are disease-resistant varieties and there are traps that make pest control much simpler.

The diversity of apple varieties is staggering. They're like the tomatoes of the fruit world. Skin colors include red, yellow, gold, orange, and green. Some varieties are great for eating fresh, while others are better used cooked. If you're not eating apples fresh off the tree, you can make cider, juice, or sauce from them. Whatever apples you leave behind the deer will gladly take care of.

■ *When to Plant*

Plant bare-root (no soil on the roots) trees in late winter or early spring as soon as the ground is thawed and dried out. These trees are usually shipped through the mail from nurseries to your home in time for planting. Plant container trees from a local nursery anytime in spring or summer. If you are planting just a few trees and are not particular about the varieties, container trees are more expensive, but easiest to purchase. If you are planting unusual varieties or many trees, stick with bare-root trees.

■ *Where to Plant*

Apples are widely adapted, but need full sun and well-drained, fertile soil that's slightly acidic to grow their best. Don't plant in a low-lying area where ground water might accumulate or late frosts are likely to occur. Apples don't grow well in soggy soils. Planting on a gentle slope is best to avoid wet soils and late frosts that might kill the blossoms in spring.

■ *How to Plant*

Cultivate the soil, removing sod and weeds. Amend the soil with compost and plant trees as far apart as their ultimate height. Dwarf trees grow to 12 feet tall, semidwarf to 15 to 25 feet tall, and standard-sized trees up to 40 feet tall. Some specialized varieties, such as columnar apple trees, can

be planted as close as 2 feet apart. Dig the hole for bare-root trees deep enough so the roots aren't bent when they're placed in the hole. If the tree is a grafted variety (the top of the tree is a different variety than the rootstock), make sure the graft union (bulge on the tree trunk) is 2 inches above the soil line. This will allow the dwarfing rootstock to keep the tree short, but allow the desired variety to grow above-ground and produce the apples you desire. Some varieties are now on their own rootstocks, so they don't have a graft union. This means if the tree dies to the ground, the shoots that emerge from the roots will be the same variety as the top.

Many apples will produce a crop on their own, but most produce more apples if grown close to another variety that the bees can cross-pollinate. If no other apples are in your neighborhood, it's good to grow at least two trees of different, compatible varieties.

■ Care and Maintenance

Keep the area around young trees weed free and well watered, especially for the first few years of life. Add compost around the trees in spring, and based on the growth rate, supplement the compost with an organic fertilizer, such as 5-5-5, to stimulate growth. You should have about 1 foot of new growth on your apples each year.

Dwarf apple trees will start producing fruits within a few years after planting. Standard or large trees may take up to five years to produce a good crop, depending on the variety. Apples will naturally drop fruit during the June drop because the tree often sets more fruit than it can mature. After the June drop, you'll have to thin even more fruits to get fewer, but better-quality apples. Thin clusters of apples to one cluster of two fruits, every 6 inches. If the tree produces too many apples, branches may break from

the weight load and the tree may not bear as well the following year.

There are many insects and diseases of apples. Apple scab, cedar-apple rust, fire blight, and powdery mildew are some of the main diseases. Controlling diseases usually isn't a big issue until the trees starts fruiting. Growing disease-resistant varieties such as 'Liberty' and 'MacFree' takes off the pressure of having to spray frequently to keep the fruits looking good. Insects such as apple maggots, codling moths, and plum curculio can damage apples so much they look like cratered moons, and Japanese beetles can defoliate a mature tree in a week or two. Clean up fallen apples well in autumn, use traps to control and monitor the pests, and use sprays to kill the insects at the most opportune time to avoid frequent spraying.

Protect young tree trunks in fall from bark-chewing mice and voles by placing a tree wrap around the trunk. Remove the wrap in summer so wood boring insects can't hide and tunnel into your tree. Use fencing to protect young trees from twig-eating deer.

Prune apples in winter so the trees stay open in the center. Remove any water sprouts (straight shoots from the main branches) or suckers (shoots from the roots or base of the tree trunk) at any time. Prune off dead, diseased, or broken branches whenever necessary. Prune so upper branches don't shade lower branches and are evenly arranged around the main trunk. Remove thin, crowded branches that reduce the airflow and light penetration. Airflow helps reduce disease problems, and good light penetration helps apples in the center of the tree color better.

■ *Harvesting*

Start checking your apples for ripeness once the fruits have their mature color and are full sized. If the apple separates easily from the tree when it's pulled and the skin is firm, it's ready to pick. Your tree will probably produce so many apples that tasting them is another good way to tell they're ripe. Some early varieties may have firm flesh and a tart taste, while later-maturing varieties may be sweeter, but have a softer texture. Later varieties are often good for cooking and processing.

■ *Additional Information*

While 'McIntosh' and all her crosses are the queens of apple varieties in the Northeast, there are many other old and new varieties worth trying. Most home gardeners should look for dwarf or semidwarf, disease-resistant varieties. It's best to taste different varieties from your neighbors' trees, farmers' markets, or grocery store to get an idea of the flavors you like, then research that apple and how it grows in our region.

Some newer varieties that have become popular include 'Gala', 'GoldRush', and 'Honeycrisp'. Older varieties are often geared toward specific uses. 'Northern Spy' makes a mean pie. 'Winesap' makes a sweet-tart flavored juice. 'Cox's Orange Pippin' is good for cider making and cooking. 'Mutsu' is a good storage apple; this Japanese variety is often sold under the name 'Crispin' (renamed for the American market).

Some crabapple varieties such as 'Dolgo' produce large-sized fruits that are great for fresh eating. Columnar varieties such as 'North Pole' produce an 8-foot-tall tree with no side branches. Fruits form along the main trunk. Columnar apples are great for a very small yard.

BLUEBERRY

I don't know why more people don't grow blueberries (*Vaccinium* spp.).
They're one of the easiest and most beautiful fruiting shrubs to grow in our
climate. They have few pests and diseases, can withstand our cold winters,
and can produce healthy fruits for thirty years. What else could you ask for in
a berry bush? I love walking out during blueberry season and picking a
handful of ripe berries for cereal, fruit salads, or just munching. I've
grown small blueberry varieties as landscape plants around our home. Not
only are the dark green leaves, white flowers, and blue fruits attractive, but
the leaves turn red, like a burning bush, in fall. It's gorgeous!

■ *When to Plant*

Plant bare-root (no soil on the roots) or container blueberry bushes in late
winter or early spring. If you are just growing a few bushes around your
yard, buy container plants from a garden center and plant after all danger of
frost has passed. If you are planting a large number of blueberry bushes,
buy bare-root plants and plant when the soil has dried out. There is a wider
variety and they are less expensive.

■ *Where to Plant*

Grow blueberries in full sun and well-
drained, acidic soil. Blueberries have
fine roots, so a loose, sandy loam soil
is best.

■ *How to Plant*

Amend the soil with compost before
planting. While most soils in our
region tend to be naturally acidic,
blueberries need an even lower pH
between 4.5 to 5.0 to thrive. Add
sulfur to the planting hole, based on a
soil test, to lower the pH to this level.
Set plants in the hole at the same
depth they were in the container.
Space the plants depending on their
ultimate height. Highbush blueberries
(*V. corymbosum*) grow up to 6 feet
tall, half-high blueberries (hybrids

between *V. corymbosum* and *V. angustifolium*) grow 3 to 4 feet tall, and
lowbush blueberries (*V. angustifolium*) grow 2 feet tall.

On clay or wet soils, consider building a raised bed prior to planting the blueberries. The raised bed will keep the roots from rotting in cold, wet soils.

Care and Maintenance

Since blueberries have such delicate roots, mulch the soil around the plants with a 6-inch layer of sawdust, pine needles, peat moss, bark mulch, or shredded leaves. This will keep the soil cool and moist, prevent weed growth, and protect the roots from damage. Fertilize each spring with compost and an acidifying fertilizer that would be used for rhododendrons or azaleas.

Blueberry bushes won't need pruning the first few years other than removing dead, diseased, or broken branches. Once they start fruiting, remove canes older than six years old and create a natural progression of six to eight young, medium, and older main canes in the bush for best production. Remove any root suckers or old, twiggy growth.

Blueberries have few insect and disease problems. If the pH isn't low enough, the leaves will turn yellowish. Simply adding sulfur will help. Birds love blueberry fruits. Place bird scare devices around plants or throw netting over small bushes to protect them. Deer will graze on young bushes, so protect them with fencing.

Harvesting

Blueberries ripen at different times in mid- to late summer, based on the varieties. Select early-, mid-, and late-season varieties to extend the harvest season from July into September. Don't be tempted to pick blueberry fruits when they first turn blue. I've found they have a tart flavor and often need a few more days to mature to their natural, sweet taste.

Additional Information

Select at least two different varieties to get the best production. Most varieties of highbush and half-high are hardy in our region. 'Patriot' and 'Blueray' are early-maturing highbush varieties. 'Bluecrop' is a vigorous midseason variety. 'Jersey' and 'Elliot' are good late-maturing highbush varieties. Some good half-high varieties include 'Northsky', 'Northland', and 'Northblue'. Plant lowbush blueberries in the landscape as ground covers. They grow only 1 to 2 feet tall.

BRAMBLES

Brambles (*Rubus fruticosus*) is the general name given to plants in the raspberry and blackberry family. I think they're essential to grow in the yard. Because the fruits are so perishable, and so expensive in the store, only fresh fruits from your garden will do. These little jewels of fruits come in red, yellow, purple, and black and grow like weeds. I often go scouting in abandoned fields for patches of wild brambles to harvest. They are one of the first species to colonize a pasture after the animals and man leaves. That tells you how opportunistic they can be.

In the yard, they can be tamed into a productive hedge. I use raspberries and blackberries along borders to keep animals out (ever try walking through a blackberry thicket?), and grow them in spots where other plants won't thrive. The key is to keep them inbounds with proper planting, pruning, and trellising.

■ *When to Plant*

Plant in late spring a few weeks before your last frost date. Purchase bareroot (no soil on the roots) plants through the mail or container plants at the local garden center. Container plants can be planted anytime into early summer.

■ *Where to Plant*

Brambles grow and fruit best in full sun, but can produce in part shade as well. Unless confined in a raised bed, keep them away from other flower or vegetable beds, since the roots will send new shoots up all around the area. I like to plant brambles in beds surrounded by lawn. That way, any shoots that escape the bed can be mowed down easily. Plant in well-drained soil and where there is good airflow. Plant away from wild brambles so insects can't spread diseases to your new plants. Don't plant in soils that recently had tomatoes, peppers, or potatoes, because these vegetables harbor diseases in the soil that will attack brambles.

■ *How to Plant*

Select certified disease-free plants and amend the soil in the bed with compost. Plant brambles 4 to 6 feet apart in rows spaced 5 to 10 feet apart. Plant at the same depth the brambles were in their pots.

■ *Care and Maintenance*

Brambles love organic matter in the soil. Amend the soil each spring with compost to keep it fertile. Mulch the planting bed with a 4- to 6-inch layer of organic material, such as straw, chopped leaves, or sawdust. This will keep the soil evenly moist and weed free. Brambles have two different

growth habits. July-bearing plants will produce a first-year cane from the ground (primocane) that will grow 4 to 6 feet tall. That cane will overwinter and in the second year will become the fruiting cane (floricane) that produces fruit in July. Once it finishes fruiting, it will die, so prune this cane to the ground. New everbearing plants will grow similarly, but the first-year cane will actually fruit in fall and the same cane will fruit again the following year in July. You can prune these plants like July bearers, or just cut down the entire bed in fall after the first fruiting. You'll eliminate the summer crop the next year, but will have a larger fall crop. You can also pinch the top few inches of bramble primocanes in summer after fruiting to promote more side branching and fruiting next year on those canes.

Most raspberries and blackberries need a trellis to keep the canes upright. The simplest trellis to construct involves some posts and heavy-gauge wire. Place 6-foot-tall posts at the end of each row and secure a 4-foot-long board across the top, 3 to 4 feet off the ground, perpendicular to the post to form a T. String wire on each end of the T-board and down the row to the T-board on the other post. This will create a fence that keeps the brambles growing upright when they're fruiting and prevents them from flopping over.

Black and purple raspberries grow more in clumps, rather than spreading like red and yellow raspberries and blackberries, so they can also be tied to 6-foot-tall stakes spaced 4 feet apart for trellising.

Brambles do have some insect pests that attack them. Spider mites and aphids will attack leaves, causing them to curl and turn yellow. Spray insecticidal soap to control them. Raspberry cane borers will tunnel into the stems of canes. They girdle the cane in two places and lay their eggs between the girdle marks. This causes the cane tip to wilt and die. Simply remove the wilted cane a few inches below the lowest girdle mark and place in the trash. Unless the damage is severe, your brambles should be fine. Japanese beetles love bramble leaves and fruits. Control these pesky beetles with traps, Neem oil, and beneficial nematodes sprayed on the lawn area around the brambles.

Avoid disease problems by planting certified disease-free plants and removing wild brambles from the area. Virus diseases, in particular, will make plants less vigorous and the fruits smaller and crumbly. On wet soils root rot is sometimes a problem. Grow plants in raised beds to avoid this disease.

■ Harvesting

Brambles have delicate fruits. Preferably harvest in the morning when the fruits are dry and cool. Wait until the fruits mature to the color for that variety. If ripe, brambles will easily drop off the plant when touched. Place the fruits in a shallow tray and don't stack them or they will turn to mush. I know because I've done that enough times. Pick often or the fruits will drop to the ground. If kept healthy, bramble plants can be productive for five to eight years.

■ Additional Information

Most raspberries and blackberries mentioned here are hardy to USDA zone 4. 'Latham', 'Nova', and 'Killarney' are hardy, July-bearing red raspberry varieties. 'Caroline' and 'Polana' are good fall-bearing red raspberries, while 'Fall Gold' and 'Anne' are two good fall-bearing yellow raspberries. 'Bristol' and 'Jewel' are two black raspberry varieties. 'Royalty' is a purple-fruiting raspberry.

'Illini' is a hardy blackberry variety. 'Triple Crown' features thornless canes and is hardy to USDA zone 5. 'Prime Jim' is an everbearing blackberry that produces fruits in summer and fall.

CHERRY

I remember as a young boy riding in my uncle's bucket loader as he hoisted me up to pick bushels of cherries from his tree. I still remember the stained smiles my cousins and I had from eating and picking those cherries (*Prunus* spp.). Cherry varieties are either sweet (*P. avium*) or sour (*P. cerasus*). While sweet cherries are mostly eaten fresh, and sour, or pie, cherries are mostly used for cooking, don't let the names fool you. Sour cherries taste great eaten fresh off the tree too. Sweet cherry trees are taller, less hardy, and more prone to diseases than sour cherries. They thrive in USDA zone 5 and warmer areas in our region. Sour cherries are naturally smaller trees and can survive into USDA zone 4.

Cherry trees are also beautiful landscape plants. Dwarf varieties make perfect flowering trees in spring, with the added bonus of getting delicious fruits in early summer. Some varieties are self-fruitful, meaning you won't need to plant another, different variety to get fruits.

■ *When to Plant*

Plant bare-root (no soil on the roots) cherry trees in early spring as soon as the ground can be worked. You can find a wider selection of trees, less expensively, by buying bare-root trees through the Internet rather than purchasing container trees at local garden centers. However, if you're planting just one or two trees, buying a container cherry tree locally and planting in spring is easier.

■ *Where to Plant*

Cherry trees need full sun and well-drained, fertile soil to grow well. Plant on the top of a slope to avoid late-spring frosts. Cherry trees are more susceptible to root rot diseases if they're grown in heavy clay soil. If clay soil is your only option, plant in raised beds to help with water drainage.

■ *How to Plant*

Cherry trees come in standard-sized trees (25 to 40 feet tall), semidwarf (15 to 25 feet tall) and dwarf (8 to 12 feet tall). Plant trees as far apart as their ultimate height. Dig holes twice as wide as the rootball and deep enough so the graft union (bulge on the tree trunk) is 2 inches above the soil line.

■ *Care and Maintenance*

Keep a 4-foot-wide area around the trees weed free by mulching with an organic material, such as straw. Keep the straw away from the trunk to avoid rot diseases. In late winter, prune sweet cherries to a central leader

system and sour cherries to an open center. Remove dead, diseased, or broken branches at any time. Once the tree is established and scaffold branches are equally distributed around the trunk, pruning consists of removing water sprouts (straight shoots from the main branches) and suckers (shoots from the roots or base of the tree).

Fertilize in spring with compost or an organic product to correct any nutrient deficiencies, based on a soil test.

Poorly drained soil can lead to a number of soilborne fungal diseases such as fusarium wilt and root rot. Look for disease-resistant varieties and keep the soil well drained. Birds love cherries and you'll need to place netting or scare devices around the trees when the fruits begin to ripen. Protect the trees in winter with a tree guard wrapped around the trunk to prevent mice and voles from girdling the bark.

■ *Harvesting*

Cherries start producing fruits about three to five years after planting. They usually ripen in June to early July in our region. Pick fruits when they can easily be removed from the branch.

■ *Additional Information*

Some good sweet cherry varieties to try in our region are 'Kristin', a hardy variety from Norway; 'Black Gold™', a new hardy, self-pollinating variety from Cornell University; and 'Stella', a good hardy, early-bearing Canadian variety.

Some good sour cherry varieties that are self-pollinating so don't require another variety are 'Bali', a very hardy variety from Canada; 'Mesabi', which has sweet fruits even for a sour cherry; and 'North Star', which grows only 8 feet tall.

CURRANT & GOOSEBERRY

Here are two related fruits that are loved by Europeans and Brits, but rarely grown in this country. But that's changing. Currants and gooseberries (*Ribes* spp.) grow easily in our climate; need only one bush to fruit; produce an abundance of tasty fruits for fresh eating or making jams, jellies, and preserves; and are mostly problem free. What else can you ask for in a fruiting bush?

Currants come in varieties with white, red, or black fruits. Red and white varieties are great for fresh eating, while black currants make a healthful juice and are used for making cassis, the French liqueur. Gooseberries have green or red fruits for fresh eating or making pies and preserves.

One reason gardeners haven't grown currants and gooseberries in the Northeast is these plants carry the white pine blister rust disease that is not lethal to currants and gooseberries, but is fatal to white pine and related trees. However, newer varieties are resistant to the disease, and while bans on growing these berries have been lifted in many areas, you should check your state Department of Agriculture about buying and growing currants and gooseberries in your state. It is recommended to keep *Ribes* plants at least 1,500 feet away white pines.

◼ When to Plant

Plant currants and gooseberries in late spring or early summer as soon as the ground can be worked. Purchase bare-root (no soil on the roots) plants if you're growing many shrubs, or container plants from a local nursery if you're just growing a few plants.

◼ Where to Plant

Currants and gooseberries grow best in full sun and well-drained, slightly acidic soil. They don't tolerate wet soils. If late-spring frosts are a problem in your area, consider planting them on a north-facing slope to delay the opening of their flowers in spring. Currants and gooseberries make excellent edible landscape shrubs, so consider planting them along a house or garage with other flowering shrubs.

■ How to Plant

Amend the soil with compost and plant shrubs 4 to 6 feet apart in rows spaced 6 feet apart. Plant at the same depth as the shrub was in the pot. Currants and gooseberries have shallow roots, so water regularly, and mulch with a 2- to 4-inch layer of straw or bark mulch to keep weeds away and keep the soil moist.

■ Care and Maintenance

Add compost and 1 cup of organic fertilizer per shrub in spring to keep the plants growing well. Prune to create three to four main canes evenly spaced around the plant. Remove small, twiggy growth; dead, diseased, or broken canes; and canes older than four years old. Currants and gooseberries fruit best on two-year-old canes.

Currants and gooseberries have few pests. I've noticed currant worms on my bushes, but sprays of *Bacillus thuringiensis* (B.t.) usually control them. Watch for aphids and spray insecticidal soap to control this pest. Chipmunks sometimes like eating my gooseberries, but I just share them since I get so many. If you aren't so generous, use fencing to keep chipmunks out. Look for disease-resistant varieties to avoid powdery mildew and white pine blister rust.

■ Harvesting

Harvest currants and gooseberries in late summer when the clusters of berries are fully colored. If you allow them to stay a few more days on the bush after full coloring, they taste even sweeter. Wear gloves when harvesting gooseberries if your varieties have thorns on the canes.

■ Additional Information

'Hinnomaki Red' and 'Hinnomaki Yellow' are two favorite gooseberry varieties. They are both powdery mildew resistant. 'Pixwell' has smaller thorns and green fruits. 'Pink Champagne' is a delicious white currant and 'Red Lake' a common red variety. 'Titania', 'Ben Sarek', and 'Consort' are all disease-resistant varieties of black currant.

GRAPE

Whether you're growing them for juice, wine, or fresh eating, grapes (*Vitis* spp.) are great home garden fruits. They're self-pollinating and productive, so you can grow just one vine. Grapes can be trained to grow in a small space or can be trained over a pergola or arbor. They require little care besides pruning, can grow on less than ideal soils, and fruit for up to twenty-five years or more. I often recommend people grow them because they fit in small spaces, easily allowing you to have table grapes right outside your door.

With some newer varieties adapted to the Northeast, we now can grow more seeded or seedless table grapes for fresh eating and even wine grapes.

■ *When to Plant*

Plant bare-root (no soil on the roots) grape vines in spring as soon as the soil can be worked. Plant container grapes in spring or early summer so they have enough time to get established before winter.

■ *Where to Plant*

Grapes need full sun and well-drained soils to grow their best. They grow best in loose, loamy soil but can grow in clay. Plant on a south- or east-facing slope to allow the leaves to dry out quickly, reducing the amount of disease on a plant.

■ *How to Plant*

Prepare the soil by removing any grass or weeds and tilling deeply. Plant grapes 8 feet apart in rows spaced at least 6 to 8 feet apart. Dig a hole twice the diameter of the rootball of the grape plant and as deep as it was in the container. Place a stake in the hole to support the one-year-old cane. Keep well watered the first year. Mulch around the base of the plant with a 2- to 3-inch layer of straw or bark mulch.

■ *Care and Maintenance*

Grapes can be grown on a fence (trellis) or a structure such as a pergola. I like to use the four-armed Kniffin system for trellising grapes. Here's how it works.

Drive 7- to 8-foot-long metal or wooden posts into the ground so they stand 6 feet tall. Space posts 10 feet apart in the rows. Brace the end posts with wire attached to an anchor in the ground. Run two strands of heavy-gauge wire 3 and 5 feet above the ground along the row, attaching it to every post.

After planting, prune the vine to one cane and attach it to the bottom wire. After the first winter, top the main cane at 6 feet tall and attach it to the top wire. Cut back all side shoots, but leave four to six buds on the shoot near each wire. The third winter, tie two canes going in opposite directions to each wire for a total of four producing canes. Prune them back to fifteen buds. Remove all other canes, but leave one bud on one shoot on each side of each wire for replacement canes. Remove the fruiting canes the following winter and allow the replacement buds to grow into the new side canes. Repeat each year.

For an arbor, train a single-stemmed cane up each post until it reaches the top of the arbor. Allow a single side cane to develop into the main canes to grow across the arbor. Allow them to grow across the top and cut the one-year-old canes back to two buds each winter to stimulate new growth.

Fertilize grapes with compost each spring. Use netting to discourage birds from eating ripe fruits. Keep good air circulation to avoid rot diseases on the fruits. Control Japanese beetles with traps and Neem oil sprays.

■ Harvesting

Grapes start producing harvestable grapes the second or third year after planting. Harvest bunches for fresh eating once the grapes color up. You can pick over a period of a few weeks, as clusters ripen at different times. Wine grapes are picked based on sugar levels (called the Brix level) and need testing to be picked at the right time.

■ Additional Information

Some good seeded table grape varieties include 'Bluebell' and 'Concord'. Some good seedless table grape varieties are 'Somerset', 'Edelweiss', and 'Reliance'. For making wine, try some of the new varieties from Minnesota, such as 'La Crescent', 'Marquette', 'Brianna', and 'Frontenac'.

PEACH

Peaches (*Prunus persica*) take a little more work and care than other tree fruits, but, boy, are they worth it! I remember when I first ate a tree-ripened peach on a warm summer day. The juices flowed down my chin and my face was covered with a smile. Although peaches are less hardy than apples and pears, there are some good varieties that grow well in our region—even in colder areas. Peach trees are generally hardy to USDA zone 5, but some survive zone 4.

Peaches are either clingstone (flesh clings to the pit) or freestone (flesh separates easily from the pit). Freestone varieties are easier to use in processing and cooking. Peach trees naturally grow short, and some can even fit in a container!

■ *When to Plant*

Plant bare-root (no soil on the roots) peach trees from a mail-order nursery or container peach trees from a local garden center in early spring or summer as soon as the ground can be worked.

■ *Where to Plant*

Plant peaches in a full-sun location with well-drained soil. Peaches don't grow well in heavy clay, so if you have clay soil, consider planting in raised beds. Peaches also bloom early in spring and are susceptible to late-spring frosts. Plant on a north-facing slope so the flowers open later and are less likely to be killed by frost.

■ *How to Plant*

Plant standard-sized peach trees 15 to 20 feet apart and dwarf varieties 8 to 10 feet apart. Dig a hole twice as large as the rootball, and plant so the graft union is 2 inches above the soil line. The graft union is the point where the variety was grafted on to the hardier rootstock. Make a shallow trench or moat about 1 foot away from the trunk to catch water to keep the roots moist.

■ *Care and Maintenance*

Keep the trees well watered and weeded. Mulch with shredded bark or straw, keeping the mulch away from the trunk to avoid diseases. Fertilize with compost each spring. Peach branches should be growing 12 to 24 inches a year. If your tree isn't putting on this much growth, consider adding an organic fertilizer in spring to stimulate more growth.

Prune peaches heavily in late winter to stimulate new growth and better fruiting. Prune to an open center, and prune off branches so air can freely move around the center of the tree. Remove dead, diseased, or broken

branches and any water sprouts (straight shoots from the main branches) or suckers (shoots from the roots or base of the tree) at any time.

Avoid diseases, such as leaf spot and peach leaf curl, by growing resistant varieties and cleaning up fallen fruits and pruned branches where diseases may be harbored. Spray horticultural oil in late winter before the trees leaf out to prevent damage from insects, such as scale and mites. Cultivate around the soil in early summer to destroy the overwintering forms of various caterpillars that attack peaches. Protect trees from girdling by mice and voles in winter by wrapping them with tree wraps. Protect container peaches by storing them in a cool basement or garage in winter.

■ *Harvesting*

Peaches begin bearing fruit a few years after planting. Fruits start ripening in July and can produce into September, depending on the variety. Let the fruits turn from green to peach color and gently tug at the fruits to see if they're ripe. Ripe fruits will pull easily off the branch. Keep picking or ripe fruits will drop to the ground, get bruised, and rot.

■ *Additional Information*

Peaches are self-pollinating, so you can grow only one tree. In small yards, select trees on dwarfing rootstocks or natural (genetic) dwarfs. 'Champion' features freestone fruits with white flesh. 'Hale Haven' ripens in September and has a freestone, yellow flesh, good for canning. 'Saturn' is a unique donut-shaped, white-fleshed, freestone variety. 'Reliance' is one of the hardiest varieties available and has yellow-fleshed, freestone fruits.

PEAR

The soft, sweet flesh of a homegrown pear is almost a meal in itself. Of course, I'll eat them with cheese or in salads, too, but eating pears fresh is the way to go. Unlike other fruit trees, pears like to grow tall and straight in the shape of a pyramid. The ones that grow best in our region are European pears (*Pyrus communis*). These are hardier than peaches, but not as hardy as apples. Asian pears (*Pyrus pyrifolia*) will only survive in warmer areas (USDA zone 5) of the Northeast.

Pears can make beautiful landscape trees as well, especially when planted in a narrow space where they can grow tall, but not wide. They can grow to 25 feet tall, although dwarf varieties will be about ten feet shorter. The beautiful white flowers in spring give way to a multitude of fruits in midsummer. Pears are unique because you have to harvest while the fruits are still firm and let them ripen indoors.

■ *When to Plant*

Plant bare-root (no soil on the roots) pear trees from a mail-order nursery or container pear trees from a local garden center in early spring or summer as soon as the ground can be worked.

■ *Where to Plant*

Plant pears in a full-sun location with well-drained soil. If you have clay soil, pears are a good choice, as they're more tolerant of heavy soils than other fruit trees. Plant on a slope to prevent late-spring frosts from killing the flowers.

■ *How to Plant*

Plant standard-sized pear trees 15 to 25 feet apart and dwarf varieties 12 feet apart. Dig a hole twice as large as the rootball, and plant so the graft union (bulge on the tree trunk) is 2 inches above the soil line. The graft union is the point where the variety was grafted on to the hardier rootstock.

■ *Care and Maintenance*

Keep young trees well watered and weed free in a 4-foot circle around the tree. Add an organic mulch, such as shredded bark or straw, to keep the soil cool and moist. Prune the tree to a central leader or open center. An open center is better if your variety is susceptible to fire blight disease. It makes removing infected limbs easier. Prune in late winter to shape the tree, creating scaffold branches equally distributed around the trunk. Remove dead, diseased, or broken branches; water sprouts (straight shoots from the main branches); and suckers (shoots from the roots or base of the tree) at any time.

The biggest problem for pears is fire blight disease. The branches look like they've been scorched by fire. The disease can spread quickly and kill a tree. Select resistant varieties and prune out fire blight whenever you see signs of it. Place tree guards on trunks to protect the bark from girdling caused by mice and voles.

■ Harvesting

Harvest European pears when they are full sized, but still have a firm flesh. Let them ripen in a warm room indoors. If left on the tree until soft, the flesh will be mushy. Harvest Asian pears when the stem separates easily from the fruits when tugged. Asian pears are eaten like apples.

■ Additional Information

You'll need at least two different varieties of pears to get the best production. They usually ripen in late August or September in our region. 'Bartlett', 'Clapp's Favorite', and 'Seckel' are common varieties that are hardy to USDA zone 5. For colder areas of our region, try 'Patten', 'Luscious', and 'Summer Crisp'. 'Shinseiki' is a hardy dwarf Asian pear variety to grow.

PLUM

There are so many varieties of plums available it's hard to grow just one. I've grown the American plums (*Prunus americana*) in my USDA zone 4 garden, mostly because of their hardiness. European plums (*Prunus* x *domestica*) are less hardy, but are self-fruitful. Japanese varieties (*Prunus salicina*) can grow only in warmer parts of our region. There are also tart-tasting native plums and plums crossed with other stone fruits, such as apricots and peaches. Pluot® refers to a complex apricot-plum cross that has predominantly plum bloodlines. Aprium® is also an apricot-plum cross, but has mostly apricot breeding in its makeup.

Most plum trees are small (12 to 15 feet tall), are productive, and have juicy fruits with green yellow, red, or purple skins and sweet or tart flesh. Plums are good for eating fresh or for using to make jams and jellies.

■ When to Plant

Plant bare-root (no soil on the roots) plum trees from a mail-order nursery in early spring as soon as the ground can be worked, or plant container plum trees from a local garden center in spring or summer.

■ Where to Plant

Plums grow best in full sun and well-drained soils. American and European varieties tend to tolerate heavy clay soils better than Japanese varieties. Plant on a south-facing slope unless you have late-spring frosts. Then, it's best to plant on a north-facing slope to delay blooming in spring.

■ How to Plant

Plant standard-sized plum trees 15 to 20 feet apart, semidwarf varieties 12 to 15 feet apart, and dwarf trees 8 to 10 feet apart. Dig a hole twice as large as the rootball, and plant so the graft union (bulge on the tree trunk) is 2 inches above the soil line. The graft union is the point where the variety was grafted on to the hardier rootstock.

■ Care and Maintenance

Keep plum trees well watered and weeded. Keep a 4-foot area around the tree clear of grass and weeds during the trees' early years and make a moat to catch water around the tree. Mulch with shredded bark or straw, keeping the mulch away from the trunk to avoid diseases. Fertilize with compost each spring. American and European plums should grow 12 inches a year, while Japanese plums should grow 20 inches a year. If trees are growing at less than this rate, consider adding an organic fertilizer in spring. If trees are growing at more than this rate, hold back on additional fertilizer. If a tree grows too much, it produces lots of young growth, which is more susceptible to diseases.

American plums grow in a pyramidal shape and require little pruning other than removing overcrowded branches. European varieties should be pruned to an open center, allowing for more light and air penetration into the center of the tree. Japanese plums should be pruned to a central leader system. While most pruning should be done in late winter, prune out dead, diseased, or broken branches; water sprouts (straight shoots from the main branches); and suckers (shoots from the roots or base of the tree) anytime.

Plums are susceptible to a few insects and diseases that can cause severe problems. Black knot fungus causes black growths on branches that can eventually kill the branch. Prune out diseased branches in winter below the growths, sterilizing the pruners with a 10 percent chlorine bleach solution between each cut. Choose resistant varieties and clean up dropped fruits and leaves to avoid other diseases. Plum curculio is an insect pest whose eggs hatch into worms in plum fruits. Collect this pest by placing a tarp under the trees and shaking the trees in the morning while the curculios are sluggish. They'll drop onto the tarp and can be easily killed. Protect the tree trunks from girdling by mice and voles with tree wraps.

■ Harvesting

Harvest plums when they have matured to the correct color for that variety and come off the tree easily with a gentle twist. American and European plums should be left to ripen on the tree, but shouldn't be left too long because the flesh will become mushy if overripe. Japanese plums can be harvested early and will continue to ripen indoors.

■ Additional Information

'Toka', 'Waneta', and 'Underwood' are good American plum varieties. 'Superior', 'Damson', and 'Stanley' are widely planted European varieties. 'Santa Rosa', 'Shiro', and 'Early Golden' are good Japanese varieties.

RHUBARB

When I was a kid, I remember picking stems from my grandfather's rhubarb (*Rheum rhabarbarum*) plant, coating them with sugar, and munching away. The juicy sourness was balanced by the sweet sugar. You don't need a ton of sugar to make rhubarb edible. Rhubarb makes a great sauce by itself with a sweetener (I now use honey) or combined with strawberries that are ripening about the same time rhubarb is ready to pick. The crunchy, sour flavor of rhubarb blended with the sweet flavor of strawberries is a perfect match in cobblers, pies, breads, and sauces.

Rhubarb is a tropical-looking perennial vegetable that grows 2 feet tall and wide. It can grow for years in your garden with little care. All you'll need is one or two plants and you'll have all the rhubarb your family can eat.

■ *When to Plant*

Plant rhubarb in spring or fall while the soil and air are cool. In spring, plant as soon as the ground can be worked and has dried out. Rhubarb grows best at temperatures under 80°F.

■ *Where to Plant*

Rhubarb grows the fastest and produces the largest stems if it's planted in full sun. However, I've grown plants in part shade and they grow well, just slower. Rhubarb is an ornamental plant, so consider placing it in a perennial flower garden or in front of a shrub border.

■ *How to Plant*

Rhubarb loves organic matter. Before planting, amend the hole with a generous amount of compost or composted manure. Plant young plants bought locally or through the mail, so their crowns (the place where the roots and shoots meet) are 2 inches deep. Space plants 6 feet apart. Mulch with compost or bark to keep the soil evenly moist and cool.

■ *Care and Maintenance*

Keep plants well watered and weeded. Apply compost in spring to encourage more growth. Remove any flower stalks that form by cutting them at the base of the plant, so your rhubarb will send more energy into leaf and root growth. Flower stalks are more likely to emerge when plants are stressed by water, heat, or overcrowding.

Rhubarb are carefree until about six to eight years after planting, when they can become overcrowded, producing smaller stems and flowering early. If this happens, divide the plants in spring, making sure each division has a generous number of roots, and replant in a sunny spot in compost-amended soil. Rhubarb have few pest problems.

Harvesting

The part of rhubarb that is used in cooking is the leaf stem. Remove the leaves and compost them. The leaves are actually mildly poisonous, but the stem behind the leaf is fine to eat raw or cooked. Don't harvest rhubarb the first year after planting. In the second year, only harvest for one week in spring, removing only the thickest stalks. Use a sharp knife to cut the leaf stem at the base. The third year, harvest all stalks larger than 1 inch in diameter for two months in spring. Use the stalks fresh or chop and freeze them for winter use.

Additional Information

'Victoria' and 'MacDonald' are two good varieties with green stalks and red overtones. 'MacDonald' grows particularly well in clay soil. 'Canada Red' has good flavor, but the stems are less attractive.

STRAWBERRY

I know it's summer when I can harvest strawberries (*Fragaria* x *ananassa*). The sweet, juicy red fruits signal the beginning of the fruit season in my garden. I'm always amazed at how fast they grow and ripen. From small plants popped in the ground the previous year comes a full bed loaded with green fruits that ripen to red almost overnight with warm weather.

When you see the price of fresh strawberries in the grocery store, you'll be enticed to grow some of your own. Strawberries are great because you can grow them almost anywhere. They produce in a garden, a small raised bed, a container, or even a hanging basket. While most gardeners are familiar with the traditional June-bearing varieties that produce in early summer and then are done for the season, newer varieties, called day neutral and everbearers, produce fruits from summer until frost. Day neutral varieties like 'Tristar' bear fruit almost continuously, while everbearers like 'Ozark Beauty' set fruit two or three times a season. Most strawberries produce runners or aboveground stems that have babies attached to them. These babies root in the soil and your strawberry plants will quickly fill out a row, bed, or the garden if you let them.

I also like to grow small, clumping types called alpine strawberries (*Fragaria vesca*). These produce small red or yellow fruits with an intense, sweet strawberry flavor. They make perfect kids' garden plants because they produce fruits all summer long, which are like hidden treasures tucked in among the foliage.

■ *When to Plant*

Plant strawberry plants in spring or early summer as bare-root (no soil on the roots) plants bought through the garden center or mail, or container plants bought locally. This allows the plants to get well established before winter's cold arrives. Alpine strawberries can also be grown from seed; sow indoors six to eight weeks before your last frost date and sow into the garden in spring after all danger of frost has passed. It's a less expensive way to grow many alpine strawberry plants.

■ *Where to Plant*

Strawberries need full sun and well-drained, sandy, loamy soil to grow their best. In all but the sandiest soils, consider building an 8-inch-tall, 2-foot wide raised bed. The raised bed warms up and dries out faster in spring. Plus, it's easier to weed, fertilize, and care for the strawberries when they're grouped in a raised bed.

■ *How to Plant*

Amend the bed with compost prior to planting. Level the bed, removing any stones or large debris. There are many planting patterns you can follow. I like to plant June-bearing varieties in a matted row system. Space plants in the middle of the raised bed 2 feet apart in rows spaced 4 feet apart. Plant so the crown of the strawberry plant (the place where the roots and shoots meet) is right at soil level. If it's buried or too shallow, the plants may die.

Day-neutral or everbearing varieties grow a little differently. They don't send out as many runners, so they're best planted on a raised bed in staggered double rows. Space plants 12 inches apart in a double row spaced 8 inches apart on the bed. Space beds 4 feet apart. Space alpine plants 1 foot apart in beds or rows.

■ *Care and Maintenance*

In the June-bearing beds, remove any flowers that form the first year, so the plants can get established and get ready to produce a big crop next spring. As the runners form on June-bearing plants, select six to eight of the baby plants and space them to fill out the 2-foot-wide row.

For day-neutral or everbearing varieties, remove the flowers for the first two to three weeks, then let some fruits set for a small fall crop the first year. Alpine strawberries don't produce runners. Remove flowers for the first two to three weeks, then let them set fruit.

In spring, apply a balanced organic fertilizer, such as 5-5-5, to beds. Sprinkle it around plants but don't hoe it into the soil, because it's easy to disturb the shallow-rooted plants. Keep plants well watered, especially after planting. Keep weeds away by hand weeding small patches and then mulching with a layer of straw.

This straw can also be used as a winter cover. Strawberry plants grow best if protected in winter with a 4- to 6-inch layer of straw placed over plants in late fall. Remove the mulch in spring as soon as the coldest weather has passed and new growth appears. Use the mulch in pathways to keep weeds away and protect the fruits from splashing mud.

June-bearing plants will tend to overcrowd the bed with their growth, so they need to be thinned, or "renovated," each summer. Overcrowded beds produce fewer berries. Renovation involves removing extra plants and cutting back the strawberry foliage, allowing new spaces for strawberries to grow and fruit next year. For small beds, hand clip the strawberry foliage to 3 inches tall after the harvest is finished. On larger beds, use a lawn mower to mow the bed. Collect and compost the clippings. Remove older, diseased, or weak plants to create a 1-foot-wide row of berry plants in the center of the bed. Keep the beds spaced 4 feet apart. Add fertilizer to stimulate new growth and remove weeds as you clean up the bed. If you renovate your June-bearing bed well each year, your strawberries can remain productive for three or more years before you'll have to pull them out and start over. Eventually they will succumb to diseases.

Day-neutral or everbearing varieties will need little renovation since they produce few runners. They stay productive for a few years. Alpine strawberries will eventually need dividing once they get overcrowded. However, mine have lasted years with little extra effort.

Strawberries have a number of disease, insect, and animal pest problems. It's important to start with disease-resistant varieties to avoid common problems such as red steel and viruses. The soft fruits are very susceptible to gray mold, fruit rot, and slugs, especially during wet weather. Keep beds thinned well so air can circulate freely and dry out the bed and fruits. Pick and destroy any moldy fruits to prevent mold from spreading to other fruits. Slugs will eat holes in ripening fruits. Use traps, iron phosphate bait, or copper flashing on containers to stop them. Use row covers to protect plants from damage by strawberry bud weevils, which sever blossoms from the plant. Keeps weeds away from the beds to reduce the population of tarnished plant bugs that feed on and deform developing fruits.

Birds and chipmunks love ripe strawberries. Place wire cages over small patches and bird netting over bigger patches to prevent damage.

■ *Harvesting*

Harvest June-bearing varieties the next June after planting. Start harvesting day-neutral or everbearing varieties about three months after planting. Pick frequently. Fruits will overripen quickly and attract diseases and pests. Pick the berry just above the top of the fruit, or cap, by pinching the stem with your fingers.

■ *Additional Information*

Plant early-, mid-, and late-season varieties of June-bearing strawberries to get a longer season of harvest. 'Earliglow' and 'Annapolis' are two early varieties. 'Cabot' and 'Jewel' are two good midseason varieties. 'Sparkle' and 'Winona' are two good late-season varieties. 'Tristar', 'Tribute', 'Evie 2', and 'Seascape' are all good day-neutral varieties. 'Alexandria' is a good alpine strawberry variety.

RESOURCES

While this book gives you a great overview and lots of details on what to plant and how to plant it, the great thing about gardening is there's always room to learn more. In this resources chapter you'll find information on vegetable and herb seed companies, fruit tree and berry nurseries, educational resources such as the Master Gardeners, and websites that will help you go to the next step in your garden. It is certainly only the tip of the iceberg of gardening information, but these resources will help you learn more about gardening in the Northeast.

In compiling these resources, I have focused on seed, plant, and product companies that are either located in the Northeast or sell varieties that pertain to our region. I'm a big proponent of supporting local and regional businesses. Not only does it help your community and neighbors, but in the gardening world it makes sense. Many of the seed and fruit companies used trial varieties in their test grounds before offering them. Chances are if it grows well in their test gardens in our region, it will grow well for you.

Finally, a word about the Master Gardener associations. Master Gardeners are trained volunteers who help home gardeners with gardening problems. They receive training, usually through the state land grant university, and then give back a certain number of hours to the community in various gardening volunteer activities, such as answering gardening questions on the phone or at events, working at local schools on gardening activities, or helping in beautification projects around town. They are a great resource for the beginning gardener needing answers to obvious, and not so obvious, questions. I've listed contact information for these associations in the Northeast. State universities also have websites with lots of pertinent gardening information for your area. They offer a wealth of information.

Vegetable and Herb Companies

While buying seeds and plants from local garden centers and nurseries is a quick and convenient way to get your vegetable and herb plants for the season, sometimes you might want to try some unusual varieties from mail-order catalogs. Many vegetable and fruit companies now offer good how-to information and even videos on their websites, so they are also an educational resource. Some of these companies will have their seeds on seed racks in garden centers in spring as well.

BAKER CREEK HEIRLOOM SEEDS

2278 Baker Creek Road
Mansfield, MO 65704
417-924-8917
www.rareseeds.com

Baker Creek features a catalog with hundreds of color pictures of heirloom vegetables and herbs from around the world. They are also the owners of Comstock, Ferre & Company in Wethersfield, Connecticut. You can order online or visit the store.

THE COOK'S GARDEN

P.O. Box C5030
Warminster, PA 18974
800-457-9703
www.cooksgarden.com

This business still holds true to its Vermont roots of offering a wide range of vegetable and herb seeds, especially of unusual salad greens from Europe.

FEDCO SEEDS

P.O. Box 520
Waterville, ME 04903
207-873-7333
www.fedcoseeds.com

This cooperative offers a full line of vegetable and herb seeds for our region, as well as an extensive list of fruit trees, berry bushes, and cover crop seeds.

HARRIS SEEDS

P.O. Box 24966
Rochester, NY 14624
800-544-7939
www.harrisseeds.com

This New York–based company offers a wide range of vegetable and herb seeds and plants, as well as some fruit trees and berries.

HIGH MOWING ORGANIC SEEDS

76 Quarry Road
Wolcott, VT 05680
802-472-6174
www.highmowingseeds.com

This Vermont-based seed company offers organic seeds and many heirloom vegetable and herb varieties.

JERSEY ASPARAGUS FARMS

105 Porchtown Road
Pittsgrove, NJ 08318
856-358-2548 (Walker Farm, asparagus seeds or plants)
www.jerseyasparagus.com

This New Jersey–based farm specializes in and produces seeds of the Jersey hybrid asparagus varieties.

JOHNNY'S SELECTED SEEDS

955 Benton Avenue
Winslow, ME 04901
877-564-6697
www.johnnyseeds.com

This company features vegetable and herb seeds and some berries. It breeds its own varieties and has organic seeds and cover crop seeds as well.

NOURSE FARMS INC.

41 River Road
South Deerfield, MA 01373
413-665-2658
www.noursefarms.com

Nourse Farms offers a broad selection of small fruits, including currants and gooseberries, as well as asparagus, horseradish, and rhubarb plants.

PINETREE GARDEN SEEDS

P.O. Box 300
New Gloucester, ME 04260
207-926-3400
www.superseeds.com

This Maine-based company sells a wide variety of vegetable and herb seeds. They feature small packets at reduced prices.

RICHTERS HERBS

357 Hwy. 47
Goodwood, ON LOC 1AO, Canada
800-668-4372
www.richters.com

This Canadian company features a wide selection of herb seeds and plants. It has lots of unusual varieties.

SEED SAVERS EXCHANGE

3094 North Winn Road
Decorah, IA 52101
563-382-5990
www.seedsavers.org

This seed-saving nonprofit organization also sells seed. It has a beautiful color catalog of a wide variety of heirloom vegetables and herbs.

STOKES SEED COMPANY

P.O. Box 548
Buffalo, NY 14240
800-396-9238
www.stokeseeds.com

Based in the United States and Canada, this company has a complete line of vegetable and herb seeds.

TOMATO GROWERS SUPPLY COMPANY

P.O. Box 60015
Fort Myers, FL 33906
888-748-7333
www.tomatogrowers.com

Although based in Florida, I included this seed company for its amazing selection of tomato varieties. If you're interested in experimenting with tomato varieties, this is a catalog for you. It also features pepper and eggplant varieties.

VESEYS SEEDS

P.O. Box 9000
Calais, ME 04619
800-363-7333

This is another company based in the United States and Canada that features a good selection of vegetable and herb seeds.

W. ATLEE BURPEE & COMPANY

300 Park Ave
Warminster, PA 18974
800-888-1447
www.burpee.com

A historic seed and plant company, Burpee features a wide range of varieties of vegetable and herb seeds and plants through the mail. You'll often find Burpee seeds on seed racks in garden centers as well. Burpee also sells fruit trees and berry plants.

WOOD PRAIRIE FARM

49 Kinney Road
Bridgewater, ME 04735
800-829-9765
www.woodprairie.com

This Maine-based specialty company features organic seed potato varieties and some other vegetable seeds.

Fruit and Berry Nurseries

While the preceding list of vegetable and herb companies includes many businesses that also sell fruit trees and berry bushes, the following nurseries have the most extensive offerings for our region. Always check the hardiness zone and compare it with your location on the map on page 7 before buying a tree. The hardiness zone number of the tree or bush should be the same or lower than the zone in your area.

EDIBLE LANDSCAPING

361 Spirit Ridge Lane
Afton, VA 22920
800-524-4156
www.ediblelandscaping.com

Although located farther south of our region, this nursery offers an amazing variety of traditional and unusual fruit and nut trees and berry bushes, along with some vegetables and herbs.

ELMORE ROOTS NURSERY

631 Symonds Mill Road
Elmore, VT 05680
800-427-5268

This small Vermont nursery features cold-hardy fruits and berries.

FEDCO TREES

See listing under Vegetable and Herb Companies.

MILLER NURSERIES

5060 West Lake Road
Canandaigua, NY 14424
800-836-9630
www.millernurseries.com

This New York–based nursery offers a wide selection of fruit trees, berries, and some vegetables. It also has nut trees and unusual fruits such as hardy kiwi.

NOURSE FARMS

See listing under Vegetable and Herb Companies.

ST. LAWRENCE NURSERIES

325 State Highway 345
Potsdam, NY 13676
315-265-6739
www.sln.potsdam.ny.us

This small nursery features cold-hardy apples, pears, plums, and many other fruits. It also has native edible shrubs and nut trees.

Master Gardener Associations in the Northeast
Maine Master Gardeners: http://umaine.edu/gardening/programs/master-gardeners

Massachusetts Master Gardeners: www.masshort.org/Master-Gardener-Program

New Hampshire Master Gardeners: http://extension.unh.edu/Agric/AGMastGD.htm

New Jersey Master Gardeners: http://njaes.rutgers.edu/mastergardeners

New York Master Gardeners: www.gardening.cornell.edu/education/mgprogram

Rhode Island Master Gardeners: www.urimga.org

Vermont Master Gardener: www.uvm.edu/mastergardener

University and Nonprofit Websites
Cornell Gardening Resources Vegetables: www.gardening.cornell.edu/vegetables/index.html

Rutgers University Home, Lawn, and Garden: www.njaes.rutgers.edu/garden

University of Connecticut Home and Garden Fact Sheets: www.ladybug.uconn.edu/factsheets/index.html

University of Maine Gardening and Horticulture: www.umaine.edu/gardening

University of Massachusetts Vegetable Gardening Fact Sheets: www.umassgreeninfo.org/homegarden/veggies.html

University of New Hampshire Home and Garden Resources: www.extension.unh.edu/resources/category/Home_and_Garden

University of Rhode Island Home Garden Fact Sheets: www.urimga.org/fact_sheets_index.html

University of Vermont Fruit and Vegetable Cultivation: www.uvm.edu/extension/yard/?Page=vegetables.html

Other Resources
Edible Landscaping Newsletter with Charlie Nardozzi
www.garden.org//ediblelandscaping

Northeast Organic Farming Association
www.nofa.org/index.php

The Northeast Organic Farming Association is a nonprofit organization of over five thousand farmers, gardeners, landscape professionals, and consumers working to promote healthy food, organic farming practices, and a cleaner environment. NOFA has state chapters with separate websites. A similar group, Maine Organic Farming and Gardening Association (MOFGA), is in Maine.

GLOSSARY

acidic soil: A soil with a pH below 7 on a scale of 1 to 14. Most vegetables grow best with soils in the range of 6.5 to 7.2.

alkaline soil: A soil with a pH above 7 on a scale of 1 to 14. Most vegetables grow best with soils in the range of 6.5 to 7.2.

annual: A plant that grows from seed to flower and fruit in one growing season, then dies. Peas and beans are good examples of annual vegetables.

antioxidants: Cancer-fighting compounds present in many fresh fruits and vegetables. Tomatoes, broccoli, blueberries, and watermelons are just some of the fruits and vegetables known for high antioxidant levels.

***Bacillus thuringiensis* (B.t.):** Bacteria that attack caterpillar-family insects such as cabbageworms. The insects must eat the bacteria to be killed by them. A strain called San Diego attacks potato beetle larvae.

balanced fertilizer: A fertilizer that has close to equal amounts of nitrogen, phosphorus, and potassium, as indicated by the numbers on the product, such as 5-5-5.

bare root: Describes a tree or shrub that doesn't have soil attached to its roots. Fruit trees and berry bushes are commonly shipped by mail in this condition, usually while the plant isn't growing or is dormant.

beneficial insect: An insect that attacks harmful insects in the garden. Ladybugs and lacewings are examples of beneficial insects.

biennial: A plant that grows only leaves the first year, overwinters, sends up a flower stalk and forms seeds the second year, and then dies. Parsley and carrots are biennial vegetables.

blanch: To exclude the light from a vegetable, such as cauliflower or leeks, so that it stays white and tender. Also, to dip vegetables in boiling water for a few minutes to preserve their color and flavor before freezing.

bolt: To form a flower stalk prematurely, usually due to some form of stress such as lack of water, overcrowding, poor fertility, or high temperatures.

broadcast seeds: To spread seeds over an area, covering the whole surface instead of sowing in rows. This technique is usually used with small-seeded vegetables, such as carrots and lettuce.

central leader: A fruit tree pruning system where the main trunk is maintained and branches are trained to grow along the trunk equally on each side. This system is used on pears and some plums.

cold frame: A device made from plastic, glass, wood, or metal, usually in a box shape, with a clear top, that protects plants from cold and wind. It can be used in spring to protect young seedlings or in fall to extend the harvest of mature plants.

compost: Decomposed plant material that is used as a soil amendment to help with water drainage and retention and nutrient uptake.

cool-weather crop: A vegetable that grows best during cool weather, such as broccoli, spinach, radish, or pea.

cover crop: A system where plants, such as winter wheat, are seeded in fall with the purpose of growing through the winter to prevent erosion. This crop is usually tilled in spring to add organic matter to the soil.

crop rotation: The planting of vegetables in the same family in different parts of the garden each year to deter insect and diseases from building up in any one section of the garden.

cure: To expose newly harvested vegetables, such as winter squash and sweet potatoes, to warm temperatures to toughen their skin to help them survive longer in storage and taste better.

day neutral: A plant that will fruit anytime during the growing season despite the length of day. Some varieties of strawberries are day neutral.

diatomaceous earth: A pesticide made from the tiny skeletons of ancient sea creatures that is effective at controlling soft-bodied insects such as cutworms.

direct sow: To plant seeds directly in the garden rather than planting them in pots and transplanting later into the garden.

disease resistant: Describes the ability of a variety to withstand certain diseases. A disease-resistant variety rarely gets a certain disease, while a disease-tolerant variety may get the disease, but usually can survive and still produce a crop.

drip irrigation: A watering system that uses plastic tubing and small emitters to deliver water in small amounts consistently to a plant's root system.

edible landscaping: The technique of designing and planting a yard with plants that are edible as well as beautiful. Blueberries and Swiss chard are examples of edible landscape plants.

fish emulsion: An organic fertilizer made from the byproducts of the fish-processing industry. It is high in nitrogen.

floating row cover: A white, cheesecloth-like, spunbonded fiber material that is used to protect plants from frost and block insects and animals from attacking a crop. It is reusable.

frost date: The time between first and last frost dates are generally considered the length of your growing season. They vary by a number of days each year depending on the weather, but are used as general guidelines for planting and harvesting certain crops.

germination: The sprouting of a seed.

graft union: The intersection where a desired variety of plant is physically attached to a rootstock of another variety with desired characteristics such as disease resistance. The graft union usually looks like a bulge on the stem of the plant near the roots.

green manure: A plant that is grown specifically to be tilled in during the growing season to add organic matter to the soil.

harden off: To get plants growing indoors used to natural wind, temperature, and weather conditions by gradually exposing them to the outdoors, increasing the amount of time over a one-week period. After that period they can be planted in a garden without any setbacks.

hardiness zone: A nationwide system based on the average winter minimum temperatures for an area. Your zone number helps you determine what trees and shrubs can safely be planted in your region. See the Northeast region zone map on page 7.

heavy soil: A soil with mostly clay that is hard to turn and work.

heirloom: A variety that was generally grown before the Second World War. You can save the seeds from these varieties and they will grow the same variety next year.

hill: To mound soil up around a plant such as potatoes (to increase production) or corn (to stabilize the plant).

hoop house: A simple form of a greenhouse, usually a metal, wooden, or PVC structure with clear plastic sheeting. It allows crops to be grown earlier and later in the season by protecting them from frost.

humus: Plant material that has decomposed to its final stage. Compost is loaded with humus. Humus helps plants take up nutrients and improves water drainage and retention in soil.

hybrid: A plant that results when two varieties are purposely bred together to get a desired characteristic, such as increased growth or fruit size. Hybrid seeds cannot be saved and grown again because the offspring will not all have the same characteristics as the parents.

insecticidal soap: An organic pesticide derived from the fatty acids in soap. It is safe and effective against aphids, mites, and other soft-bodied insects.

interplant: To plant a small-sized, quick-maturing crop, such as radishes, near a larger-sized, slower-growing crop, such as broccoli, in order to maximize the planting space.

leggy: Describes a plant that grows unusually tall and thin, often due to lack of light.

legume: A plant that has the ability to take nitrogen from the air and use it to grow. Beans and peas are examples of legume vegetables.

live trap: To remove a pest animal using a trap that doesn't harm it. Animal relocation should always be done carefully and after consulting with your state fish and wildlife agency.

mulch: To use a material to moderate the soil temperature, prevent weeds from growing, and conserve soil moisture. Mulches can be organic, such as straw, untreated grass clippings, and leaves; or inorganic, such as plastic.

mycorrhizae: A beneficial fungus that forms a symbiotic relationship with plant roots to help increase water and nutrient uptake in the plant. It only needs to be applied once for perennial plants, but yearly application is necessary for annual plants.

Neem oil: An organic pesticide derived from the seed of the Neem tree. This oil deters a large number of insects, including Japanese beetles, from feeding and reproducing.

organic gardening: A method of gardening that utilizes a systematic approach of feeding the soil using natural materials such as compost and manure, and encouraging natural predators while avoiding certain pesticides. Techniques such as rotating crops, growing resistant varieties, and planting cover crops are key to organic gardening.

organic matter: Any material that was once alive. Organic matter is added to gardens in two forms: raw materials, such as straw, and processed materials, such as compost. Organic matter is essential for feeding the microbes in the soil, which will help plants grow.

overwinter: To protect a crop so it survives the winter weather.

perennial: A plant that regrows each year, either from its woody top or its roots.

pH: The measure of a soil's acidity and alkalinity on a scale of 1 to 14, with 7 being neutral. An acidic soil is below 7, while an alkaline soil is above 7. Most vegetables and fruits grow best with a soil pH range of 6.5 to 7.2.

plant crown: The area where the stem and roots meet. On some plants, such as strawberries, it is the place where new growth emerges in spring.

pollination: The transfer of pollen within a flower or between two flowers so that fruits will develop.

pyrethrum: An organic insecticide derived from a species of chrysanthemum flower. It is considered a broad-spectrum insecticide, meaning it will kill many good and bad insects and is harmful to honeybees.

raised bed: A garden area that is elevated so that the soil warms faster and dries out more quickly in spring. A temporary raised bed is mounded up each spring, usually to a height of 8 inches and a width of no more than 3 feet. A permanent raised bed is bordered by a long-lasting material, such as stone, rot-resistant wood, or bricks, so doesn't need to be reformed each spring.

resprout: To grow again after being cut. This term is often used when talking about greens that can be cut to the ground and will regrow for another harvest.

rhizobia: Nitrogen-fixing bacterium that is common in the soil, sometimes forming nodules on plant roots.

rootball: The mass of soil and roots that is usually enclosed in a burlap sack or plastic nursery pot in a tree or shrub purchased from a garden center.

root cellar: A structure built to store fresh vegetables and fruits through the winter under optimal temperature and humidity levels.

rootstock: The roots of a tree that has qualities desirable for good growth, such as disease resistance or vigor. On fruit trees, the rootstock is the lower portion of the trunk and roots and often has a grafted variety on top of it with the desired fruit quality.

rototill: To turn over the soil using a special machine with metal tines. While rototilling is often used to create a garden bed in spring, too much tilling can cause harm to the soil structure.

season extending: Using materials such as a floating row cover, plastic, or a cold frame to protect plants from the cold and thus grow plants earlier or later than normal for your region.

self-pollinating: Describes a variety's ability to transfer pollen and produce fruits without the need of insects, another variety, or a similar plant around. Some fruit tree varieties are self-pollinating.

self-watering container: A container with a reservoir of water in the bottom that keeps the soil moist. You may not need to add water to the resevoir of a self-watering container for up to five days, depending on the weather.

side-dress: To apply fertilizer during the growing season to encourage new growth and continued fruiting.

soil test: An analysis of a collection of soil samples to determine the soil's nutrient, organic matter, and pH levels.

soaker hose: A watering hose that is meant to be laid on the soil surface. It has tiny holes through which water seeps out slowly to moisten the soil.

spinosad: A new organic insecticide derived from bacteria. It kills a wide range of insects, including caterpillars and the young of some beetles. It is safe for beneficial insects, but toxic to honeybees.

straw and hay: The dried stems of grain or grass crops in the form of bales that are used as an organic mulch in the garden. Straw is made from grain crop stems and is weed free. Hay is cut from grasses and various other meadow plants and is generally cheaper and more readily available, but may contain weed seeds. Along the coast, salt hay or marsh grasses can be used as mulch.

succession planting: The planting of a new crop of vegetables in the same space as one that has just been harvested. This practice allows a gardener to maximize gardening space and produce more vegetables.

sucker: A shoot that arises from a dormant plant bud on the root of a tree, perennial, or shrub. On fruit trees, suckers will be close to the trunk and should be removed annually. For raspberries, suckers may emerge some distance from the main plant and should be removed if growing in the wrong place. On tomatoes, the term sucker refers to a shoot that grows between a side stem and the main stem. If you want to keep your tomato plant small, remove the suckers as they emerge.

taproot: A main central root that grows straight down into the soil. Carrots, parsley, and fennel are examples of vegetables with taproots.

tendril: A small, modified leaf that twirls around to attach itself to other structures or plants. Peas and watermelons have tendrils.

thin: To remove seedlings that are growing too close together by snipping them with a scissors or your fingers. You can thin indoor seedlings when growing young plants for transplanting or thin plants in the garden. For vegetables such as radishes, carrots, and beets, thinning is essential to getting a crop.

transplant: A young seedling that is ready to be planted in the garden. To transplant is to plant the seedling in the ground.

tree wrap: A plastic or metal material that is wrapped around tree trunks in fall to protect them from animals such as mice and voles, which chew the bark over winter.

true leaves: Usually the second set of leaves formed by a newly emerged seedling. They resemble the mature leaves of that plant.

untreated grass clippings: Grass clippings collected from lawns that have not been treated with chemical pesticides. Using grass clippings from treated lawns as a mulch in the garden can potentially harm your plants.

vertical gardening: Growing plants vertically as a way to save space. Some plants, such as peas and pole beans, naturally grow vertically, while others, such as melons and cucumbers, can be trained to do so.

warm-weather crop: A crop that grow best during warm conditions. Beans, tomatoes, peppers, eggplants, cucumbers, squash, and melons are examples of warm-weather vegetables.

water drainage: The ability of a soil to drain water. It's important to plant your berries, fruits, and vegetables in an area that has soil with adequate water drainage. If the soil stays saturated for too long, the roots of the plants may die.

well-drained soil: A soil with good water drainage that doesn't stay wet for long periods of time.

PHOTOGRAPHY CREDITS

Cover Photography and Illustrations
Cool Springs Press would like to thank the following contributors to *Northeast Fruit & Vegetable Gardening.*

Front Cover Main Image
Macintosh utility apple (*Capsicum annuum*), Shutterstock.com

Cover photography provided by Tom Eltzroth
Blueberries (*Vaccinium ashei*), Cabbage (*Brassica oleracea*) Carrots (*Daucus carota*), Corn (*Zea mays*), Onions (*Allium cepa*), and Potatoes (*Solanum tuberosum*).

Interior Photography Credits
Charlie Nardozzi: 10, 12, 102, 106, 115, 116, 128, 145, 157, 158, 164, 185, 189, 199, 207, 212, 224; Ed Rode: 86, 92, 93; Greg Grant: 8, 11, 17, 20, 24, 28, 30, 39, 40, 43, 47, 48, 50, 51, 52, 54, 56, 69, 87, 90, 125, 127, 149, 150, 181, 235; Joe Lamp'l: 22; Lorenzo Gunn: 210, 228; Liz Ball: 203, 211, 216; Mary Ann Newcomer: 94, 220, 227; National Garden Bureau: 152; Neil Soderstrom: 29, 34, 36, 49, 55, 63, 64, 82; Robert Bowden and Leu Gardens: 9, 16, 19, 23, 68, 74; William Adams: 57; Tom Eltzroth: 27, 96, 98, 101, 105, 109, 110, 113, 114, 119, 123, 124, 126, 131, 132, 135, 139, 140, 143, 144, 145, 148, 155, 156, 161, 163, 165, 166, 169, 171, 172, 175, 176, 178, 180, 182, 191, 192, 195, 196, 200, 204, 209, 214, 215, 219, 223, 231, 232; Goodshoot/Jupiterimages: 58; iStockphoto.com: foued42: 44; iStockphoto.com/Michael Pettigrew: 71; iStockphoto.com/Kristen Johansen: 186; Jupiterimages: 33, 42, 59, 79, 120, 136.

INDEX

MEET CHARLIE NARDOZZI

Charlie Nardozzi is a nationally recognized garden writer, speaker, and radio and television personality. He has worked for more than twenty years bringing expert gardening information to home gardeners through radio, television, talks, online, and the printed page. Charlie delights in making gardening information simple, easy, fun, and accessible to everyone.

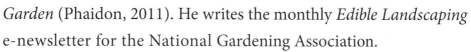

He is the author of *Vegetable Gardening for Dummies* (Wiley, 2009) and *The Ultimate Gardener* (HCI Books, 2009), and he contributed to the cookbook *Vegetables from an Italian Garden* (Phaidon, 2011). He writes the monthly *Edible Landscaping* e-newsletter for the National Gardening Association.

Charlie lives and gardens in Vermont where his gardening talents translate into other media as well. Charlie writes and produces the *Vermont Garden Journal* on public radio, hosts gardening tips on the local CBS-TV affiliate in Vermont, and is the former host of the nationally broadcast PBS *Garden Smart* television show.

Charlie also knows the value of teaching kids about gardening. He has partnered with companies and organizations such as Gardener's Supply Company, Cabot Cheese, Stonyfield Yogurt, Northeast Organic Farmers Association, and Shelburne Farms on kids' gardening projects. Charlie is also a widely sought-after public speaker for presentations to flower shows, master gardener groups, and garden clubs across the country.

See his website (CharlieNardozzi.com) for more information.

A book for any gardener, anywhere.